CRIMES AGAINST HUMANITY

The Under Jurisdiction Series

BOOKS IN THIS SERIES

Fleet Inquisitor (omnibus)
Fleet Renegade (omnibus)
Fleet Insurgent (omnibus)

Blood Enemies
Crimes Against Humanity

CRIMES AGAINST HUMANITY

The Under Jurisdiction Series

SUSAN R. MATTHEWS

CRIMES AGAINST HUMANITY

A Baen Books Original

Baen Publishing Enterprises
P.O. Box 1403
Riverdale, NY 10471
www.baen.com

ISBN: 978-1-4814-8371-1

Cover art by Dominic Harman

First Baen printing, January 2019

Distributed by Simon & Schuster
1230 Avenue of the Americas
New York, NY 10020

Library of Congress Cataloging-in-Publication Data

Names: Matthews, Susan R., author.
Title: Crimes against humanity / Susan R. Matthews.
Description: Riverdale, NY : Baen Books, 2019.
Identifiers: LCCN 2018041837 | ISBN 9781481483711 (trade pb)
Subjects: | GSAFD: Science fiction.
Classification: LCC PS3563.A8538 C75 2019 | DDC 813/.54--dc23
LC record available at https://lccn.loc.gov/2018041837

Printed in the United States of America

10 9 8 7 6 5 4 3 2 1

CONTENTS

CONTENTS

"Crimes Against Humanity" is dedicated to
Belknap "Finnie" Fenroth and the
Vreeslander commerce raider *Skipjack*.

Fictional smictional, I love you, Captain.

FOREWORD

by Susan R. Matthews

Jurisdiction is slowly descending into a loose confederacy of states—Judiciaries—from the federal model that's served it so well for so long (with allowances for recent developments, of course). Not everyone was all that committed to the integration of institutionalized torture as an instrument of State, and now that each Judiciary is free to start tweaking, some of them are making adjustments—no more Ship's Inquisitors, and no more bond-involuntary Security slaves.

This leaves a certain number of professional torturers out of a job and tainted by association with what was legal then and is now still legal in some Judiciaries, but not in others (you can see the problem). While the Jurisdiction is shaking apart—relatively slowly, if not painlessly—the refugees of the no-man's-land that's known as Gonebeyond space are slowly coming together as a nation of their own, with a different model of governance. Consensus-based. Tripartite division of powers, maybe.

As a loose association of dirt-poor settlements Gonebeyond is vulnerable to exploitation, and wide open to criminal predation. Bench Intelligence Specialist Jils Ivers thinks that her associate Karol Vogel is on the right track in his efforts to facilitate nation-building.

One of the first challenges Gonebeyond faces is developing a framework for policing its own house. Another is forming some official means by which Gonebeyond can open trade relations with the very Bench from which many of its members had originally fled to escape persecution, prosecution, punishment: some way to gain recognition as an autonomous political entity, dealing on equal terms with the confederated Judiciaries.

Some Judiciaries are more open to this effort than others, and Haspirzak Judiciary in particular has taken the bold step of sending one of its own Bench judges to Gonebeyond to watch, learn, and represent a formal liaison between Gonebeyond and the Bench. Bat Yorvik's very existence in the role of Bench Judge is an important indicator of the social changes taking place under Jurisdiction. Under the mentorship of the Third Judge at Haspirzak Judiciary he's the first man to be promoted to the senior levels of the Bench in a long, long time.

The Langsarik Coalition owes its existence to Hilton Shires' ability to negotiate, coordinate, and ultimately lead an ad-hoc police force whose mission is to eradicate predators from Gonebeyond, denying them their bases for operations, taking the war to where they live. In this novel Hilton appears as a battle commander, a leader of stature equivalent to that of the Flag Captain of the Langsarik Fleet itself.

So there's a whole lotta changing going on around here. A now-out-of-work Inquisitor offers his services to the Langsarik Coalition, but Andrej Koscuisko doesn't like him, because the evil and despicable and hateful Dr. Danyo Pefisct, tormentor of Joslire Curran prior to *An Exchange of Hostages* (found in Baen omnibus *Fleet Inquisitor*) and all-round Bad Egg, was responsible for the extra-judicial torture of a man Andrej loved—loves—at Fleet Orientation Station Medical, way back when. The Langsarik Coalition wants the field hospital Dr. Pefisct brings with him, and Andrej can't kill Pefisct under the terms of the foundational Nurail Covenant: feud stops at the border. He's not going to give up his fantasy of skinning Danyo alive without a fight, however.

It turns out that Yogee Gascarone, Gonebeyond's new, self-selected Surgeon General, is a man Andrej knew from their days together at the Mayon teaching college, before Andrej lost his argument with his father and reported to FOSM to learn the duties of a Judicial torturer. That's not all.

Security Chief Brachi Stildyne was not always the man we have come to know and maybe like a little bit. An ex-bond-involuntary Security troop has got some things to say to Stildyne about Stildyne's behavior before he got to the *Ragnarok*, and things could get awkward.

This is a problem because people are looking to a future in which the Malcontent's thula *Fisher Wolf* is going to start looking for reinforcements as people start to have real lives. Janforth is a good candidate for evaluation; but only if *he* can be persuaded not to skin *Stildyne* alive. There's more. There will be more ex-bond-involuntaries in Haspirzak, meaning more coming to Gonebeyond, meaning more challenges in how to manage them. The wolf-pack—the crew of the *Fisher Wolf*—has experience. The Malcontent's thula is one obvious place for people to go for their initial re-entry into lives as free men.

There's a-gonna be Confrontations. Reconciliations. Evolutions. But don't worry: this novel is fundamentally all about Things Getting Better.

This is more of an ensemble novel than an All Andrej All the Time book. I've got some new people to deploy, and at least one old friend— the Bench specialist Jils Ivers—plays a significant part in the action. In addition to Judge Bat Yorvick, Yogee Gascarone, and Janforth (the bond-involuntary from Haspirzak), there's the cargo handler Medith Riggs, who has previously figured in the short story "Into Gonebeyond" (on the Baen website and in the Baen ebook collection *Free Stories 2017*, a free download at Baen Ebooks) and the novella "Stalking Horse" (in the Baen omnibus *Fleet Insurgent*).

This novel is the eighth in a series, and people have Histories. You have my solemn pledge that everything I think you need to know to fully plunge into the action of this novel (without skipping the narrative groove, as it were, for an exposition dump) is in this novel.

Since there can't but be references, howsoever oblique, to backstory, I've set a notes section at the back of the book pointing you to where to go to Read More About any given reference I've been able to extract. I may not have gotten them all, but I've done my best. Feel free to contact me at *www.susanrmatthews.com* for more information.

I hope you enjoy this novel!

CRIMES AGAINST HUMANITY

The Under Jurisdiction Series

CHAPTER ONE

Inquiring Minds

Givros sat on the floor of a cell with his arms around his shins hugging his legs close to his chest, reviewing the facts at his disposal. He was a soldier of the Biramie mercantile cartel in Gonebeyond. He didn't know who was holding him, or where he was, or what had become of his working partner. He didn't know how long he'd been here. His beard was maybe four days old, but he couldn't trust that—such things could be manipulated. But most of all he wondered what had gone wrong and how.

He'd set up a rendezvous with his best contact from the Witt organization, a fair-haired woman of moderate height, deep brown eyes, and an accent that he'd assumed was Dolgorukij. They'd met in Port Delgacie, at a beer hall that had been safe the time or two before when his go-with Pilad had used the location with another working partner. They always worked in pairs, and seldom with the same person twice in a row. Things were more secure that way. Personal trust relationships were formed, but there could be no collusion.

And yet betrayed they had been, drugged, unable to struggle or to fight, extracted as calmly as any Biramie enforcer ever moved in on a target of interest. That was a hint: they'd been targeted by professional muscle. There'd been a lot of them, at least four men; that was no hint in and of itself.

When he'd woken up after the unplanned nap that had overwhelmed him on the loading ramp of some anonymous freighter, after he'd been given a meal, he'd been brought—by entirely different people—before a man of the short wiry hard-muscled kind he'd seen amongst Nurail hominids at one point or another.

Black hair down to his shoulders, curling. Dark eyes, an ugly look on his face, with a list of questions which the man asked in sequence— ignoring Givros' own questions, protests, demands—before nodding to some Security to return Givros to his cell. More Nurail, he thought.

But why would Nurail have targeted him? The Biramie cartel had no quarrel with Safehaven, none worth attending to. Safehaven didn't bother them. They didn't prey on Safehaven. All had been well, and it wasn't as though Nurail were above a spot of light smuggling or transportation of stolen goods for a modest cut of the proceeds.

Then after a while they came for him, brought him before a different interviewer, asked the same questions. Then again, with yet another interviewer, but the same questions, as though they'd completely lost their notes. He thought he'd slept; he'd found himself on his back on the cot they'd provided, once.

There was a toilet bolted to the wall, he'd used it, chemical digestion of waste matter—all very clean and tidy. He'd eaten. The food was plain but plentiful enough, and the briefings Biramie gave each of its operatives advised sleeping, eating, drinking what they were given to maintain their fitness to resist: yes, all of that could cover introduction of drugs, but it was more efficient to flat-out drug a person and if they were to be drugged it would happen anyway.

Who'd given them up? Their contact? Witt was the paradigm of honorable dealing in the trade: was that only because Witt's organization had never made any mistakes, never been betrayed themselves by treachery from within? Or had Givros' partner been a hostile implant, had she been working for Witt, had she been in collusion not with Biramie but with the contact they'd come to meet, was their Witt contact even a Witt contact?

Now security came once again to Givros' plain windowless cell. Was this the fourth time? The fifth? He couldn't remember exactly, anymore. He'd been unable to count the turnings in the narrow corridors, to build a mind-map of where he was, but still he had a sense that they were going in a different direction. Once they reached the interview room that, too, was different.

The only table was a small one. There was only one chair, facing the door. In the middle of the room stood a wooden tee-frame with its cross-post notched in two or three places and what looked like rope restraints draped across them like long bracelets; it rested in a peculiar foundation of raised slats, but it wasn't very tall.

Although Givros couldn't guess what torture would come, he knew as certainly as ever he'd known anything that he was to face torture now. By this time they knew he'd been lying, if they didn't know—couldn't know—exactly where the false information he'd learned so thoroughly had been hidden in his answers. He'd had a script. He'd been well coached in it.

They stripped him naked, well, that came as no surprise, it had been one of the preliminaries of almost every torture session he'd acted in himself. Then they bound him. They were careful with the exact placement of his knees, and the way they fastened his arms outstretched to the cross-bar of the tee-frame that had clearly been carefully designed for maximum awkwardness. Maximum discomfort. They went away: and now, Givros told himself, now the torture would come.

Nobody came. Time dragged on. He tried to shift his weight up off of his knees because the pressure was all wrong, or else it was exactly right to dig against the underside of his kneecaps with a diabolical precision that grew more and more painful with every breath. Like peeling his kneecaps up and away from his knees from underneath, but slowly, so slowly, every moment an inexorable increase in his pain.

Whatever it was they thought that he could tell them, they were apparently in no hurry to get the information. That was their mistake, because codes and coordinates changed at random intervals for security purposes, and much of what he knew would be outdated within days of his capture. He didn't know how many days it had been. For the first time Givros started to worry about that.

Yes, his script referred to a fixed target, so that the organization would be alerted immediately if anybody reached out for contact, since the only place the target was identified was in the script. And yes, contact would be acknowledged and pursued, to try to trap a would-be attacker who had already wrested the information out of a compromised soldier.

But even that information had to change. Any enemy that could take two of them from different places at once need only compare the harvest of information from two points, and they'd know they'd been deceived: because two agents on different missions would never be reporting to the same controller.

Then they'd know he was still lying. Then they'd come after him with enhanced techniques and the knowledge that they'd been duped. They'd be less likely to believe each new iteration of his story, more likely to probe harder and deeper. Was that why they were doing this?

Time dragged on and on and on. Someone came in; Givros felt the draft across his bare back, his neck prickling with apprehension. Doses? Doses put through. His awareness sharpened immediately, and he groaned aloud, hearing the near-sob in his own voice. But nothing happened. He concentrated on staying absolutely still, because any shift in his weight, howsoever slight, was a change in the pressure on his knees, and it was agony. He could feel his heart beat in waves of anguish, he could feel every breath he took in the trembling of his body.

Someone came in again. How long? How long had it been? And this time along with the doses—he knew what they were, in general if not in particular, there would be wake-keepers to ward off the deadening effects of stress, pain-maintenance drugs perhaps, to maintain the sharp edge of his anguish—there was a man. He wore plain clothes, but of the very best quality, and he wore them with an air of emphatic autocracy.

Bending, slightly, to look down into Givros' face, he raised one booted foot to rest it against Givros' body. An involuntary fit of shuddering seized Givros, because it hurt, it hurt, it hurt. Leaning down to speak close, the man balanced his weight against Givros' thigh. "Do you care to tell me what I wish to know?"

Givros screamed, fighting to stop screaming, fighting for his voice, because he couldn't tell anybody anything while he was screaming, no *yes*, no *no*, no *fuck you with my fist down your throat and your mother twice on rest-days*. Nothing. He couldn't catch his breath: surely they knew it? Surely they had to let him talk if they wanted the answers to their questions?

"I'll wait," the man said. Straightening up—pushing off Givros' thigh with his heel just above Givros' knee, Givros moaning with pain and frantic fear—the man went away, and all before Givros could catch his breath and find enough control over his body somehow to speak in words that made sense.

"Nothing to say—give over—"

But he knew he was lying. He had plenty to say. Just nothing the man hadn't already heard. All he had to do was stick to the story, somehow, and he *would* stick to the story, because the longer he held to it the better the story would stick. And because this was torture. He wasn't going to give. He owed it to himself. He would not give them the satisfaction. He'd outlast them. Biramie would reward him, he'd live like a merchant in small-heavies for the rest of his life.

Unless—unless his partner hadn't kept her mouth shut, had turned, had told, during those long stretches when he'd been left alone. Biramie wouldn't know which of them had betrayed their secrets. Biramie would kill them all, if these people didn't do it first. These people wouldn't. They'd release him. What would he have to show? Wounds? He had none. Injured knees?

How could they know what pain he was in, would he himself ever have been able to guess, wouldn't he have assumed a man with a story as weak as his had to be was covering for collusion, and get some answers of his own from such a man before leaving him to die a slow and dishonorable death?

When Givros heard the door opening behind him again he shouted as loudly as he could, hoping his words were comprehensible with his voice as rough and quavering as it was. "I'll talk, I'll talk!"

"Oh, very well," the man behind him said. Coming to the front. Familiar, somehow. "If you must, I suppose—" He slowed down, on his way past. Givros remembered the boot pressing down on his thigh and trembled violently.

"Andrej," somebody said, someone with a voice as rough as shards and sharp chips of concrete fractured in an explosion. "Focus, your Excellency."

There was a sigh. The man walked on to seat himself in the single chair, completing his thought as he went. "—but I *have* been enjoying this. Mister Yalta." Yet another person was there, behind Givros. He was handling Givros' ankles. Givros froze, in terror of more pain and not ashamed to be. That would be Mister Yalta, then, since the harsh-voiced man had followed the first one past Givros. Unfastening Givros' ankles; bringing them together with something cold and heavy. A chain. Why wasn't he shrieking? Givros wondered. Because there were drugs, obviously. They knew he couldn't talk when he was screaming, as well as he did.

More doses. Pain-ease, to Givros' surprise. Wake-keepers, clearly, from the way the fog cleared from his mind; that was a mistake on their part, Givros told himself, grimly. He found a tiny particle of strength, enough to be amused at their error. He could think. So he could deceive them.

The man took a lefrol out of an inner pocket of his plain tunic. The Voice held a firepoint, to light it; then put the firepoint down on the little table, where Givros could see it. A standard ploy, display the brutal instruments of torture, frighten the prisoner; it wouldn't work on Givros, because he'd used the stratagem himself. There was a rhyti service on the table that Givros hadn't seen before, and a flat-file docket that the man opened up.

"This is a record of the answers you have given to persons who wished to spare you some hours in my company. I will ask you these questions. You will answer them. The magnitude of the unpleasantness Mister Yalta will inflict on my direction when I decide that you are lying is something I cannot recommend, and I do not direct him to provide a taste by way of illustration, because I confidently expect you to do your best to deny me what is mine by right. So. We begin. Your name."

Familiar, somehow. With pain-ease came the memory: faces a Biramie soldier was to recognize on sight, *know these people*. A blond man with almost colorless blue eyes, his hair falling over his forehead, pushed out of his eyes with an impatient gesture of his hand, which sported a cyborg brace. Witt. Witt, himself? Witt, in Gonebeyond, doing his own inquiries? No. Witt was obsessed with Andrej Koscuisko, and Koscuisko was a Ship's Inquisitor. Witt wasn't in Gonebeyond Space. Andrej Koscuisko was.

That dropped the odds in Givros' favor even further toward null; but he would fight. He would resist. It was his duty, his determination, his survival, and now it was his opportunity as well. If he kept the truth from Andrej Koscuisko—if he held firm even face-to-face with Black Andrej—he would be celebrated, lauded, held in awe, and he would be invincible. No one in the history of Biramie had ever survived Koscuisko: the victory was his to win, if only he could hold on to his story.

They were several days traveling on a Langsarik deep space carrier out of Port Delgacie before the first of the prisoners had been ready to have a meaningful conversation with him. Once his prisoner had been well started things had gone very smoothly, but Andrej was still having trouble making up his mind about whether that was the preferred outcome.

Givros sat bound into a heavy chair, now, not so much to restrain him as to keep him from falling out of it. His knees would take their time—there was a lot of bruised bone capsule, frayed connective tissue, sheer physical insult to recover from, and he might always know by the ache of it when the weather was going to turn: but the conservative approach had served Andrej well. He was no longer required to inflict thus-and-such a degree of damage in order to satisfy the Protocols. It was no longer the case that the prisoners would be expected to die or to be killed.

The scroller on the right of the flatfile docket strobed politely at him, once. Follow-up question from the woman heading this team, the one he thought of as Miss Crownéd from the heavy braid she wore wrapped around her head like the wheat-crown of an unmarried Dolgorukij woman of gentle blood. *Location holding slaves.*

Andrej frowned—he was going to have to suspend the debriefing until tomorrow, if Givros' kidneys were not to suffer irreparable damage from more doses of the babbler than Andrej wanted to administer—but put the question. He wasn't sure he had until "tomorrow," whenever that was. *Fisher Wolf* was due to leave the protection of its berth within the freighter and make for the Couveraine vector on its own.

"We know slaves are not held at Couveraine itself." Brachi Stildyne had had more chairs brought with the one Givros was in; one for Yalta, and one for himself. He was sitting behind Andrej making little all-but-subsonic sounds in his throat when he thought Andrej was getting distracted. "Where are they held, before they are brought to market?" Hundreds of them, Andrej had been told. Captured from small independent settlements, selected for marketability, carried away.

Stildyne could bear torture rooms because his childhood had left him relatively unmoved at the sight of suffering and able to shield himself from empathy. Yalta was careful not to take advantage of an opportunity to increase suffering, but his uncomplicated pleasure in the work of his hands could be difficult for Andrej to bear. He and Yalta shared the appetite. Andrej remembered what it tasted like, the joy of inflicting atrocious agony in the service of the Bench for the sake of pure gratification.

The days were over. He was out. Not free; he could not have forgotten exactly who he was had he tried, but any work he did now for Nurail spymasters came with clear expectations that the dirty work would be done as cleanly as Andrej could do it.

He was free to almost hope Givros would lie. Then Andrej would meet Yalta's eyes and Yalta would put the shaft of the semi-rigid cane he held across the front of Givros' knees gently enough—just as a reminder—to be followed up with a correction, if Givros didn't heed the warning, a sharp swift brutal stroke that would be so strict and stern in Givros' condition that it would make the predator in Andrej's nature jump with eagerness for Yalta to strike again.

If Andrej could not in fairness let Yalta strike again, at least perhaps just press the cane more firmly against the exquisitely painful creases that the penitence-board had put deep beneath Givros' kneecaps, or perhaps just rub a little bit two and fro to remind Givros that he should answer candidly. Truthfully.

Andrej had learned that Yalta could be relied upon to not exceed the boundaries Andrej established for him. Yalta was a natural sadist. He'd sought out the Malcontent for the protection of those around him, praying for some way in which he could serve the Holy Mother's purpose as she had made him. The Saint shielded him from criminal excess, and kept him—and everybody around him—safe.

Holding pens. Pens at Holding. It was hard to extract meaning from Givros' whispered words; he was long past any normal conversational exchange. *Market prep, Biruck.*

"Do better," Andrej suggested. "Where are these holding pens? Where is Biruck?" The prisoner didn't deserve Yalta's appetite, or Andrej's. He'd fought hard and stubbornly against the tortures Andrej had inflicted; but a man whose entire energy was fixed so firmly on withstanding terrific pain had little attention left to guard against the action of a speak-serum.

It was the babbler drug that had betrayed Givros. Andrej could have had this exhausted, fearful submission in time on the strength of the penitence board's torture alone, but it would have been unnecessary prolongation of suffering, and there were time constraints.

He could see Yalta's fingers tighten ever so slightly around the cane in his hand, but Andrej gave a minute little shake of his head. Givros was not attempting to defy him. Givros was simply thinking very hard. *Freighter standing off Holding and Couveraine. Biruck. Holding camp. Holding. Danais vector. First harmonic, short hop.*

Andrej waited. He didn't like to think of what conditions might be like in a place Givros had called a "holding pen." He knew the history of the Dolgorukij Combine, and of the Sarvaw nations particularly. There'd been slave camps, holding pens, brutal "market prep." One of his own ancestors had been responsible for some of the worst atrocities against a captive population that Andrej had dreamed possible— before he'd joined Fleet and gained bitter knowledge of reality.

His scroller strobed once more. *New vector for* Ragnarok *to map. Thank you, your Excellency, done for now, stand down and come away.*

So they were done. It was time for Givros to have stronger pain-ease, then, and be taken to the freighter's infirmary. Andrej wouldn't do the examination and initial therapy himself: he'd never made a mistake with a prisoner-turned-patient, but negative proof was no proof, and a man who knew his vulnerabilities did not take chances.

"Mister Yalta," Andrej said, knowing that Yalta could take the message from Andrej's tone of voice. "Med-team, if you please." Behind him Andrej could sense Brachi Stildyne, standing up, stretching. Yawning.

"I'll go frighten up something to eat," Stildyne said, because he'd know Andrej was going to want to stand in the shower for as long as it took to wrestle the wolf that made him who he was to heel. "See you in gather-room?" Where they'd join the wolf-pack, who'd once been his bond-involuntary Security assigned. That would be good. He was fond of them, and deeply in their debt. "Bring a bottle."

Before Andrej had come to Gonebeyond, he and Stildyne had been nine years together and more, officer of assignment and chief of security. During the hell-days of Captain Lowden's command, Stildyne and the others had elected themselves Andrej's protectors against his own ferociously self-destructive drunks, the psychosis of self-hatred that consumed him every time he'd lost himself to his own bestial appetites in Secured Medical.

It might well have been no more than their own hatred of Captain Lowden for the casual floggings he imposed on them, or for Lowden's murder of their crewmate Lipkie Bederico by slow torture: at least at the beginning. They had all become more than that to one another.

"Give me an hour," Andrej said. Above all there was Brachi Stildyne, his self-same on the model in the great Dolgorukij saga of Dasidar and Dyraine—his shield-wall and close companion to be honored as his best and closest friend, comfort and counselor, each unto the other till the end of time as the Holy Mother had blessed them into each other's keeping. Tikhon and Dasidar had formed a bond, in the Saga, that had forever after defined the culturally honored and honorable ideal of passionate masculine romantic friendship for all of the Dolgorukij nations.

Tikhon had survived Dasidar by years; and although it was Andrej who had the wealth and the blood of a Dasidar—Stildyne who possessed the great heart of a hero—Andrej had had to face the fact that Dolgorukij outlived most hominids in years Standard, and Stildyne's background would come to tell on him as he grew older. It was what it was. He wished Stildyne—and all the wolves in the pack—would step out of harm's way, but that wasn't who they were.

The Malcontent's debriefing team traveled with specialty medical personnel who knew what sorts of things could happen to people. They took charge of the prisoner, now semi-conscious in a well-dosed haze in which there was no pain and no fear.

Yalta had taken up the cane and the penitence-board before the medical team arrived, discreetly. Respectfully. "Well done, Mister Yalta," Andrej said quietly. "As always. I appreciate your support." It freed him from having to seek trained hands from other sources, and he was determined never to call upon the men he'd stolen from Jurisdiction and the *Ragnarok* to do him such service ever again.

Yalta bowed, formally, and left the room. The cleaners would come. No blood to be washed away, this time, but equipment was to be removed, the room returned to strict anonymity. Andrej made his way to his quarters to wash and change, so that he could go and take a meal with his people.

Standing at the lip of the forward cargo loading ramp Medith Riggs chopped off on the final line item of the manifest with an only slightly exaggerated gesture of self-satisfaction, because she was temporarily by herself in *Fisher Wolf*'s main cargo bay and she had good reasons to be satisfied with herself. When a person completed a complicated task in a better-than-anybody-else-could-have-done-it manner she had a right to acknowledge it, if only to herself.

Her client ship was the Kospodar thula *Fisher Wolf*, an elite armed courier out of the Arakcheyek shipyards in the Dolgorukij Combine; and what it was doing out here in Gonebeyond space was a peculiarity in its own right, but none of her business. Its crew, the ex-bond-involuntaries that Andrej Koscuisko had sent out here into the safety of no-man's-land, had a more obvious and understandable reason for being where they were: keeping clear of Jurisdiction, yes, obviously.

It was coming to be the fashion in the Nurail and Langsarik shipping communities in which Medith worked to call the crew of the *Fisher Wolf* its "wolf-pack," because "former bond-involuntary Security troops once assigned to Ship's Inquisitor Andrej Koscuisko Jay Eff Ess *Ragnarok*" got to be too much to keep saying over and over again. She'd been working cargo load for the *Fisher Wolf* for nearly two years now and she knew them, the wolves, their Security Chief Stildyne, and their Cousin Stanoczk who was Chief's lover but also incidentally the Malcontent agent responsible for their custody of *Fisher Wolf*.

Knew the lot, but the other man less so, the one that the wolves were having a hard time figuring out how to refer to amongst themselves. That one was Andrej Koscuisko, because as bond-involuntaries calling Koscuisko anything but "the officer" or "his Excellency" was apparently a violation of their conditioning and she wasn't going to think about what that had once meant to them even though it didn't anymore.

They weren't being punished by their governors for failure to do exactly as they were told in exactly the right way any more, because Koscuisko had removed their governors. The ingrained expectation of punishment was harder to manage, but it was getting better, over time, and she knew, because she'd been there. So they called Koscuisko "Doctor." And "Koscuisko." Sometimes "oor Anders" when it was the Nurail Robert St. Clare talking, but never "Andrej." It was a work in progress.

One way or the other, Medith minded her own business and kept out of theirs. That was the code of the cargo handler's guild, to the extent that there was one in Gonebeyond space, and it had worked well enough for her—apparently—that she'd gotten to be just about the A-number-one expert in stowing cargo on the only thula in Gonebeyond, a challenge redoubled by the existence of the shielding for a main battle cannon that ran the length of her main cargo bay and complicated things.

Courier ships didn't port main battle cannons. Main battle cannons were for cruiser-killer battlewagons like the *Ragnarok*. What it was doing here was anybody's guess, but none of her business, so it really didn't matter either way. She collected her billable hours and her pay packets, and watched the experience mount up in her master personnel record; time on a courier like *Fisher Wolf* was worth three times as much as that spent on a small family freighter, because of the complexity of the task.

Fisher Wolf had certainly provided her with complex tasks in the past. This one appeared to be a clinic of some sort, to go by its manifest; and how it had gotten to *Fisher Wolf* was its own added bonus in cargo complexity, because the family freighter *Perigot* that she'd picked up on Delgacie had unloaded on the deep-space freighter *Sampran*, one of the real behemoth-class freighters, and a cargo handler usually didn't get close to one of those until they were quite a bit older than she was.

She hadn't been surprised to find *Fisher Wolf* waiting, because the wolf-pack had been hiding out at Delgacie with the family freighter and they went together. She hadn't had to stow the special cargo they'd picked up there. It wasn't that she didn't know they'd brought prisoners with them; just that she knew how to keep clear.

So her part of the task load was accomplished. She could retreat to her hammock in the main cargo bay where she liked to sling it, because the cargo bay was her domain and she didn't care to bunk with the wolves though she'd bunked all together on real family freighters before.

The forward cargo bay was clear of special cargo, now, so she could go there too, and not be bothered by the rest of the crew supervising cabin refresh and catching up on their regularly scheduled maintenance and generally meddling as much as possible in other peoples' tasks like ship's crews everywhere. Access to some of the thula's weapons systems were through main cargo bay. Lek Kerenko sang to himself when he was working on the swivels.

She could hear him now, through the open hatchway down into

one of the swivel gun nests which she didn't really know were there exactly. She'd never met a swivel gun before she'd met *Fisher Wolf*. Working on machinery made Lek happy. He'd start out quietly enough, but when he got involved in his music—and apparently forgot that there was someone in the cargo bay trying to stow crates and concentrate—he got louder.

She wasn't familiar with the tune. No chance at the words, but it wasn't Standard, so it was Dolgorukij of some sort obviously. Sounded a little bit like *churn all the knobs and the furnace's gone cold again, the farmer's in the dell and the dog's run home.* There was a chorus. *Pay day buy some clay and go try to sculpt a garden, there's runions in the oven and it serves them right.*

Since she'd stepped back from the lip of the cargo bay to consider her hammock-slinging options she didn't see people coming, but clearly there was someone else outside on the tarmac and closing. Singing as well. Clear voice, mid-range, same sort of sounds in the language; *yay, hay, some would say it's a sort of stupid way to get a cherry-apple-ba-ba-nana, any, any, day.* Koscuisko, then, which was clearly even more of a surprise to Lek than it was to her, to judge from the way his head popped up out of his swivel gun nest.

Hadn't heard Koscuisko sing? That couldn't be it. Hadn't heard Koscuisko sing when he wasn't drunk, maybe, because he wasn't drunk now, as far as Medith could tell. She hadn't been surprised to see him coming to greet his friends on *Fisher Wolf*, when they'd got here. Special cargos frequently meant Andrej Koscuisko, because he was apparently Safehaven's go-to guy for developing special information when things got especially urgent or complex.

Here he was, though, with Pyotr trailing, as he paused at the foot of the cargo loading ramp and called up "Permission?" as though it were a little bit of a joke. Maybe he *was* a little drunk, but he was unquestionably in a good mood, which meant he'd been finished with his task for long enough now to have worked past it.

"Granted," she called back. Heard a little bit of a lilt in her own voice, descending tone, gran-*ted*, and shook herself mentally. Lek's tune had been ear-catching. She'd be stuck with it for the rest of the day, now. "Come aboard, Doctor." She could reasonably give permission to join her in the cargo bay. That much lay within her area of responsibility, and besides, Pyotr had given her the nod.

"Good-greeting, Riggs," Koscuisko said, as he came up the ramp, satchel in hand. "*Fisher Wolf* is off for the next place soon, as I am told, and I wouldn't want to omit my thanks to you for your care of the surgical suite. It is for a combat support hospital. I don't know if that detail is of interest to you or not, but I'm grateful regardless."

He called her "Riggs" because she'd given him her *possibly affronted but you don't know any better* face when he'd called her Miss Riggs, for the first last and only time. She hadn't taken it personally—Garrity had explained that Koscuisko simply had a formal habit that way—and he hadn't called her "Miss" anything since then. It wouldn't have hurt her to let him, she'd decided; people came from all sorts of backgrounds, in Gonebeyond. Some backgrounds were more different than others, and assumptions were made.

It was value-neutral, most of the time, but just now Medith thought she heard an assumption, and she determined that it was an unwarranted one from the very faintly disconcerted expression she could see on peoples' faces. Whether they had actually grown more expressive in the time she'd known them, or she'd simply gotten better at reading them, she hadn't decided; but there it was, one way or another. Koscuisko hadn't told Pyotr this bit of his intentions, obviously enough.

"Thank you, Doctor, but I'm coming with." She'd had the conversation with Stildyne, one they'd had more than once now. Stildyne would warn her about something in adequate detail for a rational and informed decision and suggest she step off and wait for the next job to turn up. She would decline on the grounds that a variety of work environments was required for her professional development. Stildyne would look at her for a moment or two and decide not to push his argument.

She already knew there was a war on at Couveraine, a small quiet one of limited scope; nobody had tried to conceal that from her. She also knew that cargo handlers generally speaking were less likely to be shot at than other people, though if ships were blown up, so was everybody on them, which went without saying.

Pyotr coughed, gently. Koscuisko looked back over his shoulder. "What would we do without a cargo handler, your Excellency?" It was the first time she'd ever heard them call Koscuisko that; and it startled her as much as it seemed to startle Koscuisko, though he was much better at recovering than she was. "We're looking forward to seeing where she's going to put the job on the list of qualifying experience toward her next promotion. She claims there's a list. No reason to doubt her."

It wasn't a *your Excellency* of *excuse me, we think we'd like.* Certainly not anything like a *please may we your Excellency sir.* It was a plain *ah, actually we've already settled that without you, because that's in our task set, thanks.*

"There is a special column for 'hazard of being shot at?'" Koscuisko asked thoughtfully. "Intermittent metallic sideways precipitation at speed, high-impact low-ballistic missiles?" One thing she had to give him: he thought faster than many, weighed nuances, adjusted expectations, chose a response. Very much in control of himself that way. "It is not for me to say, of course, yes. Please my excuses accept, Riggs. With only one exception I endorse the judgment of these gentlemen absolutely. I go away now, covered in confusion and chagrin, happy of your help in unpacking the hospital."

There was some kind of an undercurrent of a shared stream of thought in there somewhere. The wolves had been bond-involuntaries, and Koscuisko had been Ship's Inquisitor, so they'd seen him at his worst. They apparently thought well of Koscuisko all the same, and Medith had a solid notion that it wasn't simply gratitude for freeing them of governors. Koscuisko had reservations about that, but it was an old issue, and it was between them, and she wasn't going in the water.

"Happy to take a delayed retransmit on that, Doctor." The basic impulse had been positive. *That* she didn't reject. It was always nice to be appreciated.

So Koscuisko smiled, and went forward to stow his personal effects in the best cabin. Pyotr smiled and went back with him. Lek stood head-and-shoulders in the swivel gun nest looking after Koscuisko for a moment thoughtfully. A year in Gonebeyond, and they were all still dealing with adjustment to life without little monsters in their brains; mostly very well, with the occasional explosion.

The most important person in a bond-involuntary's life was their officer of assignment, well, apart from each other, of course. That's who Koscuisko had been. Nobody had told Koscuisko where to go, no, there hadn't seemed to be any particular resentment of Koscuisko that she'd detected. But they might have just successfully and politely told him where to get off, which Medith took to be a milestone.

Lek dropped down out of sight into the swivel gun emplacement to pick up where he'd left off in his maintenance checklists, singing quietly to himself; and Medith went to sling her hammock in cargo bay forward, amongst the crates of Koscuisko's surgical suite outbound for Couveraine.

Danyo Pefisct—Chief Medical Officer, Ship's Inquisitor, on board of the Jurisdiction Fleet Ship *Sondarkit*, returning to his ship of assignment from down-leave—popped the last dose of a high-end if highly illegal restorative into his mouth, breaking the seal between his back teeth and sighing with satisfaction as he felt his senses sharpen.

The Captain, it seemed, wanted to see him the moment he returned to the ship. He needed to be alert, since he was hardly rested. It had been a good down-leave. Haspirzak Proper, where the Third Judge had her Chambers, was always good down-leave for Danyo, because the headquarters of the completely legal Witt business empire was there, and Chancellor Witt gave the absolute best parties in known Space.

Anybody who smelled the fragrance of sweet briar-root and lilacs on his breath would know what he'd been eating. That was part of the cachet, enjoying black-market Controlled List drugs ordinarily subject to some of the strictest pharmaceutical controls there were. Conspicuous consumption was a Witt hallmark; and if the drug was part of a torturer's tool-kit, what of it? Danyo was a Judicial torturer, wasn't he?

For prisoners in Secured Medical the medication was good for forcing the most tortured souls to full awareness of their agony. Which meant that for anybody else it was simply the best thing after a night of possibly rather over-done revelry. And that in turn meant that Danyo's mind was sharp, his thinking clear, his recall of the unusual events at Witt's feast-table last night perfect if not perfectly comprehensible.

There had been a woman seated in the place of honor to whom Witt had presented Danyo, rather than the other way around: Bench Intelligence Specialist Jils Ivers. So far as Danyo knew, she was the first Bench specialist he'd ever met—one of a few silent and shadowy agents of the Bench answerable to the First Judge alone and none other, with powers of extraordinary discretion to intervene in any crisis as they saw fit in the service of the rule of Law and the Judicial order.

But now that the First Judge was simply one among her peers, to whom did a Bench specialist report? Was Ivers at Witt's party because she was looking for a job? She'd made remarks to Danyo about *his* job, under cover of the dessert course. Incomprehensible suggestions with respect to the employment potentials in Gonebeyond space for Ship's Inquisitors who had become redundant to requirements.

Through the clearwall window of the shuttle Danyo watched the activity in *Sondarkit's* open maintenance atmosphere as he neared; and brooded. He'd heard about Inquisitors who'd run away to Gonebeyond, and he'd told Ivers so. Chancellor Witt followed the careers of Fleet's Inquisitors like celebrities, and had all the best gossip. Danyo himself owed his privileged position on Witt's guest list to his Inquisitorial rank.

Why would anybody trade the privileged billet of Chief Medical Officer, Ship's Inquisitor, for a resource-starved bare-bones clinic in Gonebeyond space, he'd asked Ivers. He'd heard all about what had happened to Beele, when she'd deserted. And the point, Ivers had replied, just as the after-dessert course had started coming around, was that people *had* heard from Doctor Beele. Danyo hadn't known quite how to take that: had it been a threat, or merely a warning? But he'd set it aside for further contemplation.

As his shuttle crossed the containment barrier into the *Sondarkit's* maintenance atmosphere to dock, Danyo saw there was a visiting ship, drawn up to one of the larger loading platforms. It was larger than most courier ships, perhaps half the length of a light freighter; with a vaguely menacing profile, something like a famous aquatic monster out of the scaries in which Danyo had delighted as a child. Primitive, efficient, and beautiful in its savagery. Danyo recognized it. The Kospodar thula *Haspirzak*, named for its Judiciary.

There were people gathered on the thula's loading slip. Some of *Sondarkit's* crew members were clustered around what looked like a pile of bivvy-kits. Danyo frowned. Seven men. He recognized them: they were his bond-involuntary Security slaves, and their only reason for existence was to do as he told them. Whatever. Whenever. Immediately, and without question.

They were criminals, each subject to trial and execution for their crimes. They'd been young, strong, fit, and above all psychologically resilient enough to survive being placed under Bond, survive careful conditioning to a rigorous standard of performance until they knew each requirement and expectation as thoroughly as agony and fear could instruct them.

Each of them with a surgically implanted "governor" linked into the pain centers in their brains that could cripple them with agony for hours if they gave him the slightest hint of reluctance, resistance, hesitation in doing as they'd been told. He knew. It was his responsibility to monitor their behavior constantly, to bring any lapses to their attention, and let the governor and their conditioning do the rest. They were nothing more than instruments of torture. They were his property.

And they were out of uniform. They weren't wearing the poison green piping at the cuffs and the collar of their overblouses, the unique distinction of a bond-involuntary. They were not standing silently at attention-rest in perfect order awaiting instruction lawful and received.

They were moving amongst the cargo crates, instead, talking, laughing, their posture loose and relaxed as that of any free man; and when they saw him they laughed, they pointed, and one of them made an obscene gesture that would earn any man on board this ship some disciplinary action, regardless of their status.

They were on Safe. So much was clear. Fleet gave Safes to bond-involuntary troops who had survived to the end of their full thirty-year sentence, to lull their governors into a state of suspended animation for the time it took to arrange remedial surgery. Once they'd been worn on a cord around a man's neck. Now they were simply injected into the muscle beneath the skin.

Safes were the only explanation. As for the gesture, there were other crew on the slip, *Sondarkit* and Haspirzak Judiciary alike; but nobody seemed to have seen it, and one or two of *Sondarkit's* own crew were smiling. Danyo didn't know what was going on: but he knew he didn't have to subject himself to this kind of undisciplined behavior.

He was to go directly to the Captain's office? Fine. Maybe he'd have a thing or two to say about bond-involuntary troops behaving like drunken hooligans with impunity. Was this what Ivers had meant to suggest? Bond-involuntaries being removed from his authority and supervision?

By the time he arrived at the Captain's office Danyo had an approach that satisfied him, and walked through the opening slants of the door with his hands clasped behind his back, his head lowered in thought. The attitude had worked well for him en route. He hadn't had to waste any powers of concentration on not-seeing the expressions on the faces of the crew he passed in the corridors, whether smugly satisfied, maliciously happy, or indifferent in a hostile sort of way.

"I've just seen the strangest thing, Captain—"

No use. The person behind Fonderell's desk wasn't Fonderell. A rather young man in a perfectly tailored Judicial uniform, blond, an open expression in his clear blue eyes. It wasn't the knee-length overblouse worn by a judge in Chambers; it was simple, modest, practical, and deep dark green. The official, if informal, dress worn by a Bench Judge Presiding. But the man was a man, and there hadn't been a male deemed fit to exercise the rule of Law at its highest levels for so long it might as well have been mythological.

"Will this be Doctor Pefisct, Captain Fonderell?" the young man asked, clear-voiced, calm, with the very most subtle shading of *and not before time* imaginable. "Present me, please."

"Yes, your Honor." Fonderell was on his feet, standing to one side of the desk, with the First Officer beside him. Doing a much more creditable version of "attention rest" than Danyo's own bond-involuntaries, just now, though almost anybody would have done. "Doctor Danyo Pefisct, our current Chief Medical Officer. Doctor Pefisct. This is his Honor, Bat Yorvik. Haspirzak Judiciary."

Danyo knew what was expected of him, and advanced to a formal two paces to bow. "Your Honor. My apologies for my late return." Yes, he was late. So what? Nobody had told him there'd be a Judge waiting for a word. "Captain. First Officer." Judges were introduced by the title of their courts; only Bench-level judges received the simple "Haspirzak Judiciary." So it was true that Yorvik was Bench-level. Remarkable.

And the fourth person in the room, the one nearest the door, the one he hadn't noticed—in his concentration—on his way in? The Bench specialist with whom he'd shared Witt's high table. Ivers. "Please be seated," Yorvik said, to the Captain, to the First Officer. Looking around him for a chair Danyo found none ready to hand, and nobody was offering one, either.

Yorvik had a flatfile docket in front of him on the Captain's desk, with judicial seals laid open. "I've come on the Third Judge's behalf to brief you, Doctor Pefisct, on some evolutions in the relationship between the Bench and the Jurisdiction's Fleet as a whole. These changes have a significant impact on you, and it was the Third Judge's wish that you be apprised in person."

Yorvik might have been admonishing a plaintiff's representative. He might have been ordering his mid-meal. He was giving Danyo nothing to go on.

"You may be aware that the budget for the Fleet is in renewal discussions?" Yorvik asked; but didn't wait for a response from Danyo. Of course not. "And Haspirzak is not among the wealthier of the Judiciaries. We must carefully reconsider the cost versus the benefit of Fleet support, in order to ensure continued funding for programs and expenses properly within the Third Judge's purview to maintain."

Social benefit programs. Public-funded hospitals. The renowned Gelisar gardens, the jewel of Haspirzak Judiciary, to which Chancellor Witt made such generous and regular contributions, as befit any public-spirited pillar of the business community. "Your Honor," Danyo acknowledged, politely, because Yorvik had paused, clearly waiting.

"Good. Now. The Third Judge has identified several measures which, when implemented, will allow for continued full Fleet support. There is an agreement that the Inquisitorial function is no longer necessary or useful, with today's progress in drug-assisted interviewing techniques."

No, Danyo thought, keeping his face respectfully expressive of mild interest alone. *The Third Judge has never liked Ship's Inquisitors. That's what it's all about.* Yorvik turned a leaf in his docket. "I believe you may have seen the Haspirzak thula in the maintenance atmosphere, when you docked? We'll be relieving *Sondarkit* of responsibility for now-redundant Fleet resources, released by Captain Fonderell on direction."

They weren't Fonderell's resources. They were *his*. Danyo clenched a figurative fist around the outrage in his gut to shut it up, until later. "Ah, sorry, no," he said. He wasn't on notice. He could lie to a judge all he wanted to. He knew the parameters of prohibited degrees of deception as well as any man, even a boy judge. "Might one presume you mean my bond-involuntaries, your Honor?"

He wasn't fooling anybody. There wasn't a shadow of a grin anywhere on Yorvik's face that Danyo could detect, and yet he knew that Yorvik was smiling. Damn him. "The Third Judge has taken two significant measures to reduce unnecessary costs. The first is the granting of revocation of Bond to all souls currently under Bond in Haspirzak Judiciary. So in the strictest sense, Doctor Pefisct, no, they are no longer bond-involuntaries, and therefore not yours."

It was no secret that bond-involuntaries were expensive. The surgeries, the training, the indoctrination; the replacement cost, because the failure rate was high. There was the additional cost to the Bench for every one who survived his sentence, as well: accumulated pay with interest compounded over thirty years; full pension benefits; free transport on any Jurisdiction hull on demand.

Ivers had suggested that there was to be a surplus of Inquisitors. He couldn't say she hadn't warned him, howsoever obliquely. "One is heartily glad for them," he said. "I wish them all the best." They wouldn't get it. He couldn't imagine any of those people being able to go home, not in any real sense. They'd be too marked by their experience. And who could say whether their homes even wanted them back, when they'd been torturer's assistants all this time? "The function of Ship's Inquisitor to be made redundant, that's your next point, yes?"

He had to be more careful. He was being rude. But he had a right to feel frustrated, surprised, even angry that such unilateral action had been taken with regard to men with whom he had shared a challenging assignment, without notifying him. Maybe they'd have told him up front, if he'd come back to *Sondarkit* when he'd been supposed to.

Yorvik had turned another page. There was a form, there, a printed version of a record Danyo had seen on-screen on one occasion or another; an important form, duty assignment, duty station, rank, accompanying salary. "Haspirzak Judiciary, and I'll be very blunt here, has no further use for Ship's Inquisitors. The Third Judge sees no reason why Fleet need continue to fund a senior officer whose fundamental medical qualifications are restricted to executing the Protocols."

So he was to lose his job, as Ivers had hinted. Danyo could see the sense of it, from Haspirzak's point of view. That didn't mean he could reasonably be expected to like it; and he opened his mouth to say words like *violation of employment contract* and *recently reconfirmed at grade and rank* and things of that sort, but he didn't get the chance. Maybe just as well, he thought.

Yorvik was so calm. Even mildly sympathetic. *Nothing personal,* Yorvik's tone of voice seemed to say. *Strictly efficient use of tax revenues.*

"There are already senior medical officers on board every Fleet ship with the experience and abilities to perform the role of Chief Medical Officer, and most of them are being paid close to grade for Ship's Surgeon already," Yorvik said. "Your role and responsibilities are to be re-evaluated, Doctor Pefisct, and a placement found for you within Infirmary at the level and specialization appropriate to your medical qualifications."

Now he was doomed. He was to be reduced in grade, reduced in authority, broken all the way down to junior-most officer in charge of virology, except there was no dedicated virologist in Infirmary on the Jurisdiction Fleet Ship *Sondarkit*. There was a specialist, a senior technician, but she'd had the benefit of years of continuing education, which meant Danyo had no hope of supplanting her. He'd been a good student; he would have been a good virologist. But with no practical experience since his graduation? He didn't have a chance.

He'd be slotted into general clinic duty. He'd done no other hands-on medical work since he'd first taken up his Writ to Inquire: which would logically be cancelled, as the next step, if it hadn't been revoked already.

They'd have to give him some credit for service in that role, but he knew what the service allowances were because he was responsible for finding ways to deny people promotion—or at least that was how he'd always approached it, kind of a game—and it was a three-to-one conversion for general practice. He'd be a supernumerary junior clinician. His senior technicians made more money than that, and had more authority in clinic. He'd lost everything.

"Do you have any questions about the impact of these changes on your future in Fleet?" Yorvik asked. His voice had gentled, as if to present himself as a compassionate man. Maybe he *was* compassionate. It wasn't every day a man was kicked in the stomach and then into the sewer, deprived of Infirmary command, robbed of the rank and authority that was his by right as a Fleet officer as well as a Judicial one. "If not. Resources will be made available to you to answer any concerns that may arise going forward. I'll be on my way, now, Captain."

Yorvik stood up. Fonderell and First Officer were on their feet in an instant. With calm and deliberate tread, with calm and benevolent eye, Judge Yorvik left the room, nodding at each of them in turn. The Bench specialist turned as he passed to follow him, blank-faced, without a word spoken. To go back to his ship, a Kospodar thula, an elite courier, Haspirzak Judiciary's own. Taking Danyo's bond-involuntaries with them. He might as well be taking Danyo's career.

"This must come as a considerable shock," Captain Fonderell said, returning to his usual side of the desk, sitting down. "If I'd known beforehand, I would have told you. It's as much of a surprise to us as to you, I'm afraid, unless you're better connected than we are, of course." Fonderell wasn't gloating, Danyo decided, for what that was worth. There was no fellow feeling in his voice; no concern for a comrade or a peer; but no gleefulness either. Much.

Fonderell had something more to say, apparently. "We'll be making a temporary appointment to the position of Chief Medical Officer, per regulation. In light of the fact that she's been second-in-command here, even before your arrival, I'd anticipate calling on Doctor Maparone." Of course. Why not. It didn't matter. "We won't be making a shipwide announcement until you've had a chance to transition with her. We're due at Quanto in six days. You can take some additional leave there, if you'd like. Come back to new quarters and a fresh start. All right?"

New quarters. From the suite of the Chief Medical Officer to what could only be the tiny room of an officer so junior as to be subordinate to any senior technician on board, in a practical sense. Danyo thought fast.

"Thank you, Captain." He supposed he was lucky they didn't expect him out by end of shift. Six days? That would give him time to sanitize his quarters carefully, to make sure he wasn't leaving anything interesting behind. "I'll start to build a transition plan as soon as I've unpacked. I'm not sure there's a standard procedure in place for decommissioning Secured Medical. I'll try to find out."

He owed Chancellor Witt a thank-you note. He'd been Witt's guest, he'd spent the night, he'd attended a gala, it would be only polite. He'd mention expecting to see Witt at Quanto, and maybe Witt would even come himself—it wasn't every day a suddenly surplus Ship's Inquisitor suggested a meeting.

Witt had shared secrets with Danyo before: his extensive entertainment library of highly illegal black-market records of Judicial torture, for instance, or his casual presents of repurposed drugs from the Controlled List. There was an entire shadowy world to the Witt organization that almost certainly extended into Gonebeyond.

He had six days to get through somehow. Then he'd be able to talk to some officer from Witt's organization, offer his professional services, strike a bargain. He wasn't going to end up working some Bench specialist's angle in what amounted to a charity hospital out in the back of beyond. Witt would have much better use for him than that; and in return Witt would make arrangements to get Danyo free and clear of Fleet forever.

CHAPTER TWO

The Langsarik Coalition

Jils Ivers had flown the Haspirzak thula from Haspirzak Proper—from the JFS *Sondarkit*—to Psimas, where seven former bond-involuntary troops were to undergo surgery to remove their governors and begin a two-year process of becoming free again. Three days. From there she, and Judge Bat Yorvik, were to travel on into Gonebeyond space.

She meant to embed herself with the Langsarik coalition's military action against the criminal Biramie organization. Yorvik was coming to observe the execution of a coordinated and cooperative police action as a representative from Haspirzak Judiciary; and begin, perhaps, to lay the foundation for a legal relationship that would help define Gonebeyond as a politically autonomous force in its own right.

They had to change shuttles at Psimas, because Yorvik's assignment was an informal one and the thula was a powerful symbol of Judicial dominance. The Third Judge—whose mission this was, at heart—meant to tread very carefully, doing everything she could to avoid the false impression that Yorvik was the advance scout for a Haspirzak takeover in Gonebeyond.

It had been rather tense on the thula from Haspirzak to Psimas with seven newly freed bond-involuntaries on board, a constant and elevated stress level from forward to fins generated by the sheer emotional upheaval they were experiencing. It'd get worse before it got better, she was afraid, and the man Janforth, for one, seemed altogether too likely to bolt before he could benefit from psychological counseling and knowledgeable emotional support.

As it happened she'd misjudged not the likelihood, but the timing. Halfway to cargo bay close, a dockmaster came out onto the tarmac of the launch-lane where Jils' courier was taking on medical supplies for whichever of the Langsarik Coalition's clinics came first.

The dockmaster had someone with her: Janforth Ifrits, with his bivvy-bag. In civilian clothes, now, and very pale, the knuckles of one hand where he clutched the strap of his bivvy bone-white; but unquestionably determined. "Your pardon, Dame Ivers," the dockmaster said. "Mister Ifrits says he's coming with you."

The dockmasters on duty all knew who she'd brought in with her. *Sondarkit's* liberated bond-involuntaries were the first to arrive at the Psimas Detention Facility, but there would be more, and now that the Third Judge had chopped off on her final agreement with Fleet she didn't care who knew it. So the dockmaster knew Ifrits was man Reborn, even if few people could truly grasp all that Ifrits and the others had endured.

Janforth Ifrits was watching Jils patiently, as if waiting for her to catch up. "Thank you, dockmaster," Jils said. "I'll take it from here." It hadn't been a day. She couldn't imagine that Psimas had had resources and preparations ready to conduct a complex surgery at such short notice.

Even if Ifrits had been first in line he couldn't possibly have had surgery, recuperated, and been released from Infirmary within twelve hours of arrival. Therefore Ifrits hadn't had the surgery. He was still porting an active governor. The only thing between Janforth and disaster was a Safe.

"Tell me what is on your mind," Jils suggested. She could see Yorvik coming across the tarmac with his kit; he'd made a detour to local judicial Chambers to set any last-minute administrative tasks in order. She could see his subtle hesitation when he saw her there with Janforth; but he went on up the passenger loading ramp into the courier without remark. Minding his own business.

The transit had been a challenge for Yorvik, Jils knew. He was the one who most of all represented the system that had enslaved those people and put them to years of torture. He and Jils had divided the hours of detailed briefings due each man between them, one-on-one with people who knew more about the business of executing the Protocols than anybody apart from the Ship's Inquisitor himself.

From what Jils had seen and heard from Bat Yorvik during their transit, she had fewer concerns than before over whether he knew when to keep his mouth shut and listen. His behavior had been nothing less than prudent and proper, just and judicious—calm and compassionate—throughout. She'd been impressed. It gave her good hope of Yorvik's future, and that of his mission.

"Free passage on any Fleet or Bench carrier," Janforth said, quoting from the list of privileges accrued to him in his new status. "This—" he nodded at the courier—"is an official Bench carrier, isn't it? And you're going to Gonebeyond. So I claim free passage. Take me with you."

He had a point. He *had* earned that right, even if Fleet hadn't taken the full thirty years off of him before releasing him to enjoy it. If it was his desire to go to Gonebeyond all she could say in the matter was to wish him every success. "All true things," Jils said, nodding. "If you'll permit me, though, my question for information only. What about your surgery?"

She was going to have a moral problem with herself if she let a man walk functionally naked into an unregulated environment with a governor that might wake up at any time, if the Safe should fail. No. She'd never heard of a Safe failing. But there simply wasn't a large enough "people on Safe for extended periods of time" sample from which to draw a statistically valid conclusion.

Except Andrej Koscuisko's Bonds, of course. They'd been issued Safes at Taisheki Station, because Captain ap Rhiannon's actions had placed them all in an impossible situation through no fault of their own. Then Koscuisko had decided to arbitrarily remove their governors in order to smuggle them out into Gonebeyond, and none of them had died during the process: but they were Andrej Koscuisko's security. There was a unique relationship. It couldn't be used in a prediction model.

"I hear there's someone in Gonebeyond who's done five of them already. At Safehaven Medical Center," Janforth said, and Jils could have closed her eyes and breathed a sigh of frustration. Koscuisko, of course. A force for chaotic disruption wherever he went, and he didn't even have to be here to create one. "He'll do it. I'll be on Safe till then. So. When do we leave?"

She could challenge Ifrits on whether or not Koscuisko would be willing to pull Janforth's governor, but she'd know there wasn't really any question. Of course Koscuisko would. And do it correctly. She heard things. She knew. "Ask inside for a berth, we'll be three days. Do you have any experience on a courier in this size and class?"

She thought she saw relief in Janforth's eyes, but it came and went too swiftly for her to be sure. Bond-involuntaries didn't show emotion. Even on Safe, his conditioning would continue to protect Janforth from discipline no longer in force.

"Ah, no. But navs-and-propulsion on a Wolnadi fighter." Bond-involuntaries didn't use personal pronouns because they didn't have a legal identity. It was just the first of many things Janforth had to un-learn. "Appreciate the opportunity to qualify on a civilian craft."

Transferable skills. That was good. Sooner or later the crew of the *Fisher Wolf* was going to want to partner up and settle down, or retire, or join a cloistered religious community of some sort. Garol wasn't the only Bench specialist thinking about the future of Gonebeyond. "We'll be off in an hour," Jils said. "You can shadow on navs-and-propulsion for the duration, if you'd like. But I'd like to talk with you again, once we're on vector. If you're willing, of course."

Janforth wanted out, fine, it was his right. She didn't like his choice but that was her problem, not his. Koscuisko wasn't at Safehaven, however; he was in Couveraine, or en route to Couveraine, or would have just arrived at Couveraine, so once they were on vector she could tell Janforth that she was taking him to Couveraine instead of Safehaven. He'd be going to Couveraine one way or the other because that was where the courier was going. He could find his own way from there, after he'd talked to Andrej Koscuisko.

Maybe *Fisher Wolf* would be there as well, maybe the crew would be willing to take Janforth in and help him through the rough patches Jils was sure were coming ahead. Maybe everything would work out for the best in the end, against all odds. But the odds were long and strong and Jils didn't like them: she could only hope.

After the humiliations Danyo had experienced at the hands of Haspirzak Judiciary, the courtesies extended to him by Witt and his organization at Quanto were all the more gratifying.

He'd been met at the launch-field by a luxury groundcar, his luggage expertly managed by uniformed valet staff. The route they'd taken had turned away from busy ground transit lanes into a broad quiet boulevard generously shielded by mature flowering trees, and when they'd pulled at last into the graveled drive of a great mansion Danyo had found Chancellor Witt himself standing at the top of the grand stairs, waiting for him.

That had been hours ago. There'd been dinner, but a small one, just Danyo and Witt and a few of Witt's officers. Only seven courses, but Witt was served the finest Dolgorukij elite cuisine so they were all exquisite. It was one of the many ways in which Witt's otherwise risible obsession with Andrej Koscuisko enriched the lives of his guests even beyond the usual amusement Danyo derived from trying to guess what Witt had had done since the last time Danyo had seen him.

Had he had the follicles of his hair genetically engineered to a finer, flatter Andrej Koscuisko standard, rather than just styled? Progressed toward a more exact High Aznir accent in his voice studies? Had more work done to change the shape of his fingers, had his cheekbones adjusted again, sculpted his ears? Had the time come for him to start to work on his actual height, since Chancellor Witt had started into adulthood half-a-head taller than Andrej Koscuisko?

For once Danyo didn't even care. He was too grateful to Witt for rescuing him, for the beautiful suite provided to him, the team of servants at beck and call to cater to his every wish, the meal and the wine and Witt's deference. Witt had even made a point of bringing his new pastry-chef with him, in order to honor Danyo at table.

For the six days it had taken the *Sondarkit* to make the transit from Haspirzak Proper to Quanto, Danyo had been seething in internal outrage, careful all the while to keep the depth and intensity of his resentful fury pressed down out of the way as firmly as he could.

He wasn't sure he'd been completely successful, but he'd decided that that was in his favor. If he'd been serene and accepting, people might too easily have realized he had an escape plan ready, and Infirmary staff by and large had restrained themselves from overt gloating. Maybe they'd just been saving it for when he'd been moved into as small a berth as would be granted a supernumerary virologist. The laugh was on them. He wasn't going back to *Sondarkit*. Witt could get him out of here before Fleet knew he was gone, a deserter maybe but in Gonebeyond where Fleet couldn't touch him.

He'd drawn up a plan for the transition. He'd disposed of the outstanding documentation awaiting his approval so that his successor would have a clean start. He'd issued himself a generous supply of several expensive medications with recreational applications, and though his Chief of Pharmacy had hesitated for a very brief moment, she'd authorized them—for the last time, and they both knew it. His authority to demand such perquisites would be withdrawn completely soon enough.

Nor had he been subjected to the indignity of a search prior to his departure. That was just as well. He hadn't drawn those doses for his own use, but for currency; and in any other circumstances the discovery of the number and denominations of the generic currency markers he'd amassed over the years would have triggered an immediate Security investigation. Danyo no longer enjoyed the immunity of an Inquisitor from prosecution for almost any crime.

His duty uniform blouses—with the white Infirmary badge lined through with the red line of a Ship's Inquisitor—would have been a doubtless appreciated gift for Witt, even if Witt could only ever have worn them privately. No chance of that, however. They'd already been removed from his quarters when he returned from Haspirzak. Only his duty whites had remained. At least they hadn't stripped off his rank; yet.

All of that was behind him now. Cradled in the luxurious comfort of an armchair, deep within an intimately dimmed private room in Witt's mansion, Danyo sipped his drink with profound gratification. Cortac brandy. Danyo didn't know much about cortac, but it was Dolgorukij, and it was Witt's, so he knew it was the very best cortac brandy in known Space, smuggled away from the Dolgorukij Autocrat's household itself, perhaps.

True to Witt's obsession, the room was coded for Koscuisko with what Danyo presumed to be ancestral elegance; a baroque rhyti-service, weapons on the walls, and an icon-lamp in one corner, in front of a little shrine of Saint Andrej Filial Piety. With a relic, perhaps. Danyo wondered from time to time what Danyo's staff thought about the whole Koscuisko thing, really.

It was rhyti that Witt was drinking; perhaps because—according to all of the best rumors—when Koscuisko drank it was apparently to excess, and alone. "I have business interests in Gonebeyond, Doctor

Pefisct, you know that it is true. I do not surprise you." Witt sipped his rhyti, which was so hot that Danyo could smell it from where he sat. They were so close to each other that Danyo could have reached out to touch Witt's knee had he wished. He didn't wish.

Witt was still talking, meditatively, confidentially. "We knew that, yes, Haspirzak had things in motion that would affect you, so it was good fortune that the Bench specialist proposed herself for our little gathering. I hoped she would give you warning of things of which I have no official knowledge."

Because at Haspirzak, Chancellor Witt was scrupulously clean, a respected community leader. The Third Judge herself never attended any of Witt's entertainments, but Witt always received an invitation to her annual reception, along with representatives from the rest of Haspirzak's business community. The presence of a Bench specialist at Witt's party had been a peculiar signal: had it been an endorsement, though, or a threat of some sort?

"And I deeply appreciate it, your Excellency." There was no such civil rank at Haspirzak, but here in Quanto it was not out of place. And Witt loved the sound of it. "I'm afraid I didn't quite grasp the magnitude of the mistake they were making at the time. She'll be sorry, but that's none of my concern, thanks to you, Chancellor."

He was careful to ensure he never lapsed into cynical flattery. Honest gratitude for genuine favors was one thing, and a little flowery language went a long way. But Witt for all his ridiculous obsessions was an intelligent man, as well as an immensely powerful one. Danyo knew quite well that his value in Witt's eyes lay primarily in Danyo's position as a social token, above and beyond his usefulness in validating the authenticity of Witt's extensive library of black-market entertainment material. He was a status symbol. Any personal relationship they might have was incidental.

And Witt responded in kind, because that was how a Dolgorukij autocrat might phrase a gracious acknowledgement. "But that I might be in a position to recruit you, Danyo, that I never dared to dream. At just this time, and you just the man to make a success of my proposals. Truly the Holy Mother holds me in her heart."

He'd heard that idiom from other Dolgorukij, though the ones Witt had encountered had been from far different levels of society. "Tell me how I can be of service, Chancellor." He wasn't going anywhere until

Witt made it happen. And he was curious, though skeptical. None of Witt's previous hints over the years had carried the slightest hint of torture-for-hire, but he had never been so entirely obliged to Witt before as he was now, and Witt was a businessman.

"There is a Langsarik coalition in Gonebeyond space, Doctor Pefisct, and it signals that my activities are no longer to be allowed to proceed without let or hindrance."

Langsariks, Danyo thought. He maybe remembered something about Langsarik pirates, escaping Jurisdiction into Gonebeyond— some years back. He nodded; if Witt understood him to mean that he was more aware of exactly what Witt was talking about than Danyo actually was, that was what came of making assumptions, wasn't it?

"It is time to come to an understanding with them, and recruit their cooperation," Witt said. "You will be my ambassador, coming with an introductory gift that I have prepared. There is a salary attached, commensurate with that you currently enjoy; and there is also a hidden agenda, in which I have an earnest personal interest. Shall I explain?"

Danyo could easily imagine that any "hidden agenda" Witt had in mind for Gonebeyond involved his personal obsession with Andrej Koscuisko. "I am at your disposal," he said, encouragingly; because he was, of course. "This introductory gift, it's a field hospital? Surgical clinic?" Clearly something medical. Otherwise there'd be no point in sending a physician to accompany. "Where does Koscuisko fit in?"

"Ah, I am glad you have asked," Witt said, with a smile of somewhat sinister self-satisfaction. "There will be raids, in the very near future. Of this I am reliably informed. Field medical resources will be welcome, but there will also be the Nurail intelligence moving with the action, and they will be bringing their best field-expedient interrogator with them. They will naturally post him to the field hospital we send, so you will be in proximity. That is where this comes in."

This. Witt drew something that looked very familiar to Danyo out of the front plaquet of his overblouse, a small cylindrical object. A toothpick of a particular design and decoration, just like the one from Danyo's grooming-set—just like the one he carried habitually in his pocket. Puzzled, Danyo reached into his own overblouse; yes, there it was. Reaching forward Witt plucked Danyo's toothpick out of the palm of Danyo's hand and tossed it behind him, over his shoulder.

"One opens the cunning little cap with one's thumbnail," Witt said, and dropped the one he had into Danyo's still-upturned hand. "The virus it contains is specific to the medical profiles in Koscuisko's records, we took them from Brisinje, where he had surgery on his hand. That was two or three years ago, yes, but genetic profiles do not change."

He wouldn't have guessed it wasn't his. Holding it up to the muted light from a wall-sconce figure Danyo studied it carefully: yes, he could see a subtle little line, there towards its base.

If it was an aerosol under pressure—as he would expect—he might be able to deploy it if he assisted Koscuisko in surgery. Otherwise, all he really needed was for Koscuisko to somehow touch or inhale particles that had been contaminated by the virus. If there was the usually standard status meeting three times a day, for instance, and a person stood in proximity to the target.

"Koscuisko is exposed, Koscuisko falls ill." Danyo talked it through out loud, to be sure he and Witt were running in parallel. "If you'll excuse me for saying this in this way, your Excellency. So what?"

"So you are the virologist, it is your specialty. You are understandably perplexed by the savage progression of this infection, you fear for his life. He must go at once to a qualified hospital, and it doesn't matter whether they accept your specific suggestion—" to a hospital associated with Witt's organization, obviously—"or to any other. I will have people in place. We will take it from there."

So long as there was no potential cross-infection of related ethnicities, so long as it was truly specific enough, no one else need be endangered; and if they were, did Danyo really care? "If the virus escapes?" Engineered viruses were by definition new, young. They might do unpredictable things. There could be unfortunate over-reactions from other peoples' immune systems, more lethal than the virus itself.

"I do not mind if it is pure blackmail, *we can rush immediately equipment and medications back on the freighter that carries Koscuisko away.* I want him." There was a note of true longing there, a tender wistfulness that Danyo almost regretted for Witt's sake. Koscuisko was unlikely to requite Witt's passion in any positive sense. "I cannot truly express how much this means to me, whatever may come of it in the end."

It was a small enough price to pay for his escape, for Danyo. Maybe Witt would cut him off if he didn't make this work, but he'd be in Gonebeyond. Even if he lost Witt's support forever he'd have shown his bare ass to the Bench and pissed them good-bye.

"I think I understand." He pocketed the toothpick that wasn't. Witt would have ensured against any premature escapes, and people carried toothpicks around with them all the time. This one would become part of Danyo's existing set. He'd made good entertainment for himself from time to time by dropping it somewhere and then challenging the bond-involuntary on orderly duty with having been careless with it. He was, as Witt had said, a virologist. He could adjust on the fly. "You can rely on me, your Excellency. I'll make it work."

Now Witt nodded, rising to go to his drinks service. "I know, and thank you," Witt said. "I will see you chief medical officer of Safehaven Medical Center if I have to spend three field hospitals to buy it for you. Now. We were cheated of our evening's entertainment in Haspirzak, Danyo, because of the Bench specialist, but we are safe together now, just you and I, and this is very special material. Another drink? Very well."

And one wall of the room darkened; a holoscreen frame descended over the floor-to-ceiling bookcases with their antiquated volumes of old-fashioned paper. If they were going to be looking at "very special material" it would be old, and Danyo resigned himself to the murky images and blurred outlines that characterized evidence recovered from compromised Records in years gone past.

Witt had newer product, beautiful visuals, dimensional holovids at three-quarters scale; but they were fakes. There was a market for people who didn't care, who were willing to squint at an Andrej Koscuisko who was not quite Andrej Koscuisko and let their fantasies supply the balance of the detail. Witt showed such creative re-enactments in strictly controlled environments from time to time, but what he shared with Danyo and Danyo alone in intimate moments was the genuine article.

So here they were. The visual encoding was correct for official evidence; Andrej Koscuisko, administrative facilities, Port Rudistal. Danyo frowned. He'd seen some of this before. There was the soul in custody, Administrator Geltoi, though no longer shown by his former title on screen.

There was the purpose of the recording: Tenth Level Command Termination per the decision of the Bench for crimes committed in Geltoi's official capacity as Administrator of the Domitt Prison, Port Rudistal, during the period from and to, and so forth. By the solemn adjudication of Second Judge Sem Porr Har, Presiding.

Koscuisko's Tenth Level had dragged on for days. The copies Danyo had seen had all been Bench archive material, though, record of execution in due form; this material appeared to be unedited, which would mean it couldn't possibly be enjoyed in any three single sittings, and that it was—inevitably—going to drag. Here, for instance, Koscuisko was talking, just talking, and while Witt clearly enjoyed the native arrogance of the man for Danyo it was already a little boring.

Witt was a sensitive man. Danyo noted with regret that he'd been thinking too loudly; Witt had apparently heard him, had sensed Danyo's relative lack of interest. Because Witt leaned forward and drew in the empty air, fingers flickering in and out of a narrow beam of focused light, changing the tempo, skipping ahead.

Geltoi on four-point suspension, Koscuisko's progress clearly marked on Geltoi's body in welts that showed the force Koscuisko had put into the whiplash that had laid them down. Geltoi on his knees on the floor with his hands behind his back, wearing a sensor hood, a mask, the controller suspended from Geltoi's neck reflecting the progress of its programming. Restricted airway. Active gag reflex. Extreme visual pulses, random, searing, inescapable. Good stuff; but Witt hadn't found what he was looking for, apparently, not yet.

The things Koscuisko could do with a flensing-knife. The things he could, and would, do with the whips at his disposal. He could have simply stripped meat from bone, with that peony; with the peony the challenge was not so much making an appreciable impact, a persuasive impact, as avoiding simply killing a prisoner before three hours were up: and Koscuisko had taken days with Administrator Geltoi.

What was Witt looking for?

If this unedited material had been in the Judicial record someone would have marketed it by now. So this was what had been sent back to Fleet Orientation Station Medical, Fossum, to complete Koscuisko's certification, his qualification to be given custody of a Writ to Inquire. This wasn't from Bench offices. This was from the torture school itself. *Impressive*, Danyo thought at Witt, admiringly.

"Oh, good," Witt exclaimed suddenly. "Yes, this, this. I wanted particularly to share this with you. It is a delectable moment, have I ever seen anything its equal? I don't know."

In the Record, Danyo could see Koscuisko and Geltoi, both of them bloodied but one of them still clothed. Mostly. Koscuisko's underblouse was soiled with drying blood, his face smeared along one side where he'd pushed his hair out of his eyes or some such thoughtlessly casual gesture; he'd rolled his cuffs up well back to just below the crook of his elbow, and his trousers were no longer bloused tidily into his boots. He had a knife. He'd made an incision.

There'd only been five viewpoints that Danyo had noticed on the fly as Witt sought his desired spot. Koscuisko had managed to find an angle that obscured them all. Danyo could still guess what Koscuisko was doing, with a visceral recognition like a stone-hard lump in his throat that brought the water of revulsion into his mouth and made him afraid that he was going to vomit. That wouldn't do, of course, not in front of Witt. He had a reputation to uphold. Witt would lose respect, if Danyo showed him any weakness.

Danyo had seen patients in his Infirmary with traumatic abdominal injuries; he'd heard them. There were ways a knife in the gut could be worse than a knife to the testes. He couldn't see Koscuisko's hands, but he could hear Koscuisko talk, and at this moment even he was afraid, because he was in the virtual presence of a genuine madman, and profound psychological disturbance elevated to such a height made any sane person prepare to flee out of an instinct for self-preservation.

"You asked me before—" Koscuisko said, on record. "—what you had done to me, as though you believed I consulted anything but my own pleasure. And. No." Working his fingers, from the shift in muscle at Koscuisko's partially uncovered shoulder. Like telling beads. Like squeezing a damp cloth in his closed fist. Far too deliberate, too gentle, too controlled to imagine that Koscuisko had blocked the recorder's vision in order to relieve some of the tension in his body in the most obvious and traditional way. Danyo knew what Koscuisko was doing.

"You deserve it all, for the dead of the Domitt Prison. But I admit there is in addition something personal." Koscuisko made an emphatic gesture; Geltoi choked and tried to scream, but had no more screaming left in him. "On the night of my arrival, the ambush in the street, because someone thought I was you. I do not blame them. But Joslire died. Be grateful that I do not in the ways of my ancestors consult and roast these, Geltoi, bit by bit. You would breathe and feel until there was nothing left in your belly but the smoldering ashes."

No. Of course Koscuisko couldn't do that. It wasn't in the inventory, not under Protocol, not authorized under any circumstances—except that this was a Tenth Level Command Termination and Koscuisko could do anything he liked. Koscuisko was insane and Koscuisko was capable of unheard-of, unimagined, unimaginable atrocities. Koscuisko stood up. Geltoi's stomach was covered in blood, fresh, new, thick; Danyo was grateful for that, because it hid things.

"And I would. There is no one here to stop me. But he, the man for whose death you are responsible, he would take it as dishonor, and for that reason alone I merely suggest you meditate upon it until I see you again. Good-greeting, Administrator Geltoi."

Witt stopped the record. Danyo tried not to take a deep breath that would betray his horror; he was only partially successful, but fortunately for him Witt mistook the signal. "Oh, I agree," Witt said, one hand pressed to his chest as if to calm himself, to keep his passions in check. "It is of stunningly superlative artistry. I have seen such things done, yes, but where there is no awareness there is no real sublimity. I'm so happy I could share this with you, my friend. My dear, dear friend."

Witt was being unusually demonstrative, even considering the influence of the things he'd just watched. Danyo had been *my friend* not infrequently, *my dear friend* seldom, but *my dear, dear friend* never before. "We should toast on it," Witt said, standing up. "I have not been able with anybody else to this share." He poured the drink himself, from a separate service at a side-table. "Here is wodac. Drink with me, Danyo, to our success in the future."

Something, Witt's movement to the side table, perhaps, had set the visual display into motion again; but—Danyo was more glad than he liked to admit, even to himself—the material was changed. Quite different. There was just a room, small, rather cramped, with someone seated on a cot just inside the door working on the polish of a boot.

There was something familiar about the scene. Danyo frowned, trying to recall. Of course. Fossum. Student quarters, and that man, or that bond-involuntary rather, could that actually be Joslire Curran, with whom he'd practiced so many pleasant ways to pass the time in admonition and instruction?

Then he'd seen Curran again. That was true. The once. A mass casualty exercise at Hassert, the infirmary staff of three Jurisdiction battleships pooled to triage and treat the wounded, soldiers and traitors and collateral damage alike.

He'd never thought to have the pleasure, and he'd been delighted. But Andrej Koscuisko had been there. Koscuisko had thwarted Danyo's quite natural desire to revisit some points of discipline with his once-orderly to assure himself of Curran's sensitivity with respect to lessons learnt. Koscuisko had taken Curran's side. Koscuisko had insulted him, and denied him access. Koscuisko's captain had backed his own man, and Danyo had been defeated.

Danyo heard his own voice, now, on the holo-vid. "Curran." Somehow Witt had found a record, an actual record, of Danyo's rooms during Danyo's tenure. He could see Curran stand up, set the boot down neatly, hurry to comply. And there was his own voice again, from out of his past, innocent words, but Danyo remembered what would happen next. "Didn't you hear me, Curran? Come here. We should have a little talk."

Witt pressed an icy cup of wodac—so cold it was almost syrupy—into Danyo's hand as Danyo sat there, stunned, suddenly terrified. Witt clinked the rim of Danyo's cup with his own, smiling.

"You will not fail me," Witt said, downing the entire cup of wodac in one swallow. "I of this have no doubt. Now. Ah. I regret the necessity that must deprive me of your company, but my plan was already in motion, and the ship leaves tonight. Go with this man, my dear dear friend, and let me hear from you when you can. We will be watching."

Witt had signaled for escort, clearly; because there was someone at the door. "This person will escort you on my behalf." Witt was all business, now. "The ship on which you travel is called *Nikojek*. You go to Couveraine by way of Langsarik Station. Andrej Koscuisko is there. The captain has your briefing, and my gift to the Langsarik Coalition. If I should never see you in person again, let me just say that I have enjoyed your company, and thank you for it. Good speed to you, Doctor Pefisct."

"Thank you as well," Danyo said, standing up, with a sincere bow of salute. "And no. I will not fail you." Witt had played him a trick, a nasty trick, indicative of how deeply Witt had studied Danyo himself as well as Koscuisko. It was a useful warning. What Koscuisko would do to him if Koscuisko ever saw more of this record . . . with this weapon in Witt's hands, it was a matter of Danyo's plain survival to ensure that he delivered Koscuisko into Witt's hands, finally and forever.

En route from Psimas to the Langsarik Coalition's base at Couveraine, Bat Yorvik—who was the first Bench Judge of the male sex to have been seated at Haspirzak Judiciary in recorded history, more or less—had studied everything he could find within Bench records about the history and characteristics of Gonebeyond space, from the physical to the philosophical, the practical and the political. He knew how to study things.

One conclusion he had derived: there was really very little information. The Bench had expanded the scope of Jurisdiction by making first contact with already-cohesive communities; never something like Gonebeyond, so sparsely populated as to have been beneath the Bench's notice for so long, and inhabited by refugees with no interest in joining the government from which they'd fled. He was the Bench's first substantive overture for communication with any such community outside the defined boundaries of Jurisdiction space.

When he'd been a child he hadn't known there was any such thing as *outside the defined boundaries.* The idea was absurd; all there was in Creation were worlds either under Jurisdiction or worlds to be integrated into Jurisdiction as Fleet located them, mapping the vectors.

When he'd been a boy he'd started wondering how it could possibly be that all worlds outside Jurisdiction had been absorbed entire, to become participants in—supporters of—the rule of Law and the Judicial order.

By the time he was nearing adulthood it had come to seem self-evident that some people just didn't fit within the framework of the compulsory public education system that formed his understanding of society. Reasoning by extrapolation, there were almost necessarily worlds that might have as much to offer of value that were at the same time not interested in being drawn into an exchange under a complete and codified system of relatively inflexible rules and regulations.

It simply didn't make sense, and Bat Yorvik had decided that when he was Judge he would see if he couldn't derive a better way. Then, his determination had seemed misguided to his teachers and his counselors and his friends and his family, because men weren't Judges, not at the highest levels of the Bench. Now, as it seemed, he was to have his chance.

Gonebeyond space was a far-flung collection of communities of all sorts, many no larger than a single small group, some one or two worlds linked by their history and culture; some large enough to qualify almost as world-families—the community made up by Nurail centered around the hub of Safehaven, for instance, or the formidable Langsarik fleet recently reinforced by a tentative stream of people from its home system of Palaam eager to make amends and become families again.

Some of them were criminal, like the Biramie cartel whose headquarters was under siege and blockade at Couveraine. Some were shipboard colonies; such a one was the Jurisdiction Fleet Ship *Ragnarok*, standing at the ready between the Pavrock exit vector and the planet on which the cartel had built one of its bases. Bat had studied the *Ragnarok* as well: but until now he had never seen it, nor thought to come on board.

He'd watched the *Ragnarok* on approach, as Specialist Ivers had plotted an intercept twelve hours off the vector. He'd toured one of the Jurisdiction Fleet ships in the *Ragnarok*'s class once before—as part of his orientation as a clerk of Court at Haspirzak—so the shape and size were familiar.

Such ships were less than half the size of the huge deep-space freighters, a carapace hull above, a maintenance atmosphere below, a constant stream of ship-traffic of various sizes going to and fro—but great *Ragnarok* had been an experimental ship, the pet research project of the First Judge na Roqua den Tensa that had been, and its carapace hull was distinctive.

Black hull technology.

The *Ragnarok* had never gone to war, before Jennet ap Rhiannon. It had never even drawn its base issue of weaponry and munitions, though it had fielded a full complement of the small five-soul Wolnadi fighters whose mission was primarily to protect the ship itself. There were experimental test beds among those Wolnadi fighters as well, Bat knew, though he didn't have his hands on many of the details. Yet.

For now they were to dock and take a meeting, because the

Langsarik coalition was using *Ragnarok* as its central command post while its Wolnadi fighters were occupied in encouraging surface traffic on Couveraine to mind its manners and stay dirt-bound.

Dame Ivers had surrendered the courier's command systems to the *Ragnarok*'s Chief Engineer to guide the ship to its assigned docking slip. Bat had had four days in her company—hers, and the ship's crew, and Janforth Ifrits. It had been an honor, and an invaluable opportunity. Truly once in a lifetime, unrestricted access one-on-one to a Bench intelligence specialist willing to speak to all of his questions.

He'd talked her almost hoarse, taken a break, had a meal, and sat back down again with her to talk some more: and she'd let him. There was only one subject she hadn't been willing to discuss: where she'd come from, how she'd been tagged for the unique role of a high-level operative with powers of extraordinary discretion, why she'd accepted a job that kept her outside the normal human relationships of friends and family and elected to stand alone. Apart. With only other Bench specialists for occasional companionship.

The docking slip the courier settled into was big enough for a ship several times the courier's size, with plenty of room for the reception committee. There were people waiting. Bat knew the *Ragnarok*'s senior officers from briefings he'd studied: the Captain, the First Officer, the Ship's Engineer,

He'd been looking forward to meeting Ship's Intelligence Officer particularly, because she was one of the relatively few non-hominid souls in Fleet. A Desmodontae sky-soarer, or, in common parlance, a bat. There had been no Desmodontae in public service when he'd been a child, for which fact Bat had reason to be grateful. The teasing alone . . .

Also there were others waiting, representatives from the Langsarik coalition, or so Bat surmised. He could recognize one or two of them on sight. There was the Langsarik mission commander, Hilton Shires, tall, rangy, sharp-eyed, keen of gaze. The short dark-haired man whose curling hair fell well down on his shoulders would be the Nurail spymaster-general Tamsen Gar.

Among the others Bat noted a tall rather hawk-faced man with a dour expression and red hair, and big hands. The Langsarik coalition's Surgeon General, Yogee Gascarone, self-selected for the role—

according to Haspirzak's information—but who'd shown how much a Surgeon General had been needed by the results of his first steps in resource balancing and central inventory management of medical equipment and surplus supplies across as many of the communities in Gonebeyond as he'd gotten to, so far.

All of these people. Waiting for him. Waiting for the Bench specialist, yes, but Bat knew that Bench specialists rarely accepted formal welcomes and Ivers was going down first. Neither of them needed to duck their heads to clear the courier's passenger access door, since they were both of a height; and yet Bat was conscious of being both in Ivers' shadow and in the tri-lights at the same time.

Captain ap Rhiannon took two steps forward. Her officers stood at attention, and the other people there adopted slightly less uniform— but still formal—postures. There were crew members all over the maintenance atmosphere, but as Bat took an only partially theatrical look around for effect he could see that they'd all stopped and come to attention where they'd been standing. Eyes front.

Specialist Ivers was waiting for him at the foot of the passenger loading ramp. Wishing he'd remembered to wear his formal Judicial dress—then remembering why he'd decided not to—Bat stepped down off the passenger loading ramp and crossed the tarmac to where ap Rhiannon and her officers waited.

"Welcome to the Jurisdiction Fleet Ship *Ragnarok*," ap Rhiannon said, with a crisp nod of her head—the bow in salute, from the neck— and a subtle emphasis on the ship's formal status. *Jurisdiction* Fleet Ship. Making her position clear. "Speaking on behalf of officers and crew it is an honor to receive a Bench Judge. Let me personally escort you to the briefing room."

He was glad she hadn't said Bench Judge Presiding. He had yet to be assigned specific duties at the Bench level. Unless this was to be it, of course. He was here in a relatively undefined, if officially endorsed, capacity. The dream he'd been entertaining in transit—Tenth Judge Bat Yorvik, Gonebeyond Judiciary, Presiding—was clearly a vague fantasy for the future; he had no doubt the phrase would mean something quite different when it came, if it ever became reality.

"Thank you, Captain ap Rhiannon." According to protocol he was to address her by rank, not by her courtesy title of "your Excellency." That was because according to protocol he outranked everybody here, under Judicial ground-rules. Which in a sense he was here to represent. He wasn't here as an entry-level liaison officer. He was here as a Judge whose senior position in the hierarchy was specifically intended as a signal of the weight Haspirzak Judiciary was willing to put on the importance of his embassage. "Shall we?"

The moment he and ap Rhiannon started moving, everybody else on the platform except for the First Officer evaporated: to meet them in the briefing room. On board the *Ragnarok* it was the Captain alone who could offer the official welcome aboard. Hilton Shires—as the leading representative of the Langsarik Coalition— was senior otherwise, but every captain was supreme authority on her own ship.

The briefing room was full when they got there. It was both informal and austere. The same room that served for formal briefings had other lives as a staff meeting room, Disciplinary Mast hearings room, and senior officers' mess, to include ship's officers, its Chief Warrants, and its section chiefs. No thick carpet. No draped walls. Modular tables; adequate chairs. Bat was immediately much more relaxed.

Ap Rhiannon escorted him to a place at the table that took up most of the space in an area slightly raised on a low platform at the far end of the room, marked off with a railing: the Captain's Bar. He'd studied. But on one level at least there was no studying this ship, not just because it had begun its life as an experimental test bed built on a Fleet battlewagon model.

This was the *Ragnarok*.

That was Jennet ap Rhiannon, the crèche–bred Command Branch officer whose training and indoctrination had gone so spectacularly wrong when she'd shot her way out of Fleet Audit Appeals Authority at Taisheki Station rather than surrender crew she considered to be falsely accused.

She'd been right about that, but it wasn't protocol, and how she'd gotten one of Fleet's major depots to release an entire ship's commissioning load of arms and armaments at Emandis Station was still the subject of lively debate in drinking establishments. It was widely supposed that it had had something to do with Andrej Koscuisko.

Who wasn't here. Because Koscuisko had removed the governors from the brains of the bond-involuntary Security troops assigned to the *Ragnarok* and stolen them all from the Bench, at which point a career chief of Security had deserted his post to accompany the men into Gonebeyond, and the *Ragnarok* had followed in pursuit into Gonebeyond where it had been ever since. *Mutiny in form*, the Second Judge at Chilleau Judiciary had said—or her proxy, First Secretary Verlaine.

Who was rather unfortunately dead, of course, and long before the question of the *Ragnarok's* exact legal status had even come to preliminaries, so *Ragnarok* was in its own unique and undefined status category. The Bench had other things on its mind. Bat believed it would be years before Fleet had time to present a formal complaint, especially since Fleet was to an extent fighting for its own survival.

That was Serge of Wheatfields, Ship's Engineer, who'd been assigned to *Ragnarok* from its earliest days when it had still been in production, at least partially out of sheer guilt on the part of the Bench over a monstrous miscarriage of justice that had had to be hushed up because there were too many people with information for the cold truth to be denied.

First Officer Ralph Mendez, still proposed for his own command year after year by Fleet proponents whose recommendations were still formally marked "not received" by still-powerful political factions within Fleet's command structure. Two, of course, Ship's Intelligence and Communications, Desmodontae. The acting Chief Medical Officer, Dr. Mahaffie—nothing Bat had heard about him was off-kilter, but there had to be something, didn't there? Because this was the Jurisdiction Fleet Ship *Ragnarok*.

The entire situation was already full of color and drama, and that was even before Hilton Shires began to speak. Hilton Shires and the Langsarik pirates were their own separate saga—but Bat knew he had to be Judge, not partisan, and formally, resolutely, immune to the romance of it all.

"Good-greeting, your Honor." Shires had risen to his feet as Bat had come into the room. There were uniformed members of the *Ragnarok's* crew seated among the people below the Bar in their own dedicated section, but now that the proceedings were at the Langsarik Coalition level they offered no separate salute to their captain. There was a place at the table for her: almost the junior-most, except for the Surgeon General. "Thank you for coming all this way to meet with us. We appreciate Haspirzak Judiciary's representative as observer."

Ivers didn't have a seat at the table at all, which meant she didn't need one; also that she wasn't here in any official capacity representing the Bench as a whole, because there really wasn't one any more, in a significant sense. That didn't matter. A Bench intelligence specialist *was* an official capacity. Shires indicated a place for Bat, beside him at the table; there was a tray with water-glasses, but of even a cavene service there was no sign. Perhaps that would have been too informal, Bat decided.

Shires didn't sit down. "Before we get started, let me introduce everybody. My name is Hilton Shires, designated mission commander for this action at Couveraine." The title was a careful compromise, "commander" because any organization needed one, and linked to the specific mission alone because none of the Langsarik Coalition's component forces had ceded its autonomy. Bat nodded, gravely; Shires continued.

"To your right, representing Safehaven space as collective for the Nurail members of the coalition, Tamsen Gar, our chief of intelligence and communication. Vandrill Hoggs, the Uritag confederacy, our Executive Officer and second in command; Nambroch Zoster of the Berico Reach, logistics."

"Thank you, Mission Commander. And I'm Bench Judge Bat Yorvik, out of Haspirzak Judiciary. I've been sent to gain an understanding of Gonebeyond space." He sensed, rather than saw, the reaction to his statement; he was a man, and yet he was a Bench-level judge. *One would have thought*, he told himself with resignation, *that of all places in which one could make that statement without surprising people, it would be in Gonebeyond.* "I look forward to the opportunity to learn from you all."

"Then we'll get right to it." Stepping down from the platform, Shires took up a position in front of the wall to the left, where some charts started to tile themselves into a display. "We are over Couveraine Prime, Couveraine system, off the Pavrock vector. The Biramie cartel has enjoyed the development and use of an established base for possibly fifteen years, and does some of its most lucrative trade in its own marketplace. They're entrenched."

There was a city, set against the rising wall of what appeared to be the remains of an ancient volcanic caldera. A huge one. Bat could see a system of watercourses coming down the high slopes behind the city to braid themselves into a river washing the city's outskirts before it joined an even deeper channel that flowed out of the caldera in what was probably a significant waterfall, but there were no pictures, just notations on a map.

"This serves as their control collection point for high-value goods, and is the administrative hub of the enterprise. Our first priority is to deny this facility to the cartel, because it will at least slow them down to have to fall back on the redundancies. We hope to identify these redundancies. Our second priority is to gain access to people and documentation through which we can further trace and neutralize traffic in illegal recreationals, stolen small-heavies, and slaves."

The Bench didn't traffic in bond-involuntaries, though the Bond amounted to term-limited slavery. There were other exceptions to the Bench prohibitions: within the Dolgorukij Combine, for instance, members of a particular order had always been slaves by definition, and there was a religious exception in place to cover that. The Malcontent could hold its members as slaves. Not even the Malcontent could traffic, however.

"We've been holding both ends of the Pavrock vector for seven weeks Standard. We've recently learned that there's a second operational vector in the vicinity, and we don't think we've missed any traffic through there—it's unmapped as yet, *Ragnarok* will be working that issue—but we're going to make sure. The city's defenses are strong but not insurmountable, and we've neutralized the exo-atmospheric armaments. We're down to the city itself. First line of defense yet to get past is the containment dome."

Containment domes were for hostile environments. Insufficient atmospheres, temperature extremes, stations planted on miscellaneous asteroids without a star close enough for harvestable heat or light. The stats on Couveraine Prime indicated a perfectly adequate class-three environment for most classes of hominids.

In certain circumstances, though, a containment dome could serve as power generation and light gatherer; and, of course, a defensive barrier. A tricky one, however. Depending on the materials used they could be difficult to breach: but, once breached, there was the potential for structural components to be raining down into the city from a considerable altitude.

"The dome is vector-defined. It apparently went up in units as Couveraine was developed. This increases the complications involved with entering the city, to take control, as there are a minimum of three separate domes between the outermost perimeter and the administrative center. On the plus side, each of those domes is of relatively low height, and if we can time things right the impact from falling components can be used as resistance suppressants in their own right."

Even at a relatively low height—that of multistory mixed-use structures, for instance—something dropped from the roof would have lethal impact below. It seemed almost suicidally risky, to Bat; but Shires had to have a plan.

"We'll be taking two lines of approach on areas targeted as particularly vulnerable. Couveraine has used bunker-fired missiles against air-breathing reconnaissance aircraft, so we don't know for sure what we're walking into, but we can't wait until the value of the intel harvest has declined to nil. Support functions—"

Another screen, another schematic, a highlighted area away well to one side of the city's location, screened by a rib of rock between it and the city. "—have been bunkered. Couveraine knows we're coming, just not precise timing and location. There's our next phase, your Honor, any questions?"

Are you out of your minds, are you all going to die, don't you have loved ones. Plenty of questions, but none within Bat's purview. "Thank you, Mission Commander. I have nothing to say, except to wish every success on the enterprise."

Where was he to be, during all this? On the *Ragnarok*? Where would Ivers be? On the ground? She was conferring with someone Bat thought to be one of Shires' subordinates, quietly, head-to-head. The Bench couldn't afford to risk one of its top firefighters under actual live fire, surely. But nobody told a Bench specialist what to do. More surely than that.

The room was clearing. People respectfully declined to try to engage Bat in conversation, and clearly they had a lot of work to do. Ivers came to join him, with one of the *Ragnarok*'s junior officers in tow; Command Branch, a lieutenant. *Ragnarok* only had the one, Bat remembered.

Full complement of top-level staff, though, even if ap Rhiannon remained a brevet captain rather than the formally instated kind; one lieutenant, and a field general of artillery, who'd come aboard at Pesadie Training Command to head up an investigation that had turned out to have a foregone conclusion, and who'd stayed on with the *Ragnarok* through its "mutiny in form" and ever since. Hadn't approved of phony investigations.

That was a thought, though, Bat realized, one he'd not had at top level in his mind. General Rukota *was* an artilleryman. He'd have experience, as well as field exercise training, in getting through containment domes and capturing city commands as intact as possible. He wouldn't have made it to general without participation in police actions on a "small war" scale.

"Your Honor," Ivers said. "Lieutenant Renata Seascape is your command interface officer. You'll observe from the *Ragnarok*, and I'll see you again soon."

Yes. She was going down-planet to participate in the shooting. "I wish you all the best," he said. He could hear a little strain in his voice, because the reality of the situation—all of these focused and determined people, and he with no way of knowing whether and how many of them might be dead within days—was suddenly a little too real.

He could think of only one adequate response: it was all the more important for him to do his very best to derive a good outcome under Law for everybody who lived through this, and the survivors of anybody who did not. "Lieutenant Seascape. Do I have quarters? I should wash up." *Before the war starts.* He suddenly wished he hadn't said that in quite those words, but Seascape smiled in a friendly fashion, and bowed.

"Come with me, your Honor," she said. "I'll introduce you to your orderly, who can provide in-depth assistance on any administrative subjects. You have the freedom of the ship, saving the engineering bridge and the maintenance atmosphere, for reasons of preparation for hostilities. It'll be this way."

Should he demand to be taken down-planet, for a dirt-level view? No. He was a judge. He knew nothing about war that didn't come out of textbooks. Did he wish he was going to be an active part of this, risking his life, shoulder to shoulder with seasoned warriors?

Just a little tiny fraction of an iota. Yes. Yes, he did. But realistically he would only be in the way. He was lucky to be as close to this as he'd gotten already. He'd never really seen himself being briefed by a mission commander in a life-or-death struggle about to take place while he watched from a safe distance on a renegade Fleet warship.

To the extent that it would make him a better Judge he welcomed the experience.

CHAPTER THREE

Intervention in Force

I wonder whatever became of my old friend Koski. Yogee Gascarone had had that thought from time to time over the years. Not *my old friend Andrej*—he knew perfectly well what had become of Andrej Koscuisko, anyone who cared to pay attention to the crimes of the Jurisdiction's Bench knew that—but his friend Koski. A different man entirely.

They'd been close, at Mayon, even with the unavoidable resentments Yogee could still feel about Koscuisko's money. Yogee had had to settle for the less challenging courses of study, because he couldn't afford the tuition. He'd been lucky enough to have gotten into Mayon in the first place; but scholarships only went so far, and the truth of the matter was that Koski had been the brighter of the two and Yogee knew it.

Yogee had been the better doctor, though, because he knew more of the real-life challenges his patients faced. Koski had been plain brilliant, however, in surgery, where a patient's history was perhaps not as important as the immediate medical requirements.

"Koscuisko?" the intake clerk at the combat support hospital's control point had said, with a mildly curious look at the man with Yogee. "Oh, yes, him. Uncle you'll find out on the shingle by the river. Polluting the air. Wishing you joy of the lefrol smoke." But there'd been no malice in the orderly's voice, and no particular resentment in her manner. She'd been busy. She'd had plenty of inventory-and-issues reports to prepare, and some of it on actual flatfile flimsies. *Whatever worked*, Yogee told himself, with a shrug.

So Yogee Gascarone—Surgeon General for Gonebeyond, if largely self-elected—had made his way with his companion through newly entrenched corridors and out into the open air under the blue sky looking down over Couveraine's river, following the smell of fresh water and the faint perfume of a lefrol; and found his quarry. Andrej Koscuisko, Koski of old, when they'd been much younger; there was no mistaking him, even from behind, because he'd always been of that sort of trim and rather elegant appearance that was everything Yogee felt he was not.

He, he was a tall loose-limbed man with just that little bit too much face for his skull to manage, increasingly craggy of appearance as he aged and his once-bright-orange hair faded to auburn. "How about a few friendly shuffles?" Yogee called out. "I'm a little short of the ready, again."

Koscuisko's general air of grace and affluence wasn't his fault. That hadn't ever meant that Yogee took his winnings at cards with reluctance, no, and they were scrupulously honest winnings, there was never any temptation to cheat Koscuisko at cards because Koski had simply never been much good at four-handed relki. Yogee knew how to cherish rich friends with more money than they knew what to do with. It was nothing personal.

Startled, by the looks of it—a shift in Koscuisko's balance, the quick snap of his head to look back over his shoulder—it was that moment, Yogee could tell, before his once-classmate recognized him. Of course, it had been at least thirteen years since he'd seen Koscuisko last. Or since Koscuisko had seen him, anyway. Yogee had seen Koscuisko on the vids, that whole Domitt Prison thing. Disgusting.

"Yodge!" Good. Koscuisko had placed him. He even sounded glad, but who knew how long that would last? "Name of all Saints, Yogee Gascarone. Of course. Gonebeyond, and where else." Now, that had been unnecessary, Yogee thought, even though he could see Koscuisko's thinking and that it wasn't a malicious thing to say. Koscuisko knew perfectly well that Yogee was a good doctor. "What brings you here?"

And Koski wouldn't have expected Yogee to fit in well with any state-funded hospitals, not with the itch the whole idea of Jurisdiction had given him so long ago—even if he'd been able to find a good job. Therefore: Gonebeyond space. Logical. Insightful. Koscuisko. Annoying.

"You and me, Andrej, long time, but you can invite me for dinner some other time. I have a pressing issue to put before you." It had to be said, though Yogee felt a little wistful about the dinner Koscuisko might have been able to share. Koscuisko might be in Gonebeyond, but he was still the inheriting son of the Koscuisko familial corporation—technically, at least. There were certain to be more lefrols where the one Koscuisko was smoking had come from.

In the end, the whole thing about Ship's Inquisitors had come decisively between them, and intemperate words—but ones Yogee still stood by—had been said. So Koscuisko didn't try to embrace him heart-to-heart; but held out his hand, instead, with a tentatively offering sort of energy, clearly remembering how they'd parted as well as Yogee did.

It had been a long time. Koscuisko had paid for his filial piety. Unfortunately, there were who knew how many once-living, breathing, feeling souls who had paid a much higher price. Yogee clasped hands with him. Now Koscuisko was looking at the man Yogee had brought, with a curious and engaging expression on his face; he'd be wondering.

"Right," Yogee said, decisively. No sense in dredging up old arguments, and they were in Gonebeyond, where people came to be free of imprisonments of many sorts. "I've got a new job, have you heard? Not the point, though. Here's a patient. I'm hoping you'll take his case."

Of course Koscuisko would. At the very core, the essential center of his being, what had made Koski tick had been compassion. That was what had made what became of him all the more horrifying.

And there in Koscuisko's eyes behind the apparently honest pleasure he had in seeing Yogee again, past the layers of sin and suffering and regret and guilt, there suddenly sprang up a look of sheer delight that was pure and good and true. That was Koski. Before he'd lost his quarrel with his father; before he'd thrown his decency away.

"You? Our surgeon general? Holy Mother. Do I salute you, now, and call you sir?"

The warmth in Yogee's own heart wasn't unexpected. He'd guessed it might come, and he'd armored himself against it, because there was no getting around the fact that Andrej Koscuisko had been a judicial torturer in Fleet for all this time. Most of this time. Retired from torturing people in the service of an authoritarian and tyrannical Bench, but that didn't unwrite history.

"You call me Doctor," Yogee said. "But you also pretend to accept my authority. Here's a man who's come a long way for your help, and you're the only surgeon in all of Gonebeyond I'd trust with the particular problem." There was Janforth Ifrits, standing several steps removed and squinting in the light. Early afternoon, where Yogee had been. Two hours into midshift, in Jurisdiction time. "Have you heard what the Third Judge means to do, in Haspirzak Judiciary?"

Koscuisko frowned, with a fractional shake of his head. He looked a little perplexed about Janforth, to Yogee. Yogee hadn't seen Koski for years. He couldn't really swear to "perplexity," but he'd be able to check on his identification of Koski's expression soon, because what he had to say would certainly evoke that response.

"She's pulled every Ship's Inquisitor to save their salaries, and replaced them all as CMOs with their own seconds-in-command." So all Koscuisko would have had to do was stay on, so long as he could have managed to be at Haspirzak when the Convocation had failed.

Then he wouldn't be a mutineer and a technically outlawed man and almost certainly an immense embarrassment to his family, because to have set himself at odds with lawful order and established hierarchy would have been enough to reduce his father and his mother alike to near-terminal fits of the vapors.

He'd have done all right. A man of Koski's genuine ability would find the reduction in status from Chief Medical Officer to head of Surgery practically painless, so long as he was willing to be reasonable about it.

"And—" Koski was looking Yogee in the face, but he had Janforth in the corner of his eye. Yogee could tell. Koscuisko had always had a peculiar sort of peripheral vision: the result, he'd told Yogee once, of a lifetime spent surrounded by other people at almost all times. Fortunately this talent had not extended to any ability to read the cards of the people to his left or right.

"And their bond-involuntary Security assigned, she's cut them loose as well. Cost-cutting measure. That's the story, but there'll be no more of them in Haspirzak." Yogee watched Koski carefully, willing him to understand. Willing him not to ask questions. "This man, who is Janforth Ifrits by name, decided not to wait around for surgical remediation and debriefing and all of the formal procedures. They're using an implanted Safe, now." So Koski would know why there wasn't a cord around Janforth's neck with a Safe hanging off it.

Reaction from Koski. Fury. Conflict. Koscuisko raised his voice. "Mister Ifrits, excuse me, you, how would you best prefer I called you? My name is Andrej Koscuisko. Have we an issue to discuss?"

Yogee could see him trying to adjust on the fly, his personal outrage—that Janforth had been permitted to fly away without the most basic measures of support—as against his knowledge, still sinking in Yogee believed, that Janforth was bond-involuntary and deserved Andrej's most delicate handling. He was glad to see it. Otherwise he might have had to issue a Rebuke, and who knew what would happen then?

"My personal name is Janforth." There was a "your Excellency" there, but Janforth had bitten it off. "Couldn't stand it. Couldn't wait. Specialist Ivers was coming to Couveraine, I took advantage. Thought I'd have to find my way to Safehaven, though."

"Had you consulted with me I would have said—" but it was Koscuisko's turn to bite his comment off. "The conditions are not optimal. Do you desire I should free you of this vile thing, even as I warn you, the equipment is not so good as that in Jurisdiction, there is no one here to serve you as your guide during recovery?"

"I couldn't wait," Janforth repeated. That was the voice of determination, or desperation; sometimes there was little to separate the two. "Could not. The risk is mine, your Excellency. I gave Specialist Ivers no choice."

It wasn't quite the case that Koski had no one to help Janforth adjust to life without a governor. There was the crew of the *Fisher Wolf*. On the other hand, Koski would not consider himself in a position to make demands of *them*; because of the man he was. Obligation ran only one way, with Koscuisko. He was willing to be obliged to someone who'd done him a favor: but refused to permit the establishment of the reciprocal, of someone owing *him* a favor. It was just another one of the ways in which Koski's wealth and position had made him arrogant.

"I heard you pulled governors on the *Ragnarok*." Yogee wasn't about to let Koscuisko get away with dodging his responsibilities to Janforth, and Koski was good about responsibility. "But also at Connaught Vector Authority. Didn't I hear that? How did you cover that activity, exactly?"

Because he'd heard gossip. Running quality checks on surgical apparatus. Just the sort of thing Koscuisko had either not gotten around to yet or needed to do again, redundancy being the best policy where the calibrations of delicate surgical equipment was concerned, the combat support hospital having been set up under less than ideal conditions.

Koscuisko shot him an ugly scowl. Yogee wasn't fooled. He remembered. Koski had a hard time unleashing his inner trickster; but when he did, the joyful play of Koski's pure anarchic genius had been wonderful to behold. But then Koscuisko's expression changed, and Yogee wondered if he'd misjudged his man after all.

"It is true, as Doctor Gascarone says. I will do it, and I will do it as soon as the equipment can be brought on line, if you wish it," Koscuisko said. "And yet I would ask you to wait, because I have only just now realized. It is that we may be having a war, and I don't know when it will begin. You have medical qualifications. We will need them."

Oh. Well. Yes. Koscuisko had a point. Patients first; that was Yogee's motto. And yet in this instance, perhaps their duty to the population they were here to serve should take precedence.

Janforth went white in the face, and closed his eyes: struggling to make up his mind, perhaps. It was a terrible choice to make. When Janforth opened his eyes up again Yogee could tell he'd made his choice. "Very good, sir," Janforth said. "After."

"Come with me, then, and tour the hospital." Koski's voice was gentle. "Keep close, throughout. Permit me to keep my eye on you, and tell me if something seems to be creeping up on you. I will have a dose at the ready at all times. It is a hard thing that I have asked you to do. You have the thanks of everybody in this hospital, Janforth."

Well, people had told him that Koski had a reputation, an actual reputation, for his ability to earn loyalty in challenging circumstances. With any sort of decent luck it would make things work with Janforth: and now Yogee had to go and take a shuttle out to Pavrock Vector Control to see a man about a hospital.

⊕ ⊕ ⊕

The freighter Witt had sent with Danyo was a Dolgorukij hull, freighter *Nikojek*, Combine registry, built by Yansaloft. Danyo had to grant that his accommodations were more luxurious than those he'd enjoyed as the chief medical officer on JFS *Sondarkit*, which could only mean far more commodious than the new berth Captain Fonderell had had in mind. Not quite every luxury. Still better than those of *Nikojek's* Captain Morrisk herself; Danyo knew, because she'd given him a small dinner party when he'd come on board.

That had been ten days ago. *Nikojek* had gone to Langsarik Station, as though they thought the Coalition's headquarters were still there; and been redirected. Now he was here at Couveraine off the Pavrock vector, just as Witt had planned.

Nikojek's captain had briefed him: there was apparently a dispute being carried out in force at Couveraine between the Biramie cartel and the so-called Langsarik Coalition—which was made up of Langsariks and other people who didn't like slaving—among which number he was to represent Witt's organization. Danyo had been happy to hear that there was no expectation on Witt's part that he would be expected to pretend that Witt objected to dealing in slaves on principle.

No, Witt wanted it understood that he had dealt in slaves before— as a buyer, and on a strictly occasional basis, to acquire specific entertainers—but was willing to abjure the trade in order to do business with the Langsarik Coalition. Not quite reforming, or abandoning his wicked ways; making a pragmatic decision, rather, to concede points in order to be admitted to a trading community in the future of whose developing markets Witt wished to be included.

There was to be no mention of Witt by name, of course, or of any parent company that could be traced. Danyo was here on behalf of a bulk commodities firm dealing in wine, bappir, rhyti, jifka, in a market slot between drinking water and cortac brandy, priced to be comparable in cost to nearly free home product and sufficiently better in quality to make a most—affordable—markup an acceptable investment.

As part of Agavie's pitch, *Nikojek* had brought samples, some pre-distributed to Langsarik vector control on the way to Pavrock and some carried through to the Couveraine side of the vector. Danyo wished he'd brought brandy, because he wanted a drink, but he didn't know how many more bottles *Nikojek* might be carrying for *his* use.

Pavrock Vector Control was little more than a launch-fields on an artificial platform towed into place. The Langsarik Coalition had the vector debouch on quarantine—nothing in or out without clearance—so Witt had accompanied Captain Morrisk from *Nikojek* to Vector Control to present Nikojek's papers, and for Danyo to present Witt's offer.

There were four people waiting for them in their little conference room, which was a little awkward, because there were only five seats. He took one of them. One of the station's people—an attractive woman with a heavy braid wound around her head, Danyo had seen the hair-style on people on Witt's household staff so he assumed she was Dolgorukij—opened the meeting without much by way of a preamble.

"Good-greeting," she said. She had a clear voice, calm, soothing, low-pitched. "My name is Ekaterina Felsanjir. I've been asked to receive the proposal we understand you wish to make for preliminary evaluation, on behalf of the Langsarik Coalition. About your registration and your documentation I have nothing in particular to say because we are in Gonebeyond. Let me have the details of your proposal, please, and I will communicate on your behalf with the Coalition Command."

She wasn't wearing Langsarik colors, but she wouldn't be if she were Dolgorukij, would she? What were Dolgorukij doing in Gonebeyond? Independent contractors, perhaps. Keeping his mission firmly in his mind, Danyo rose to his feet. Witt had entrusted this embassy to him; he was Witt's proxy, here, howsoever indirectly.

"I come on behalf of Agavie Beverage and Consumables. You may have heard of us? No? Well." Danyo would have been surprised if she had. He expected Agavie was carefully positioned in a reasonably respectable but low-profile position, and for another this was, as Felsanjir had noted, Gonebeyond. "I myself am not a man of business, but a doctor. Agavie wishes to donate a field hospital to the Langsarik Coalition as an in-kind investment in the development of the Langsarik octant. At Langsarik Station they directed us here."

"And in return," Felsanjir prompted. Danyo nodded. Of course there was an *in return*.

"Agavie anticipates that you may have questions about its good faith. I won't try to hide the fact that its trading practices in Gonebeyond prior to now may not have been on strictly value-for-money terms." That was supposed to represent Agavie's admission of past predatory practices, of various sorts. Which it was willing to put behind it. "The conditions of trade within the Langsarik octant are changing. Agavie asks that its donation be accepted as a token of its eagerness to do business on Langsarik terms."

Danyo paused, looked down at the table, shifted his stance slightly to indicate a break in what he had to say. "That's the official statement. Captain Morrisk has more details here for you. So far as I understand it, the *in return* is that you receive a trade delegation, and give Agavie a fair hearing for a preferential market partnership."

And get me close to Andrej Koscuisko. Danyo had no hope that Koscuisko wouldn't remember him from that one occasion years ago, because Koscuisko had clearly developed a strong prejudice that could only have come from communication with Joslire Curran—difficult for Danyo to imagine, given how hard Curran had fought against communicating with *him*, but maybe Curran had learned that there was no point in trying to keep any secrets from his officer of assignment.

If so, Danyo knew that he could take credit for his contributions to Curran's education. Any discussion of specifics with Koscuisko on Curran's part would have been strongly prohibited communication of a personal opinion with respect to a senior officer, however. Curran had clearly needed discipline. Retraining. The problem was that if Witt shared the actual records of Danyo's first forays into developing his teaching skills with Koscuisko, Danyo was a dead man, and the death would be horrific.

Now for the first time another one of them spoke, a tall man with untidy red-gold hair and a moderately rumpled costume. "And this contribution, we're to do whatever we like with it? Send it wherever we want? Blow it up? I don't see where you've brought staff with you, a hospital's not much good without staff, is it?"

Beautiful. Was this man on Witt's payroll? "You'll admit that recruiting qualified medical staff might present some problems. To whom am I speaking, please? Doctor Gascarone? Thank you, Doctor Gascarone. That's the reason Agavie hasn't made contact earlier. We're still working to recruit qualified staff willing to abandon their lives to come out to Gonebeyond. We decided to come ahead with what we had."

There had to be only a skeleton staff. Full staffing, and the Langsarik Coalition could just as easily find a good place for the hospital and leave it there. But a few extra medical professionals could be readily integrated into an existing hospital, since Witt had counted on finding a casualty station at Couveraine. Danyo and his few staff could be a welcome augmentation of a stretched medical team in the middle of a potential mass casualty situation. *Just like last time, Koscuisko,* Danyo thought with satisfaction.

"Well, Hilton Shires might send it all back," Dr. Gascarone said to Felsanjir. "But I'm not so nice as that. You've listened to him. So what do you think, can I have it, or not?"

Whoever Gascarone was *he* wasn't Langsarik, either, and didn't seem to have the highest opinion of apparently influential people. Hilton Shires. Danyo remembered the name from the briefing Captain Morrisk had provided: the Langsarik Coalition's battle commander. Gascarone was from another polity in the Langsarik Coalition, then. Danyo made a mental note to find out which, because there seemed to be clear opportunity to exploit potential conflicts of interest to achieve his goal.

"I see no reason why not." Felsanjir seemed to share some of Gascarone's reasonable feelings about exploitation of free hospitals. "We can think of it as a quality check. A demonstration of Agavie's sincerity, if you will."

She hadn't identified her political alignment, nor Gascarone's; which was a disappointment. One Danyo could overcome. A man didn't perform his judicial function for as many years as Danyo had done without gaining a baseline degree of skill in conducting an interrogation on informal lines as well as under the Protocols, and without the person being drained for information even realizing what information they were providing. Preparing an interrogatory was as much of an art as executing it. Dr. Gascarone nodded with satisfaction; and turned to Danyo.

"You'll be called Danyo Pefisct, though, Doctor. I don't have any particular objection to people who run away from their ships when they're Ship's Inquisitors; quite the opposite, really. But it's important to let people know who you are. As much for your own protection as anything else."

No surprise on anyone's face, so they all knew exactly who he was, and their intelligence operations clearly reached at least as far into Jurisdiction space as Witt's into Gonebeyond. Danyo was annoyed. Somehow he'd expected anonymity, or at least a cover identity; had this been a plain oversight on Witt's part, or some sort of a manipulation, to keep Danyo focused on how much he needed protection?

"I fail to see—" No. Wrong approach. "I'd hoped to turn my back on all that, frankly." He could turn irritation into a more acceptable form of protest, regretful, ashamed. "One hears. One hears in particular that Andrej Koscuisko lives quite openly at Safehaven, so I thought there'd be no problem with the fact of my former life. I thought I might be excused public exposure."

Dr. Gascarone was nodding. "Yes, Koscuisko's here, and nobody's killed him yet. Because he's useful, and because everybody knows who he is, so nobody's taken by surprise if they suddenly come face-to-face in a dark corridor with the man who murdered their loved ones. That would be unfortunate. We might lose one of our best surgeons, if that happened, and his executioner would suffer banishment. We wouldn't want that. The banishment part, mostly, is what I mean."

Nothing to be done but deal with it, then. "Banishment?" It didn't mean he couldn't push back on some of Gascarone's reasoning. He wouldn't make it easy. "How can you be banished from Gonebeyond space, of all places?"

Felsanjir laughed. Gascarone smiled, and it wasn't an altogether pleasant smile. "Yeah, you're right. Sounds silly. Is silly. But it's all we've got, no army, no police, no prisons worthy of the name. People could be kicked back to Jurisdiction, I suppose, but I wouldn't wish that on anybody."

That hadn't answered the question. Felsanjir took over. "It's one year's time to arrange transport, and between one and eight years to stay away. No contact with your community, and if you don't go you're shunned. That's how. You might be surprised at the efficacy of the threat, Doctor Pefisct."

He'd be surprised if the threat had any efficacy at all. "Well, we mustn't have that, mustn't we? Very well. Doctor Pefisct it is." He knew he sounded scornful, but he couldn't think of any reason he oughtn't. "Am I to be of use here, or not? It seems a shame to me to leave an entire field hospital to idle on a freighter. At Langsarik Station they said there was a war on."

"Right, so it's hold in stasis orbit for a little while or get shot at," Gascarone said. "Which would you prefer?"

Stupid question, but Gascarone already knew that. There was something Danyo knew now: he didn't like Gascarone. So he decided to piss back at him. "I prefer to be of use," he snapped. "I won't decide for the rest of my staff. But take me down to where I can do some good. If you don't mind very much."

Gascarone nodded, approvingly. "Good man," he said. "There's one of your lot dirtside already, did you know that? Andrej Koscuisko, the very same man."

Of course he'd known that. That was the whole point of this excursion. Now Gascarone would take him by the hand and lead him to his prey. Straight to a secure posting at Safehaven Medical Center, a comfortable top-echelon billet greased and oiled by Witt's organization, by way of a short detour through Andrej Koscuisko.

It was perfect. He could get rid of the annoying and insistent reminder of the toothpick in his pocket, with its payload of a virus to take Koscuisko out. Who knew? He might get Gascarone at the same time, there'd be two men to evacuate in life-litters who would never arrive at any destination of record. He'd be clear. Witt would be satisfied. He'd be able to breathe easily.

Then he could contact Bench intelligence specialist Jils Ivers, and remind her of their conversation over dinner at Chancellor Witt's in Haspirzak Judiciary, and provide excellent reasons why he should join the administration of Safehaven Medical Center.

Jils crouched down low to ensure that the camo field cloak she wore made good contact with the ground surrounding her, scanning her environment with as few movements of her head as possible. She knew the crew of the *Fisher Wolf* were all around her, but she couldn't see them any more than they her under the camo-cloak.

If the defenders of Couveraine were looking hard enough in the exactly right places with exactly the right equipment they'd be able to detect the concealment field that surrounded Jils, compact, not extending much further than the physical garment itself. It was much easier to pick up when she was moving, so they'd moved as quietly as possible under cover of night, six hours just to cover the distance between the edge of the containment dome's probable sensor coverage and the outermost structural elements of the physical dome itself.

The predawn twilight of Couveraine city came up quickly, as close to the planet's equator as it was. The assault had to begin before the skies started to get light, because that was when the natural animal time-sense of the sleeping brain began to do its work and initiate its arousal sequence. That was an almost immutable fact of hominid biology. There were ways to get around it, of course, but so far as the snooper scans had been able to report most of Couveraine slept during the night.

Couveraine knew that the Langsarik Coalition was there. No attempt had been made to hide their presence either orbiting high above the city or bunkered in along an established perimeter that included a combat support hospital. Several unsuccessful attempts had been made to negotiate a surrender. Hilton Shires was a patient man, but information staled quickly under quarantine.

Every moment Couveraine remained its own city gave the Biramie cartel another chance to get the information that it was under siege—that any of its subsidiaries was vulnerable to compromise, should the city defenses fail—out to its network. Resources would vanish. Supply trails would disappear.

And above all, the cartel's prisoners would be moved before they could be rescued. There was no sign of the freighter *Biruck*, the one in which captives were supposedly transferred from a slaving camp at Holding to the market here at Couveraine. They needed to find Holding. The *Ragnarok* had its probes out, and Two was a genius, but time continued to slip away and hope for the captives with it.

All around the city commando teams like theirs had gathered around their targets. Couveraine's internal domes were old; its outermost walls hadn't been recently upgraded, and the area was geologically active. There'd been ground-shifts. Give the wall the right tap at the right places and they could watch the pressure faults split the interstitial fabric of the dome right up to the first of its bond-beams, and get in that way.

There would almost certainly be armed resistance. There would be fighting in the streets. But there were too many places where a vulnerability could be forced for Couveraine to have covered all of them.

She caught the whisper of movement out of the corner of her eye, tracked the shifting shape against the static background without moving her head. She knew who they were because they'd rehearsed this: Garrity and Hirsel, fleetest of foot of the lot of them, and Stildyne coming up to one side to plaster himself prone on the ground and attach the fail-safe to respond if by ill chance Garrity and Hirsel were discovered and neutralized before they'd finished their task.

They weren't. Or if they had been, the city's security were waiting for them to breach the wall in order to cut them down as they came through. Either of those two possibilities was equally likely at this point and there was no way to tell which was to prove out until they started to move. There were no communications in force; Couveraine could too easily have triangulated an intercept. This was as close to dead cold blind going in as Jils had ever been.

If she looked hard enough she could almost believe she could see the right place, at the foot of the wall, where a subtle dip in the micro-terrain before them hinted at the location of a shift in the bedrock deeper even than the foundation of the containment dome.

Stalloy was stalloy. But imbalance over time in the rock beneath their feet set stalloy against stalloy on the angle, strength against strength imperfectly balanced, and they didn't want or need the stalloy frame of the dome itself to come down—only bits and pieces of the fabric between the structural beams.

There was that distortion. There were Hirsel and Garrity sprinting swiftly away from the wall, and now Stildyne was in retreat as well. The perfect point of weakness had been tagged—or an almost-precise point, at least—and the countercharge set, backup, a lateral stress across the outer face of the dome to release the pressure that fixed the fabric in its place.

Jils waited, counting out fractional slices of time in her mind. Garrity had activated the borer on contact with the wall. It would be feeling its way through, sliding along the stress-shear patterns in the fabric of the dome until it reached the other side. It would start humming. All over Couveraine other little borers would have started singing now, on a frequency calculated to resonate with destructive force.

In the rustling silence of the coming dawn Jils heard a little sound like a pebble dropping to the ground, and couldn't tell if she'd imagined it or not. Gathering her legs under her, still careful to maintain as much contact between the camo-cloak and the ground as possible, Jils listened.

There. There it was. Another pebble. Then nothing. Nothing. But then a rock. And now the fabric of the containment dome came spalling off its face in a shower of gravel, expanding outward from the place where Garrity had set the borer, falling off on a diagonal toward Stildyne's fail-safe further away on the side of the dome. Jils waited.

There was a gust of warm air, and it carried a fragrance with it, its own smell—of the city within the dome. Not much more than a stale dust odor of stagnant air, but it wasn't the fragrance of the night outside the dome: so they were through.

Somewhere far off in the distance Jils heard the shooting start, and ran forward with her team to get through the dome and blow a hole in the next—smaller, weaker—one before the small stream of fractured fragments became a flood that would carry them away with it and bury them before they had their chance to face the city.

"Stop shaking the heterodox module," Andrej swore between clenched teeth, feeling the vibration beneath his feet, knowing that the combat support hospital had been deployed at speed with casualties incoming and was as far from state-of-the-art as even the best that Gonebeyond Space had to offer, knowing that the bunkered vibration dampers hadn't been recharged in hours. "Stop shaking the fish-eating module, the saints-rebuking module, the unfilial module, the—"

But here came the next casualty for his station, one of five, someone Andrej was afraid he recognized somehow—body recognition being challenged when the body one had only ever seen at the vertical was horizontal. The siege of Couveraine Proper had turned suddenly, viciously violent, and the "wolf-pack"—and Andrej's self-same, Brachi Stildyne—were in on the ground assault.

He didn't like it. At least this newest casualty wasn't any of the crew of the *Fisher Wolf*, all of whom he might well have recognized dead drunk or upside down. It was bad enough, no, it was even worse in the real sense of command and control, it was Hilton Shires, the Langsarik battle commander, with most of the tactical armor and a genuinely awkward amount of the skin beneath blown clear of his upper torso to the right: shoulder, upper arm, chest, bared ribs. Andrej tried to remember whether Shires was left-handed.

Fate had sent him support staff familiar with working with a battle surgeon, three to a team. There was Janforth Ifrits, still on Safe. Frodis, cutting Shires' remaining clothing away from his upper body, facing Andrej from across Shires' prone body; Caith beside him. Janforth at Andrej's right lay down cleansing pads, lifting away remnants of charred fabric and clotted blood so that Andrej could make his initial evaluation even as the evac team eased Shires onto the treatment level from the evacuation carrier, open stretcher, manual assist transport.

"Story?" Andrej asked. Shires was blue around the mouth but the cardiac indicators were clearly in strong recovery. He'd had the sense knocked out of him and it took significant impact to knock the sense out of Hilton Shires, whose eyes were starting to jump behind his closed eyelids—coming to consciousness, trying to find the footpath of his thought. Andrej smelled smoke, char, dust; the clean fresh fragrance of a just-washed open wound, blood faint, bleeding minimized. Mostly translation injuries. Mostly skin deep, except across the ribs, but that was the way of it.

Why was Shires here? None of his injuries seemed to be life-threatening—"Hit a patch of resistance near the city center," the lead man on the stretcher said. Already on the way out for the next casualty. *Because he was Hilton Shires*, Andrej reminded himself, and his presence was perhaps crucial to their success. *That was why.* "Pretty good hit, but the portable shielding mostly held. We're nearly through to the command center, it could get busy, Uncle. We're away."

The grim warning was called back over the man's shoulder because the team was already halfway out the door to pick up the next patient from triage. "Uncle," he'd said, so they were Nurail. Shires had gathered people from all over Gonebeyond, anybody he'd been able to reach who could spare resources. Most of them agreed on the subject of slavers and why they were to be destroyed. Shires had pulled together a good coalition. Shires was good at that. It was all the more important for Andrej to get a good status on Shire's immediate condition.

Shires would be in pain and Andrej let it hurt, for a very brief time, because sharp negative stimulus could sharpen the senses. For all of the struggles Andrej had with himself during an interrogation, he was a professional, and he hadn't forgotten what pain was good for in the strictly therapeutic sense. He watched Shires's eyes and Shires's grimace carefully—dose-stylus at the ready—and put through the anodyne on the rising curve of Shires's consciousness.

"Whatwhere," Shires gasped demandingly, opening his eyes. It was a moment before he could focus, yes, but it was obvious to Andrej that Shires knew almost immediately where he was, in the general sense at least. "Status report. Current location, operational control?"

Frodis was applying sterile gel carefully over raw scraped skin. Caith had the synthesizers working on the meds, because Caith knew what meds Andrej was going to call for—in a general sense, at least. Everything under control, though accelerated almost past the border between effectiveness and anarchy.

"No, let's have up some quiquonet, rather than warbitol," Andrej said. "He's Langsarik, I know him." They didn't have much by way of genetic analysis on site and they didn't have time to run stats if they had. Warbitol would have been a perfectly adequate anti-inflammatory; that was why it was the default. Quiquonet was marginally more effective for Shires's ethnicity, but Caith had no way of knowing that.

Andrej turned his attention back to his patient, a little concerned that the pain medication wasn't having the effect he wanted. Shires's concern about the mission might be suppressing the anodyne. "I don't have the answers," he told Shires, watching the gross body scans.

Deep tissue scan showed bits of armor lodged under the skin but atop the membrane that covered the muscle, where it would not be migrating until they had a chance to go back in and clean things out.

Shires wouldn't lie still for a leisurely therapy follow-up any time soon, and Andrej needed to clear the level for the next patient. Janforth was laying down the brace, Frodis on the lifts, strapping Shires's shoulder into its stabilizing web while Caith—working around them both—was wrapping Shires's ribs. "I've got you on some third-tier medication, to fight the shock. That's why you don't feel the pain you're in for later, sorry. And stims, you've got half a day, but after that it's drop or risk overdose. On these. Here."

He positioned a reckless dosage down on Shires's cheek and secured it with a gelseal. Nobody in Shires's condition could be expected to keep track of time. The gelseal wouldn't give until an almost-safe number of hours had passed. If Shires was thinking clearly enough to force the secures on the gelseal he'd be at least marginally competent to decide to take the risks of premature dosing, and nothing Andrej could do would stop him.

Signaling for transport—he wasn't having Shires trying to get off the level on his own power, he was just as likely to fall over because the therapeutic drugs had not yet come up to speed, and Andrej had no room for semi-conscious bodies on the floor getting in his way and creating clutter—Andrej closed his eyes for a moment, remembering at just the last moment not to relax against Janforth at his back. He and Janforth had no history. Janforth would neither be expecting Andrej to borrow his strength or necessarily give his acquiescence if Andrej tried.

So Andrej shifted his weight from one foot to the other for an instant's rest, instead, one side of his body at a time, and accepted the flask of hot beverage automatically, drinking of it without thinking before realizing that it had materialized out of thin air and was rhyti. Hot sweet milky rhyti.

"That's good," he said gratefully. "Thank you." That had been Janforth's doing. He wasn't Janforth's officer of assignment, but maybe behaving as though he were helped Janforth maintain his confidence in the Safe he wore to shut his governor up, and Andrej had needed the rhyti. The room had not stopped shaking. It was additional strain on everybody here, because they were constantly being forced to adjust their balance while they were focused on the task.

Opening his eyes Andrej watched the main entry for the next casualty, but they'd hit one of those rare and unpredictable slack moments in the patient flow between one round of deliveries and the next. It meant nothing; there would only be that many more people to treat to come in the next rush. That was Andrej's preferred outcome. The other reason for a temporary lull was that the next seven bodies the front-line medics had pulled out of the rubble were already dead, or too close to it to make a difference.

It was still crowded. There were support staff with crates and carts hauling away the trash underfoot, the accumulated torn steri-packs and discarded single-use dose styli, bloodied cleaning pads escaped from confinement, scraps of peoples' cut-away clothing like Shires's body armor.

Trash going out. Restocks coming in at speed because a dressing or a dose had to be where a med tech would reach for it, without the loss of precious moments required to go hunting it up. Emergency medical equipment repair and replacement, everything not absolutely essential out, every treatment kit restocked. There were bread-folds coming around, cavene in rewrap flasks, another flask of rhyti handed him by the server.

Then the main access door rocked back against its stops as a litter-team came through, with more—inevitably—to follow. Back to work, then. And there were transport teams, yes, and lift-stretchers, wounded whose injuries required immediate attention lest lives be lost; but none of the wounded were brought to Andrej, and behind them were two men.

One of them was a loose-limbed man with the look of a grimly amused hawk about him, craggy of appearance, with strands of red-gold hair amongst orange. Tired as he was, it took Andrej a brief moment to recognize him as Yogee Gascarone. He'd seen Yogee just a little while ago, yes, but he wasn't used to thinking of Yodge as the older man they'd both become over the years.

The other was a man who seemed familiar to Andrej, but at a greater remove of time or space; he heard Janforth at his side let his breath out in a hiss of hatred and disgust. Janforth had gone pale, but it was with furious contempt rather than fear or conflict. He could guess that the newcomer was someone Janforth knew, then, but from where, how long ago?

People being stared at stared back. It was basic human instinct, a trick of peripheral vision and social awareness, a survival trait. Andrej was staring, trying to remember where he'd seen that doctor before; the doctor stared back, holding Andrej's gaze for what seemed to Andrej to be a long moment, challenging and defensive at once. Andrej was even more sure he recognized the man from somewhere, and it had been a similar situation, hadn't it?

Suddenly Andrej knew. He'd seen that man at a mass casualty exercise accompanying Fleet's reduction of a rebellion at Hassert, and it had been a long time ago. He'd been assigned to *Scylla*. They hadn't been to Port Rudistal yet.

Joslire Curran had still been alive, and not willing or able to tell him why it was important for Robert to be protected from that man.

Andrej had lost Joslire Curran at the Domitt Prison, bond-involuntary, yes, but the man who'd given Andrej his first survival tools in the face of the life to which his father's dictate had condemned him. Joslire, whom he'd loved.

Joslire, who'd left Fleet Orientation Station Medical to go with Andrej to *Scylla*, who'd told him things about his past experiences at the hands of other "Student Inquisitors" that had horrified him. Joslire had never spoken again of the abuse he'd suffered at the hands of one Student in particular, but they'd met that man at another mass casualty incident, in the aftermath of another war. And that man had tried it again.

Andrej had thwarted him of his prey when the man had thought to exploit Andrej's bond-involuntary Security assigned for his amusement. That was who he thought he recognized. What had the name been? Pefisct. Doctor Pefisct. "I find myself not liking that man," Andrej said quietly, to Janforth beside him. "I think he tortured somebody I loved, his name was Joslire, he was bond-involuntary. How do you go?"

Pefisct was the reason Joslire had left Fossum before his deferment from active duty had expired, choosing to go with Andrej rather than chance another Student Pefisct. So Pefisct was the reason Joslire had come to Rudistal as part of Andrej's security; so he was the reason that Joslire was dead.

"Hate him too much to be afraid of him," Janforth said. His voice was rock-steady, solid, determined. "I'll keep my hands off. For the sake of the Covenant."

"I wish I could confidently promise to do the same," Andrej almost whispered. Yogee was near enough to hear him. He wasn't going to get into it with Yogee. It was between himself and Pefisct. "So all I have to do is not kill him for what he did between now and then. There's stocking to be done if you wish to turn your back."

Yogee was here. "I've brought you one of your own," Yogee said; Andrej heard the "Koski" fighting with the "Koscuisko" in Yogee's tone of voice, and neither winning. "We've taken the city hospital, and I want you there. Doctor Pefisct will fill behind. What, do you know each other?"

"We've met," Andrej snarled. "Frodis, Caith, keep your eye on this—person. Janforth is with me." Yogee's expression changed;

speculation, and a quick sort of understanding. But this was no time to reject any medical assistance no matter how Andrej distrusted the practitioner; and he'd be telling Yogee all about it soon enough. "City hospital, Surgeon General?"

"Good man, Janforth," Yogee said, by way of an endorsement. So there was no question about the matter. Pefisct started around one side of the emergency levels to take Andrej's place; Janforth turned suddenly to bar Pefisct's way, and stood there, staring into Pefisct's face, chest to chest with him, for a long moment. Pefisct looked confused. Then angry. Then a little genuinely, honestly afraid.

So the Safe really was doing its job. Doing it well. Janforth shouldered his way past Pefisct, who gave way. Andrej followed him. He didn't have time to think about this. There was a hospital. There would be casualties. They'd include civilians. Janforth was strong. He'd be all right.

All the same Andrej was going to want to do that surgery as soon as possible: and hope someone would speak earnestly to Janforth about the Covenant of Gonebeyond, and why he couldn't skin Pefisct alive with a dull knife.

At least not without *him* there, to participate.

CHAPTER FOUR

Rescue Mission

Bat Yorvik had never been aboard a ship during somebody's war. He'd never seen a war, and it was difficult for him to really focus on the fact that "casualties" meant "dead or wounded." To know a truth to be true wasn't the same thing as really internalizing it.

There had been a moratorium on reports from dirtside, because during the lead-up to the invasion of the city by Langsarik Coalition troops, a strict communications quarantine had been rigorously maintained. Silence. Nothing for Couveraine to pick up and use to derive information about what was meant to happen, when, and how. No accidental interceptions that would lead Couveraine to target individual teams.

There had been surface scans from the *Ragnarok* itself, looking for activity within the city; with the containment dome in place there wasn't much by way of detailed information. They didn't answer the questions Bat most wanted to ask.

He'd been haunting the officer's mess for three days, now, taking his meals, devouring the four-times-a-day scheduled briefings and whatever updates came in. The people who lived on the *Ragnarok*, whose dining room this was, had been very patient and hospitable; and, yes, he could have had his meals in his quarters—his one room—but he didn't want to miss a moment.

This was real. This was serious. He knew how to weigh and balance important issues with real impacts on the lives of people and their communities—he was a Judge, after all. This was much more immediate. It was of a different order of magnitude altogether.

There'd been no live discussion within the command and control center on the *Ragnarok* since before the shift-change second-shift yesterday—programmed, rehearsed sends from a roving location, yes, to avoid alerting Couveraine that an attack was imminent, material that conveyed no information. A repeat of the Langsarik Coalition's final communication. *In the absence of agreement to our demands we will take active measures to achieve our objectives as laid out in our last meeting.* Nothing else. For nearly a full day.

The lull had given him time to talk, which had been good. He'd found in Captain ap Rhiannon a legal philosopher of sorts. She was willing to discuss her actions at Taisheki Station, her decision to shoot her way out of the minefield Taisheki had been laying to trap her. Yes, she'd received an order in good form from the Fleet Audit Appeals Authority to surrender her ship and crew for investigation of the potential murder of a senior officer.

No, it had not—in her view—been a legal order, since the crew Fleet demanded be turned over were not guilty of any such crime and did not fall to Taisheki to process as already condemned. Those crew hadn't even been on the *Ragnarok* at the time; Bat had been a little surprised to hear that. Ap Rhiannon was perfectly clear on her main point, as firm as the most dogmatic judge could be: an illegal order was not an order.

As the captain of the *Ragnarok*—brevet or not—she was, in her analysis, competent in Law to make a decision about the legality of an order that affected the health and welfare of the ship entrusted to her care, the ship and crew for which she was legally responsible to Fleet and the Bench. There were no other questions that pertained.

Crèche-bred were raised to be sure, confident, completely binary in approach to their sworn duty; and ap Rhiannon was all of those things, absolutely. It was only that her training and education had developed an unforeseen complication. Absolute devotion to her duty transcended her compliance with directives from external authorities, if she didn't think her *instructions received* were lawful in context with the benchmark *orders legally valid and received*.

She therefore had declined to receive them, in a formal sense. And it clearly made crystalline, pure sense to Jennet ap Rhiannon; and she clearly had no second thoughts. No doubts. No uncertainty.

Finally there was a status update from Couveraine, unscheduled, immediate. Bat was grateful he hadn't stepped out to the toilets. He'd have missed the first moments, the receipt codes on the signal, the encoding of the secures on the transmissions, during which nothing but picture was available.

But what a picture. Stand-up briefing in a small room with windows all around, windows through which Bat could see into what looked like a warehouse full of activity—medical staff, coming and going, technicians escorting ambulatory patients, the people running past the window in the background on their way from one emergency to another.

Hilton Shires was wearing what Bat could recognize as a medical stabilization underblouse beneath his jacket, the sort of thing emergency medical people used when a man couldn't be bandaged up and made to lie down. It was dirty.

Bench specialist Ivers was there, the hair on one side of her head flattened down at an odd angle—blood-caked, then, Bat guessed. Torn clothing, dirty faces, bandages in odd places, Doctor Gascarone standing next to a man in much-distressed hospital whites who was as pale as Bat had ever seen a man—Dolgorukij, then, he guessed. Which would mean Andrej Koscuisko. Bat put that thought away for later.

There was the man Shires had introduced at Bat's first briefing, the Nurail communications officer—also described to Bat, recently, as Safehaven's spymaster general.

"Captain ap Rhiannon," Shires said, but the encoding was still stabilizing, the blue telltale lights were bright, yes, but the final audio sort had been steadying when Shires had started to talk. "Where's Rukota?"

No, that was an aside, as Shires looked around him. A man came forward to stand in the front rank; there were easily ten people in that glassed-in room. There must not have been any bombs in the immediate vicinity, Bat guessed. Otherwise there'd be no glass wall intact, unless it had been hardened past the point usually required in hospitals, and they didn't seem to be in a combat support hospital, either. Were they?

"Thank you, General Rukota." Shires folded his arms across his chest—maybe hesitating just a bit, as if his ribs hurt—and started off. "Please share this message on distribution, all participating forces. Port Couveraine has surrendered, and is cooperating with coalition forces in pacifying the city. Cleanup parties comprised of mixed personnel are going house-to-house looking for casualties and pockets of resistance."

Bat saw the back of someone's head crown briefly across the visuals; someone bearing a tray with flasks of cavene. Bat could see the steam rising as Shires took a cautious sip before he continued. "Any news on the vector for Holding?"

"Located," ap Rhiannon said. Bat hadn't seen her come in, but of course she'd have been called for. He'd been concentrating on Shires. "Identified. Vector calculations confirmed, vector secured on this end. I suggest we send *Fisher Wolf* on ahead, it's our fastest, and three armed couriers to follow to secure the debouch if required. Probes don't detect any vector control on Holding's end. Intelligence seems to indicate no hostile presence. No sign of freighter identified as holding slaves in transit."

"Well. Now. Here's the thing." Another sip of cavene, and a stifled cough; drinking too fast. "Couveraine says the cartel's gone from the slave base at Holding. Not evacuated, deserted, and all of the prisoners left behind. Abandoned in place. I need the hospital that Agavie sent ready for transit, as soon as an advance party sends an all-clear."

Abandoned? Hundreds of people, Bat's briefing said. Abandoned with what supplies, what resources? "Understood," ap Rhiannon said. "Limited medical staff in reserve, however."

Yes, that would be a problem. The Coalition forces had sent medical teams, and the *Ragnarok* had not been excepted. The hospital that the Agavie trading firm had sent as a token of good-will was still stowed on the freighter, ready to send to Holding; but there were limited staff accompanying, Bat understood.

Shires looked to Dr. Gascarone, and then at his cavene; passing the discussion over. "We won't be needing all these people now that the shooting's stopped," Gascarone said. He appeared to have plaster in his hair and all down the side of his hospital whites. "And we can peel off some support staff, with Couveraine's people to fill behind. That hospital of Agavie's, I've discussed it with Doctor Pefisct, we can staff a refugee camp. I hope that's all we have to worry about."

Pefisct? Wasn't that the Ship's Inquisitor he'd spoken to on JFS *Sondarkit* in Haspirzak, not altogether very long ago? What would Pefisct be doing in Gonebeyond? Oh. Of course. A deserter. Ivers had talked to him about Witt, and Witt's organization. The Third Judge had had some interesting information as well, but Bat had always been at the other side of an active criminal investigation.

"Casualties?" Shires prompted. Dr. Gascarone nodded, if a little reluctantly. "Combat teams running roughly eight in ninety-six, very reasonable, really. Not ready to report a fatality count, Mission Commander." The scene through the windows was busier than eight in ninety-six, Bat suspected. Civilian casualties. "Mortality less than that, of course, and I will say it doesn't seem to be in excess of standard parameters. So far. I think."

People had died. Bat had known that people would. He didn't know any of them, but still the news was more shocking—put in impersonal terms, hard statistics—than Bat had realized it would be.

"Occupation troops to join us, at this time," Shires said. "Sending *Fisher Wolf* out on priority through Pavrock vector. Let me just express my appreciation for your weaponer, Captain, General Rukota's been invaluable. Okay, that's it for now. Thank you, everybody."

And that was it. "Your Honor," ap Rhiannon said to him. "Any questions?"

As a matter of fact there were. The Langsarik Coalition had taken over an autonomous settlement, one run by a criminal cartel, yes, but the cartel was criminal under Jurisdiction commerce codes and there weren't any such things in Gonebeyond.

On the one hand, Bat was completely behind shutting down slave markets, and the effort clearly had a broad base of support. On the other hand, the Langsarik Coalition had taken police action against a community that wasn't doing anything illegal because there wasn't a legal code in Gonebeyond to define what was and wasn't lawful behavior.

So where was the Langsarik Coalition getting the validation for its course of action? And didn't this point the way to the kind of civil unrest that was all but inevitable when unwritten concepts of legality were set in opposition to each other, and wasn't the regulation of trade to avoid civil unrest the very foundation of the Jurisdiction's Bench, and hadn't that led in time to problems?

Maybe it was. And maybe it wasn't. One thing was for sure: between Agavie's offer of negotiation with, and Couveraine's unsuccessful resistance to, the Langsarik Coalition, there was almost certainly example after example of conflicts similar in kind if not in criticality that would have to be resolved, adjusted, adjudicated, for Gonebeyond to go forward as a responsible polity, with protection for its people and prosperity in its future.

Andrej Koscuisko stood in the surgical suite of Couveraine's hospital arguing with himself as much as with Yogee. "Really?" Yodge demanded. "Now? You want to do this *now*? You're not fit. I won't allow it."

Andrej was tired. No, he was exhausted. Could he perform the surgery? Was he in fit condition? Could he afford to make Janforth wait to have the governor removed? He hadn't had time to accomplish that vital task before, not knowing for certain when the shooting was going to start. It wasn't really after, yet. There were patients coming in, almost all of them from the civilian population of this city, husbands and wives and children and cooks and clerks and maintenance workers.

The hospital had been staffed to a normal standard of medical support for a civic community mission. Translation injuries? Yes. Five times the normal rate? No. Ways in which he could make himself useful in the emergency treatment area? Always. Surgeries that he and only he had primary responsibility for performing? Only one.

"We didn't know Pefisct would turn up. Janforth just got away from that—object, Yogee. Pefisct tortures bond-involuntaries for amusement. He tortured one of mine." That wasn't purely pertinent. Maybe. But Yogee had to be convinced of how much more pressure it would put on Janforth to be in proximity to his tormentor. "And there'll be no avoiding him in a refugee hospital at Holding."

If the Safe was going to fail this would be just the thing to tip it over, and Andrej knew what a governor could do to a bond-involuntary without defenses because he'd made it happen. "I'm willing to do the surgery," Andrej said firmly. "He's willing to accept the risk. There'll be a start on recovery time on *Fisher Wolf*, and my gentlemen were up and about within two days. If I can take him on *Fisher Wolf*. If I can go with *Fisher Wolf*. They of all people know what he is going through."

"Ehh," Yogee said, half-turning, clearly undecided whether to just leave or continue to argue. He'd lose the argument. He and Andrej both knew it. Andrej recognized the sound in Yogee's voice, the expression on Yogee's face, the restless language of Yogee's body. Remembered it with remarkable clarity, even after all these years. They'd been so much younger at Mayon. It had been before Andrej had found things out about himself. "I don't want any more casualties."

"You don't want what happens to a man if his governor finds fault. Neither do I. I've seen it. And we are wasting time that would be better spent in recovery for my patient."

"I'm sorry about that, Koski," Yogee said, impatient but sincere. "I didn't know about Pefisct. I don't see a way around it, it's his hospital, really, and I'm worried about those prisoners. All right. Go ahead. Do you have a team? I'll be a team. I'll help."

That offer was on the face of it amusing; but also unacceptable. Hadn't Yogee done epidemiology? Not surgery? On the other hand, they'd all done baseline general practice, which had had some emergency surgeries thrown in, if of a relatively straightforward kind. Mostly simple ones. This was a simple surgery. It only had to be perfect.

"You're on vitals and anesthesia. Be prepared for sudden spikes in pain levels if anything goes wrong, I'm not an expert on governors. All I can say is that I didn't kill anybody with the prior surgeries. Can you get me some field technicians? And I'll start calibration."

He had an edge, quite apart from previous experience and solid surgical skills with recent practice. He knew how to select his own drugs. Not for Janforth. For himself. He'd had to self-prescribe for years, long years, bad years, when Lowden had been captain of the *Ragnarok* and Andrej had had to be able to jump quickly from wrestling with self-inflicted ethanol poisoning to an emergency surgery in Infirmary. He knew which stimulants worked best, most quickly, most reliably.

It took a little longer to achieve a solid sterile environment, because Andrej's clothing—and his person—were thoroughly contaminated with dust, sweat, blood, everything that went with open wounds in a hospital too far over capacity to contemplate. Couveraine's hospital itself had escaped major damage. The surgical suite remained intact, and since it always had its own power and ventilation and all the rest, it was ready to go by the time Andrej had completed his own transition from sweaty dirty tired battle surgeon to hyperalert operational surgical readiness.

Yogee had done the finals with Janforth, to save time prior to patient preparation for anesthesiology; it had been patched through to him while he was changing, because he had the ultimate responsibility for any mistakes.

Do you understand the nature of this surgery. Please tell me in your own words what we're about to do. Do you understand the risks, have they been explained to you, please state in your own words what these risks are, please state plainly whether you agree to this surgery with those risks in mind. Do you understand that the whole hospital might still collapse and bury us all, no, never mind. Please answer this question in your own words, do you elect to have this surgery at this time with the medical team that has been introduced to you.

Now not even Yogee could stand in Andrej's way. Not in honor. Not in their shared responsibility for the patient. Once the patient had demonstrated his understanding of the risks—including in this case the drugs Andrej had taken, and Janforth was more knowledgeable than most patients, he had his own baseline medical training, and bond-involuntaries were conversant with wake-keepers and all of the doses in that class—once all that was finished, it was time.

Everything was waiting on him, in the surgical theater. Andrej backed into the surgical machine that would translate his magnified manipulation of surgical flint and whisper-probe extractors into action, within Janforth's brain—the places where the best pain was, where the governor's activators lay in wait. Isolated from all external distractions Andrej ran through his final calibrations, rehearsing his approach one last time in his mind.

He had to open up the skull, pierce bone, because he was going to be pulling something out, a physical object. All of it. No single fragment broken off at the end of a single filament of the governor's long spider-like legs. He had to be certain that he knew exactly how this governor was built, and how implanted. He had to have the index-screens where he could see them. He had to be sure of what he was doing.

And now he had to get to work.

Security Chief Brachi Stildyne stood on the decking of the free-floating loading platform that the freighter *Nikojek* had deployed for

Fisher Wolf's use, watching the crew load cargo under the able direction of Medith Riggs.

Garrity was battered. Lek was bruised. Godsalt had gotten himself knocked around, Pyotr had wrenched his left foot practically off his ankle, Hirsel's head was half-shaved around the newly-sealed pink line of a beautiful tear in his scalp, and for once—in complete defiance of the usual run of things –Robert St. Clare didn't have more than a scratch or two on him. Robert had tried on a little dry cough or so, sporadically, from inhaling too much dust, but nobody had given him much sympathy.

All things considered Brachi Stildyne was pleased with the day's work. He'd pulled wrong between his hip and his thigh, somehow; but it hadn't been more than a year since he'd been shot in what Andrej Koscuisko had referred to as his fundament, so he wasn't sure that counted as damages or mere residual inconvenience. And he could walk. They were all ambulatory. Pyotr'd be wearing a boot to support the various insults he'd done his ankle, but Pyotr could navigate—or pilot—sitting down, so that was no problem for anybody but Pyotr.

They'd been rotated out for fresh troops once they'd made the mission objective and secured their piece of the final perimeter, surrounding the leadership's last remaining outpost. By that time they'd been on the offensive for the better part of four shifts. An entire day. Close to the limits of peak level combat performance.

Since they'd been first in, they'd been among the first rotated out, they'd expected that. But by the time they'd gotten to the other side of medical treatment and stabilization Dame Ivers had sent them a command redirect, a mission objective behind the lines of direct engagement. He and the wolf-pack had been out with *Fisher Wolf* to the freighter *Nikojek*, to pick up a forward aid station. Stildyne didn't think he'd ever seen one of those, and as yet there'd been nothing to see on the floating loading platform except crates.

Fisher Wolf was probably the best ship for a fast armed courier that the Langsarik Coalition had, and if there was anybody who knew more about loading *Fisher Wolf* than Medith Riggs by this point Stildyne didn't know who it would be. She was down in *Fisher Wolf*'s cargo holds even now, generally using all the space she could find to stow the forward aid station she'd pulled out of *Nikojek*'s cargo.

Godsalt and Hirsel and Robert spun their loading-lifts like Wolnadi fighters on maneuvers. It made Stildyne a little nervous to watch them, but Koscuisko wouldn't have released any stimulant drugs that would interfere with their capability to crew the thula; so they were simply one ratchet up from "all deliberate speed," and he didn't usually see it because they weren't usually in this much of a hurry.

And still it was a problem. They should be stowing their own, because a cargo handler took off as well as put on. They were leaving it to him to talk to Riggs again; cowards, one and all.

Riggs came barreling down off of the cargo loading ramp with her flatfile docket in one hand and a look of grim satisfaction on her face. "Can't quite make two shelters and a ration," she called out to him.

Two temporary Infirmary shelters' worth of cargo containers, she meant, one medium container full of emergency rations. But she'd gotten all of the potable water on board. She'd checked with him about that, but it had only been for official confirmation—she already knew that water was more important than food. "Apart from that. Final stowage. Ready to seal and go, Chief."

When do we leave. He cleared his throat, looking down at the decking. They hadn't had the conversation. "Before we go," he said; and she was immediately wary. She'd thought of this already, too. It came from her study of cargo handling, Stildyne had decided; the habit of putting things together in her mind at speed and then looking for the places where something wasn't where it ought to be.

"Yes?" That was a dare, a challenge. Stildyne had one really important advantage, though. He had years of practice telling Andrej Koscuisko things Koscuisko didn't want to hear.

"I've been on the ground at a displacement camp." That was the official term for a concentration camp full of people pushed out of their homes with nothing more than the clothes on their backs and sometimes not even those. Such an innocuous term, *displacement*, Stildyne had always admired it. "It's uglier than even me in a mirror. No. Seriously. They're full of more misery than I can describe. The worst slums in Supicor are better."

She might not know how bad that was. He wasn't getting an encouraging *I understand and comply with unstated suggestion* body language from her. Well, he'd just go on. "And these people were taken by slavers. I don't want anybody there who doesn't absolutely have to be. The wolf-pack have seen horrors, and this'll almost certainly be one."

She didn't know, she couldn't know, and he didn't want her—didn't want anybody—to have to find out. But it wasn't his call. She did right by *Fisher Wolf.* The crew had already made it clear to him that they'd do right by her. "I think I know where you're going with this," she said. She wasn't going to give him any more than that, to go on.

"We can do it without you," he said. "Not as well or as quickly, that's true. I'm only saying this once. Don't get unreasonable on me. You'll never unsee it, and we don't know what it is. You're a civilian. You can follow on with the main party. We won't think less of you for it."

Things would be better already by the time the main party arrived, if only because they'd have a better idea of how bad things were. And there was something to be said for the emotional support of being one among maybe a hundred and twenty people rather than six wolves, himself, her, Koscuisko, and the patient he was bringing on board. Out past *Nikojek's* maintenance atmosphere Stildyne could see a courier on approach now; that would be them.

"So you do the military, and I do the cargo management," she said. There was maybe a little bit of the bluster of the inexperienced there, just a hint; but she had a right, and life would knock it out of her soon enough without his help. She was young. He was sorry that she had to learn unpleasant things, but life was like that. "I promise to hide out in the cargo hold if I have to. After the cargo's unshipped."

This was not a good idea. It was a bad idea. She'd never done a war, or a displacement camp, or a field hospital with everybody doing whatever they could whether they knew what they were doing or not. But she wasn't a child, either, or his responsibility. She had to be allowed to make her own decisions, even when he thought she was going to wish she'd thought twice about it. Maybe she'd already done that part.

"I have no further arguments." The courier was landing. Stildyne watched it come to rest, its passenger loading ramp descending; Koscuisko was first off the ship, his patient following him down. Stildyne frowned; there was something he thought he recognized about that man. Then he shook it off. It was obvious. The man was a former bond-involuntary, Koscuisko had said. Stildyne recognized the man's military bearing, disciplined precision, especially following a ranking officer.

He'd come to Gonebeyond rather than wait for surgery at a formal detention facility, apparently. And he'd been on Safe, but there were reasons Koscuisko hadn't trusted that enough to refuse to perform the removal of the governor himself and as soon as possible.

Koscuisko had done it before, of course. Stildyne had seen the entire crew down for a day or so, and then ready to face life again, and even under these challenging circumstances he had to agree that the best place for Janforth was with other people who'd been where he was now. So they had their full complement, and all the cargo the thula could carry.

"*Fisher Wolf* to *Nikojek*," Stildyne said, knowing the talk-alert was listening. "Ready to clear for departure."

The wolf-pack liked to think of themselves as a high-functioning band of warriors, and they were. Still. All of those years with Koscuisko as their officer, working with Koscuisko, one community even if the power dynamic had been on Koscuisko's side. They were just as glad Koscuisko was coming with them to be first on the ground. They were all going to need all the mutual support they could get, and that included him; he wasn't even going to pretend to deny it.

His only remaining regret was that Riggs had made up her mind to come with them.

They were on vector for Holding, and Andrej was enjoying a quiet game of tiles with his self-same companion, his Tikhon, Brachi Stildyne. It was always good to play tiles between emergencies. Life had been one emergency after another for weeks. There was a lot of catching up to do.

"Have you seen our Surgeon General?" he asked, looking at the array before him on the table. Tiles weren't about hidden hands as much as pulling the perfect citation associated with each token to lay down. He and Brachi had always played the open game to even the advantages, since Andrej knew more about the Saga than Brachi did. Andrej had been raised on it, and in his milk-tongue. "Yogee Gascarone. We were at school together, Mayon Medical College. It seemed that I annoyed him by just breathing."

"Doctor Gascarone, yes," Brachi said. He put down a seamed kerchief next to a fruit tree, adjacent to a small boat: he was turning the narrative, and now Andrej wouldn't be able to deploy his rock fence because there hadn't been a need to pick stones for boundaries in the fair garden of the anxious Anariand. "Only to see him, at a briefing. I heard he brought a doctor down from the Agavie freighter that you didn't care for."

Stildyne had something on his mind. Andrej wondered if it was the challenges they'd face when they came off vector and found out for sure whether someone was waiting to destroy them, or something tangential. Either way if Stildyne was distracted he might not see the potential that playing a mead-cup had of destroying the entire narrative line, because Andrej had nothing to block the tile of winterpinks picked out in fine stitch-work on the collar of deceitful Kandril.

"Suppose you had met a man who'd tortured someone you loved," Andrej said. "That sounds risible, coming from me. I know. He was Joslire Curran's student of assignment at Fossum, before I arrived at orientation. Meaning that Joshire was his orderly. We saw him again while we were on *Scylla*, just the once. Joslire never spoke of him but twice, and the first time without naming any names."

Andrej had wondered, from time to time, whether he'd been granted Joslire's confidence from the beginning through no merit of his own, simply out of gratitude that he was not Pefisct. And maybe Joslire *had* been vulnerable when they'd first met, but they'd had a partnership, though an unequal one. Stildyne was considering his tiles. Andrej spoke on.

"Then to see that person after many years, to be surprised at how much I still hate him who knows almost nothing about him. I suppose he did his work in clinic well enough. How many people do I see every day who hate me as much, or more?"

"Fewer than you might think," Stildyne said, but a little absentmindedly. "Mostly they're kept clear. Or keep themselves clear. It's for the best." Since Stildyne was still puzzling out his next move he hadn't seen the potential triumph that awaited him if he played that mead-cup. *He wasn't talking to distract Stildyne*, Andrej told himself. *He was just talking.*

"And then to discover that Janforth Ifrits is here with us, come straight to Gonebeyond because he couldn't get away from Pefisct fast enough. Only to find Pefisct here arriving. When I compared my hatred for Pefisct to how a man would feel who had so recently suffered under him I feared the Safe would not be able to withstand the depth of the emotion."

Stildyne picked up the tile. The mead-cup token. He didn't set it down; he turned it around and around, end to end, restlessly. "I want to tell you something, Andrej," Stildyne said. "I thought I'd recognized him, and I was right. He and I were together on JFS *Chaezul*, before I was transferred to the *Ragnarok*. Bond-involuntaries were tools for use, criminals, put under Bond for punishment and expected to suffer. I wasn't the only one, but that's not the point."

Now Stildyne put the mead-cup token down. As though he'd forgotten why he'd picked it up. "Five minutes before shift-change here and there. He resented it, but that was his problem. I kept things balanced among the lot of them. Still. And there it is."

Andrej couldn't think what he should say. He'd thought he'd sensed awkwardness, when Janforth was introduced to the crew. He'd thought it had a different source.

He'd known about casual exploitation of bond-involuntaries by the people in their chain of command. He'd made a very strong point with the *Ragnarok*'s then-First Lieutenant about it, during his early days on the *Ragnarok*. He outranked Wyrlann. He could issue correction any way he liked with impunity, and Captain Lowden had thought Wyrlann's indignant complaints about Andrej were funny.

Lowden didn't take sexual advantage, not directly; the floggings he could order had been gratification enough for him, until Andrej had found a way to persuade him to stop. Which was the more contemptible? A Security Chief who granted himself sexual favors from troops unable to decline the honor? Or a Captain who tortured them for idle sport? Or a Ship's Inquisitor who did the same?

He hadn't been able to afford thinking it through. He'd needed Stildyne's support too much to preserve his sanity as things got worse and worse on the *Ragnarok* under Lowden's fiendish regime than to be able to risk analysis or pass judgment. None of the wolf-pack had ever so much as hinted at any issue with Stildyne, and that had been enough. Now it came back to him. All he had was what he'd told Stildyne once: the most important thing, the critically important thing, was that Stildyne had stopped, because he had learned shame.

The crew of the *Fisher Wolf*, once freed from Bond, seemed on much the same terms with Stildyne as ever, though Andrej didn't know what might have passed between them all during that first year in which he'd had no contact with them. It wasn't any of his business, really. Now, however, now Stildyne had spoken, and Andrej needed to respond. He didn't know what to say.

"You surprise and yet do not surprise me." Had he ever taken Brachi Stildyne for a virtuous man of principles and high moral standards, imbued with the classic Dolgorukij values which included abhorrence of taking advantage of power—in whatever sense—for sexual exploitation?

He had not. He'd taken Stildyne for a fundamentally practical man who in the greatest impracticability of his life had taught himself compassion, but for practical reasons: to best preserve expensive Fleet equipment—bond-involuntaries—for their entire range of function; and, once he had begun to suspect that he'd become vulnerable in some sense to Andrej's disapproval, to protect himself from earning it by becoming a man of whom Andrej would not disapprove.

He'd better explain. "You do not surprise me because you have once previously spoken to me on this subject. At the Matredonat, years ago." Bluntly, brutally honest, presenting the worst of himself, not to be forgiven or excused but to be seen as who he'd been as well as who he was. Andrej hadn't found it making as much difference as he might have once thought it would. And now? "And yet surprise—"

In that you speak of it. That you somehow believe I don't know exactly how such things come to happen. That you think I might not have guessed, whether or not I ever faced up to it. No. None of those things were worth their being spoken. "And yet surprised that you grant shame such power. What will you do?"

Put the mead-cup token down. That was what Stildyne ought to do. Should Stildyne be ashamed? Uniquely so? Why did he speak, if he was not ashamed? "You know, we never really had it out," Stildyne said. "Not in so many words." That wasn't Janforth Stildyne was talking about now, Andrej realized. "If I end up at the bottom of a ditch with my neck broken, ever, I'll maybe deserve it. I mean to just keep clear from him. He wants to say something, it's up to him."

Very much the same as Andrej approached his own life, Andrej realized, suddenly. He acknowledged his crimes, he owned them, he had earned hatred and contempt honestly. He apologized to nobody and for nothing. That he had done great ill was too obvious to say. That he had done so with reluctance—before, after—was no defense, and to apologize for having committed his sins with enjoyment would be hypocrisy.

I have wronged you, yes. *I regret the suffering I have caused you*, yes. *I wish that I had not*, these things he could say honestly, but *I hope that you can forgive me*—no. That was between him and the Holy Mother. If—perhaps when—he ended up at the bottom of a ditch with his throat cut, or his own neck broken, or more imaginatively dispatched, he would not be surprised, however much he would regret the loss of his life.

"All I can say is that should Janforth kill you I will resent it very much, and return the favor." Yes. Perhaps that was all he had to say. "I further speculate that there are others here on this ship who would also regret that. And that you should perhaps examine your tiles, Brachi, I do not wish to take advantage of distraction on your part."

Whatever Stildyne had done Andrej had done worse, and in full knowledge that what he was doing was a violation of moral law, although legal—and required, to an extent—under the rule of Law and the Judicial order. He was the last man alive who could sit in judgment on Brachi Stildyne: who took up the mead-cup token with an expression of mild surprise, and laid it down on the playing-field, and won the game.

Things were by no means all bad, from Danyo Pefisct's point of view. The patient load at the combat support hospital outside Couveraine was lightening up. There were actually places to sit down in triage. There was cavene and bread-folds coming out from the city, limited quantity, but at least they were hot. Danyo sat with his back to the wall eating a snack and considering.

People weren't looking at him, but it was too early to tell whether it was because they'd been contaminated by Koscuisko's hostility or just tired. They shared the fellowship of the battlefield. He could assume a welcome where and when he wanted one, because he'd been part of the emergency medical staff; that was social credit.

There was more. He was to move into an overflow clinic inside the city. He'd be working with civilians who knew very well that they were beaten, so he wouldn't have to think twice about raising his voice. It had been an unpleasant surprise to see Janforth here, but on balance that was all right too. Janforth could hate him all he wanted. They were in Gonebeyond.

Under the Covenant, Janforth couldn't revenge himself on Danyo for things that had happened before Janforth got here. And Janforth was still afraid of him. The fact that he couldn't deploy the punishment of Janforth's own governor any more didn't change the fact that they had years of shared understanding between them, of careful tutelage and salutary discipline. Danyo could find some amusement there.

During his transit to Couveraine Danyo had had a chance to study up on Witt's virus—and its persistence, once deployed. The only real challenge Danyo saw in his way lay in the actual mechanics of getting close to Koscuisko. Staff briefings would suit very well. The chances of it making other people sick—sick enough to require hospitalization—was real, but low, by Danyo's analysis.

Whether or not anybody else got sick, Koscuisko was the best neurosurgeon they had available, and would necessarily have priority for evacuation to a specialty hospital—in Haspirzak Judiciary, perhaps. All Danyo had to do was arrange the sickness, then arrange for evacuation. He had a contact, a comm drop. Witt's people would know Koscuisko was coming.

That Koscuisko wasn't actually here was a setback, but a temporary one. Koscuisko had gone off to Holding with the forward aid station that had been among the elements of the field hospital Danyo had brought with him on *Nikojek*. He'd hoped that it would be buried deeply enough in cargo that the Langsariks would be forced to send the entire field hospital—with Danyo on it—right away, but that, apparently, would have presented an anomaly.

One way or another, the Langsarik's cargo manager had pulled the forward aid station out and carried it off with Koscuisko to Holding. So Koscuisko was gone. Janforth had gone with him. Danyo hadn't asked after Janforth by name, but he'd heard enough to realize what had happened.

He'd been thinking too hard. He hadn't noticed Gascarone coming in until someone blocked his light. "Information," Gascarone said. Gascarone apparently knew Koscuisko from before; he'd apparently taken Koscuisko's prejudice against Danyo. Danyo didn't care. Danyo had the hospital that the Langsarik Coalition wanted. Gascarone had more-than-adequate reason to be polite. "We've just gotten word back from the other end. Finish up here. You and I—as well as everybody else we can cut loose—will be on freighter *Nikojek* to Holding, with that lovely juicy field hospital Agavie has been kind enough to send us."

Good. The toothpick with its hidden payload was an annoying distraction, a constant reminder of the record Witt had showed him. He couldn't wait to get rid of it. "Right away," Danyo said, stuffing the remains of his bread-fold into his half-empty flask of cavene to toss them both together. "Any details? Situation report?"

He'd been Chief Medical Officer, as well as Koscuisko. No negative assessment of his medical skill-set versus Koscuisko's could bear on the fact that they'd held equal rank and equivalent authority. He stood up, looking around him for the waste receptacle. "Er, sorry, Doctor. Habit. But are there?"

Gascarone had turned to go. "Briefing on board once we're on our way. Collect at the tactical launch-field, we'll load for transport to the freighter. I'm taking your room, nice drinks cabinet, think I've earned it and excuse me if I don't invite you. Don't lose any time, it could get ugly."

Something to go on, at least. Ugly? Well, not likely to be a very challengingly ugly, all the same. It had been explained to Danyo as abandoned human cargo, not a fighting war with complex casualties. Fattening people up was probably as demanding as it was going to get; and he'd be further establishing himself with the Langsarik Coalition as the man who'd brought them a hospital, at the same time. All good.

"I'm on my way, Doctor," Danyo assured Gascarone, following him out of the room to go collect his satchel, and get out to the ship that would deliver him to *Nikojek*; thence to Holding, and the fulfillment of Witt's purpose for Andrej Koscuisko.

It had been two days from Couveraine to the Pavrock vector debouch at Holding; another full day and the fraction before *Fisher Wolf* found a stable geosync orbit above the only sign of any occupation on the planet's surface. *Fisher Wolf* had had to make four passes through the uppermost layers of Holding's breathably dense atmosphere before they found the trace: chemical signature consistent with surface-to-space propulsion, conversion engines deploying burst thrust to clear the cling.

Stildyne hadn't seen much of Janforth in all that time. Koscuisko had wanted Janforth to keep relatively quiet on account of his recent surgery, so Godsalt had mostly been running him through mid-deep-cycle maintenance on *Fisher Wolf*'s armament: main battle cannon, and two swivel guns.

The wheelhouse was quiet, half-empty. *Fisher Wolf* could maintain itself on geosync forever, as far as anybody knew. Garrity and Robert were keeping the watch while Stildyne supervised, sitting beside Robert's comm station, watching the ship's scans build the ground-map.

Below them Holding looked like a wasteland of bare rock ribs and drift sand reflecting sunlight back into space with notable intensity. Category eleven six arid environment, limited vegetation. The temperature varied between late afternoon maxima and early morning minima on the elevated plateau; the site was southerly to the equator, so there'd be long twilight morning and evening. Frost and fire.

"He said something to me once." Robert's remark seemed to come out of nowhere, but Stildyne knew to sit and wait. It would come. Robert could be a bit oblique on approach to what he meant to say sometimes; that was all. Not like Garrity. Garrity was all straight to his point in as few words as possible, and after that nothing. "Anders. Himself. Our officer. About that deserter that came in with *Nikojek*."

Pefisct, then. There were only two people who knew what the relationship between Curran and Pefisct had been like: Curran and Pefisct. One of them was dead, and Stildyne wasn't sure about the other one's chances. Janforth might have hints, but Stildyne wasn't going to be the one to ask. "What did he say?"

Then there were two people with possibly half an idea, which might ordinarily make up one whole except that one of them was Koscuisko and if he'd intended to share any details he'd have let Stildyne know. There was no reason Curran should have told Koscuisko all about it.

Stildyne had been living with Joslire Curran for years, now—the shadow of Curran, Koscuisko's very occasional remarks. He'd grown reconciled to the presence of a ghost. It wasn't as though Curran came up in conversation all that often.

Robert, now, Robert had come from Fleet Orientation Station Medical at the same time as Curran, for a different reason of course—Curran by choice, Robert by Fleet assignment. Maybe Robert had something to say about it. Stildyne watched data scroll across one of the analysis displays on the bulkhead to the right of main screens, coalescing as it ran into a dimensional projection of the structure on the ground.

"Well, that Pefisct was there." There was a main well that apparently supplied the station with water; several subsidiaries. Pulling from an aquifer, since there'd been no rivers or lakes detected on first analysis. There were mountains, at an appreciable distance removed; bare rock. Not much water there either. Not enough to feed an underground stream system, apparently. "He wanted me to know. And to watch out. And make sure he—Joslire—was never alone with him, or me either. Alone with Pefisct, that is."

If he was going to build a slaving camp, Stildyne decided, this was right where he'd put one: in the middle of a desert, with nowhere to go. Nowhere for an escapee to hide, and easy to track, over terrain with relatively sparse flora and fauna for a basic seeker probe to have to sift through.

People might just fall down and lie there, heat prostration. A person could recover from that, if they were found in a reasonable period of time—before their brains had started to dry out and shrivel up, in a manner of speaking. They'd be recovered and ready for sale with minimal investment required for camp management.

"I got no details," Stildyne said, after a moment's silence to make sure he wouldn't be interrupting something Robert might be still thinking about saying. That tended to end discussion. Robert didn't like to be interrupted any more than Stildyne himself did, though their techniques for avoiding it were different. Robert nodded.

"Me neither," Robert said, and fed a data refinement subroutine into the data analysis flow with an adjustment of an input control. Buildings taking shape, reflecting a little more than the surface of the site itself; thermal shielding. Eight. The schematic was coming faster, now. More buildings, but they were clearly mixed purpose as well as mixed size—one little structure seemed to be the pump-house, for instance, its immediate surroundings showing a much higher level of atmospheric moisture.

"There we were," Robert said, apparently reminiscing. "Doing our assigned tasks and supporting Himself, aftermath of an all-out assault on a resisting population. There was this one senior officer, Ship's

Inquisitor, I don't remember the shipmark. He was just suggesting we go off together and have a talk when Jos—and this part I got on redirect, eventually, from Himself—got agitated."

More adjustments, then Robert continued. "Insisted that Koscuisko needed me right away. Later Pefisct seems to have tried to get Jos off by himself to demand an explanation about why I was shadowing the officer for the duration and depriving him of his fun, and Jos wouldn't do it."

That took some meditation time. Bond-involuntaries normally didn't do *wouldn't*. Not *wouldn't, won't, can't, don't want to,* none of those things. Such things were quarantined vocabulary like *please* and *help me,* put away, locked up, never to be spoken until the Day had dawned and a man was reborn, bond-involuntary to privileged private citizen. "Curran said that? To Pefisct?"

The launch-fields weren't obvious on sight, though the chemical traces were quite clear. The ground was already flat and hard. There apparently hadn't been much additional work required beyond putting in a maintenance house and bringing on an isolated power source. Robert grunted, *yes.*

"Captain called in to adjudicate, because Pefisct wanted eight and eighty for disrespect. Refresher course in proper manners. Irshah Parmin was a good officer. I never noticed being treated much differently than any other Security on Koscuisko's teams, not apart from the obvious, but people explained to me that a Bond could never really count on that."

Stildyne knew what Robert meant. Some commands stinted the rations, not the required baselines for nutritional requirements but nothing authorized by way of the occasional special meals or after-sweets. Lowden on the *Ragnarok* wouldn't authorize adequate pain management when he wasn't satisfied with the noises a troop made when they'd been sent up for two and twenty or three and thirty on a pretext.

That was something Koscuisko had stopped: not even as much as one and ten for the rest of Lowden's life, once Koscuisko had been confronted with the facts about Lowden's bond-involuntary management techniques.

"I'm guessing Curran didn't tell anybody about it." There were stray hints, points of connection, between the undefined abuses Pefisct had committed and the conversation Stildyne had had with Koscuisko about Janforth. He'd had to raise the topic with Koscuisko, but he didn't want to think about the whole thing more than he had to.

"You remember, Chief," Robert said, sounding a little distracted by the fine-tuning—additional adjustments—he was making to his incoming data. "Not asking about peoples' histories. Their lives. Their families. Almost unwritten rule, my experience limited, of course." Robert had only served on two ships, and with only one officer, in all his time under Bond. He'd been young in bond-involuntary years when his governor had died in Burkhayden, that was true.

That didn't mean Robert wasn't an intelligent man who thought about things. "But I have an idea of how easily someone who worked with bond-involuntaries could make things bad, *talk to me, tell me all about it, how did that make you feel, that's an order, how dare you hesitate, that's a violation*, and so on. I only mostly ever met up with people who were careful to mind their own business, but my dancing-master *did* teach me about doing as I was told under all circumstances, or else."

Stildyne had seen that, too. What he suspected Robert was talking about. It could be easy to escalate a trivial error into an actionable violation, if a person was wired that way. A bond-involuntary had no means of defending himself, and the governor would do the rest. Governors didn't do nuance. They only knew stress hormones.

Seen it; been part of an ad-hoc work group that had been formed up to stage an intervention. He never knew whether the warrant who'd done things like that to bond-involuntaries had ever learned how to stand up and count the number of fingers on one hand again, because so far as Stildyne knew nobody had seen that warrant again. They wouldn't have gotten away with it if an officer had been involved.

"Come on back, Robert," he said. "Remember, you can hit him for anything he tries on, here-now." That didn't violate the Covenant. "Only try not to kill him; he *is* a doctor. Maybe. Some kind of doctor. With me, here?"

Robert took a deep breath and let it out slowly. Basic response to emotional stress, Stildyne knew. "Right. Sorry. Habit hanging on. Looks like we may be picking up organic trace around this cluster, Chief, *Ragnarok* will be able to tell us more."

"But we're getting it first." Stildyne spoke up quickly, and maybe a little more forcefully than he needed to. *Fisher Wolf* could be a touchy machine. He didn't want it getting offended. "Have we got any activity tracks yet? Anything?"

They already knew the launch-field was completely deserted. There was no way off Holding: no ships. If people had been abandoned to make the best of things somehow there'd be no escape from barren desert and no surface water. It wasn't an encouraging thought.

"Nothing." Robert was thinking what Stildyne was thinking. Stildyne thought so, at least. Maybe Stildyne only thought he knew what Robert was thinking, and was wrong. That line of thinking got so complicated so quickly that Stildyne made up his mind that Robert was reading his mind and closed the door on further cogitation. "But maybe they're all just keeping out of the sun. I can hope."

He always had, Stildyne thought. *Hoped*. Robert was an optimist. If there were people abandoned at Holding, they *could* just be keeping out of the sun. Or they'd been killed. Or they were still locked up, which would make it a slower death, but one that took less time and effort for people in a hurry to get out of system. There was no sign of the freighter *Biruck*. Somewhere there were slavers with a full cargo and an urgent need to obtain some cash.

"I'll work the schematic if you want to hunt out auto-transmissions," Stildyne suggested. "I'll pretend I'm making up a scenario. Command Branch classroom training." He could do that. He'd cleared settlements abandoned by hostile opposition, in early days, and before that—in the streets of his childhood—he'd learned how to watch the signs to locate someone's cache, or hiding place, or bolt-hole.

The fact that he'd been born and raised in a city gave him a little bit of an edge on Robert in that area; only a whisper of an advantage, really—installation terrain analysis was something like a standard logic problem, and Robert wasn't stupid, for all the jokes he made on the subject of his intellect.

All Stildyne was after was a redirection of Robert's attention toward a new task that would require concentration, one in which Robert could become absorbed. Remembering was good, for bond-involuntaries, but it had to be consumed in sometimes very small doses to be safe.

"On it," Robert said, standing up to take the empty seat at Godsalt's station. Stildyne thought Robert's voice held a faint but unmistakable trace of *I know what you're doing and I'm all for it.* "Let me know when we hear something from the *Ragnarok*."

They could talk to the *Ragnarok* on vector, because *Fisher Wolf* knew how to find it. *Ragnarok* was two days behind them, though. *Fisher Wolf* had taken the vector at its very best speed all the way here to Holding but the ships coming up—the hospital freighter most notably—traveled more slowly.

They weren't going to be able to wait. There was no question of letting people continue to suffer imprisonment until the *Ragnarok* arrived; if nothing else someone needed to make a medical survey to call back to the rest of the relief fleet so they'd know what to prepare for.

Things were beginning to come together with the schematic. A large warehouse-type building showed up at regular intervals with the earth packed harder, denser, than that at other buildings; an actual warehouse, maybe, with offloaded cargo moved in and out on heavy flatbeds. Buildings that looked like warehousing on one side of the packed-earth road from the launch-field; smaller buildings, varying shapes and sizes, things that could be office blocks—dormitories— even private residences, on the other.

Now it was up to *him* to concentrate. They needed to see what they were up against before they took *Fisher Wolf* down; and they needed to get *Fisher Wolf* dirtside as soon as possible, to get the first rough outlines of the forward aid station on the ground and running.

If they were unaccountably lucky, they'd find that everything was all right at Holding. But Stildyne didn't like what he was seeing on the scans. The more he saw the less he liked it, so they had to hurry.

CHAPTER FIVE

Horrors

Lek Kerenko dropped from the thula's emergency access hatch to the ground, straightening up with a muted grunt as the muscles of his legs absorbed the impact from the ground through bended knees. They'd landed *Fisher Wolf* late in the day, during the long twilight creeping up over the desert as the sun set.

There were movers on the launch-field, but they'd elected to run *Fisher Wolf* itself down into the warehouse farm. It was a tradeoff, the risk that an organized armed party would attack the ship versus the significant savings in time achieved by having the thula's complete cargo load at the point of need.

They had all the light they needed to creep in the thula cautiously from the launch-field toward the warehouse farm, but more important was the fact that it would be full dark soon. Holding had no moon. *Fisher Wolf* had full issues of tactical gear for a standard five-soul field security team, so they had nightscopes.

Even though Riggs had deployed the protection curtain it was a dangerously exposed position. Lek Kerenko knew he didn't like it any better than any of the rest of them, Stildyne and Garrity and Hirsel. And Janforth. They didn't really know Janforth, they'd never done a grouping with him, the level of teamwork wasn't there—hadn't had years of development—but just because they were no longer under Bond didn't mean they'd forgotten how to mold themselves together into an effective team at a moment's notice.

Lek would rather have left Janforth on board. That there was something between him and Stildyne was their business, and none of Lek's. Not unless and until Janforth decided to open up to anybody, not as though Lek couldn't guess. But Pyotr was out with an ambulatory handicap and they needed Robert on board; Godsalt was *Fisher Wolf*'s tertiary backup on the pilot's station, backing Pyotr up. They could shift hull in a hurry if they had to.

It worked out. They'd had a quick chat with Janforth; *we need you on this mission but our Chief is one of us and a part of our team. You decide.*

Lek's earpiece clicked; incoming signal. "Nothing so far." Robert. "No activity. No active weapons systems." That wouldn't stop small arms, of course, handguns whose deployment required a power source of such minimal strength—especially at rest—that it was easily lost in the noise, the kinetic energy of the breeze, if there had been one, from the station out to the desert as the land cooled more rapidly than the warehouses.

Click, but at a different pitch and volume. Moving. They knew where they were going. *Fisher Wolf* had comm with the *Ragnarok*. Neither *Fisher Wolf* nor *Ragnarok*—now off-vector—could find any trace of communications activity, apart from an auto-transmission that was days old.

Both *Fisher Wolf* and *Ragnarok* could isolate two small warehouse buildings as generating heat and ground-level respiratory gasses consistent with numbers of people, too many people in too small a space. More than three hundred people. Maybe more than four hundred.

The only hopeful sign was that not all of the station's power had failed, yet, there was still power working in those two warehouse buildings, and there was enough of a temperature gradient—cooler air leaking out, if only relatively cooler—for there to be hope that environmental health systems were still functioning.

They couldn't do anything about the warehouses until they'd secured the station, and that meant taking it by surprise if necessary. They'd trained for the mission. Holding was a small station, to judge by the allowances made for the number of people it accommodated in terms of sleeping and eating like decently cared-for souls—on the other side of the road. Outside the warehouse farm.

Away from the warehouse farm, then. Into the business and

residential areas. Nothing. Garrity had forward passive defenses covered, because of the eye Fleet had given him to replace the one the Bench had absentmindedly put out; he was laying down the standard number of neutralizers as they went to guard against any passive troops in place but he also wasn't saying anything about them so he wasn't seeing anything. Standard operating procedure.

On to the communications hub. *Click.* "Comm center," Robert said, calm and warm and confidential. "Repeat loop only. No trace, live souls." *Proceed with caution.* Lek could hear it in Robert's voice because they'd known each other for years. There were auto-secures on the side entrance they'd targeted; Garrity gave the nod—*no anomalies detected*—so Janforth blew the locks, and the door opened. There. If there was anyone on station they'd be on notice, now.

Chirp-click, not from *Fisher Wolf,* going to *Fisher Wolf,* Chief. "Anything?"

Click; click. Or, in other words, *no.* So Lek went in. The auto-environs came up, lights, power to the doors, air cooling quickly as it blew through the vents at the floor. When they reached a corridor intersection all they had to do was follow the directions coming to them from the ship, short click left, two right, long straight ahead.

Fisher Wolf's clicks had suddenly acquired an accent, but Lek recognized it in some sense and led the team ahead without hesitation and without thinking. Koscuisko. Anders son of Ilex, in the Nurail parlance; Dolgorukij accent. The weight on a doubled vowel, the subtle arc of a diphthong, *left, ahead.*

Since a team moved together—and Lek was on point—they followed his lead. It didn't take long: here was the comm center's control room. Janforth was willing and ready to blow that door too, but that might damage the equipment, and as it turned out the door wasn't secured anyway.

Janforth went first. The place was empty. The arrays were all on line, but there was no data—no data to transmit, apparently. And still no bombs. As the lights brightened Hirsel set his nightscope aside and sat down at the master console station. Click-chirp. "On site," Hirsel said. "Robert. Got any traces?"

Were there traps in the channels, not physical bombs, but stealth captures, something to alert somebody somewhere that the station had been infiltrated by persons unknown?

When Robert came back there was no *click*. Communication in the clear. "None detected," Robert said. "Site on functional secure. Okay by them if someone came in to clean up their mess, I'm thinking. Your action, Hirsch, *Fisher Wolf* standing by. Good luck."

They'd leave Janforth with Hirsel. They needed Garrity's eye, they needed Chief because Stildyne had done more of this than they had—his primary mission hadn't been Secured Medical, but baseline security—and since Lek wasn't needed here, he'd go on. Back across the main axis of the station; across *Fisher Wolf*'s field-expedient launch-lane, into the warehouse farm. Heading for two small warehouse buildings with life-signs.

Just because there'd been no sign of station security in effect in the working areas of the port didn't mean the warehouses themselves hadn't been secured. They went as quickly as they could without being stupid about it.

There were probably passive defenses on all of the storage units; even out in the middle of nowhere—with nowhere to hide and nowhere to run—valuable portable goods would be secured as a matter of basic prudence. It didn't matter. They only meant to get into two warehouses, and what they expected—hoped—feared to find there wasn't anything that could be stolen and smuggled out.

They were very close when Garrity stopped, suddenly. Click-chirp. "One soul," Garrity said. "Seated, in front of main access door I guess. No visible weapons." Then Garrity—before either Lek or Chief could stop him—walked forward calmly and slowly, with his hands quiet at his sides. "Ahoi-hoi," Garrity called out, loud and clear. "I'm here to help. Can I help?"

Moving up behind Garrity, keeping well to the concealment of the terrain, Lek and Stildyne followed. Lek could see the figure, now, coming up clear in his nightscope. Slim figure; seated; hadn't moved—past an initial start, Lek guessed. Hands in lap, could be holding a book.

"There is no hope in a world without God." It was a woman's voice, a girl's voice. Calm. Clear. Confident. Resigned, and it raised the hairs at the back of Lek's neck, for reasons he didn't understand. "There is no light. I cannot look upon a world that God has forsaken."

No.

He wondered—

He had to do this, he and only he, because he thought he remembered something. He had to be wrong, he told himself, fiercely. It was impossible. It was obscene. It was a coincidence. Letting his hands drop impotently to his sides—as Garrity had done, but for an entirely different reason—Lek moved carefully past Garrity, toward the warehouse's main access doors and the figure seated in front of it. She heard him coming, but she didn't move.

"Little sister," Lek said. He had to speak Standard. If he spoke scripture, Dolgorukij scripture, Chief and Garrity wouldn't be able to understand that something beyond terror confronted them all. "Light has not died, though we do not see it. We come to help. Oh, in the name of holy God, I beg you, is all well, within?"

That phrase was hard to say, "holy God," because it was blasphemous. It was in the masculine gender, in Dolgorukij.

"There will be light when we rejoice in the Presence," she said. He was so close to her, now, that he could see her face. Her clumsily bandaged eyes. "There are others—" There, there was a sliver of horror in her voice, an almost inaudible sob of all-but-reluctant compassion. "Not in the sight of God. You may tend *them*."

Chief was behind him, now. Garrity was behind him. Garrity put his hand on Lek's shoulder, clearly puzzled, clearly concerned. Falling down to his knees Lek put one hand to the ground and bowed his head. "How many, little sister, how many others, and how many see the light?"

They wouldn't know. They couldn't guess. He couldn't tell them, either, because his voice was choked in his throat with anguish. "We were sacred in number," she said. Simply and plainly. "Others ten and twice as many, I think. You will number them. It is not for me to number the true servants of Holy God."

Something clicked in his ear again, but Lek could hear the force of the blow behind it, could almost see Koscuisko smashing his fist down on the toggle-switch. Lek had forgotten that Koscuisko was listening. "I am coming," Koscuisko said. He shouldn't. He was supposed to stay on *Fisher Wolf* where he was safe. "Riggs, I need wound management, now."

Not "now, please." Koscuisko knew what Lek knew. He wouldn't bring Riggs with him, but he'd come, there'd be no keeping him back. And Chief? Chief had been reading in the saga of Dasidar and

Dyraine, cultivating his understanding of the literature for Koscuisko's
sake. How much did Stildyne know about the Old Believers?

Chief it was who came up now to put one knee to the ground and
his fist down beside it, his other hand resting on his thigh. A much
more perfect humility than Lek had been able to manage, in his first
shock; and Chief not even Dolgorukij. "I am other," Chief said.
"Outlander. Is this the knife? Let me keep it. For a token."

Yes take the knife take the knife and feed it to the conversion engines,
Lek thought, desperately. *That thing is cursed, it's evil, it's wrong, it's
unholy.* And she might use it again against herself, to do even worse
harm. There was nothing else beneath the canopy of Heaven for her to
do, now, nothing to live for and every reason to die. *There is no light if
God has forsaken us.* Blasphemy.

The girl held up the knife she was holding, the bloodied knife, Lek
knew it was bloodied through he couldn't see the color in his
nightscope. He couldn't tell how fresh the blood might be. He could
smell it; had they been only a few hours too late? Or had she struggled
to find the will to put out her own light, since she'd been left here
outside the doors with no one to do it for her?

"Can we go in?" Stildyne asked, very gently. "Will you lead us, can
you walk?" She'd be in shock. But she couldn't be left alone. She was
hurt, though self-injured. Garrity wasn't talking, but Garrity's hand
had tightened on Lek's shoulder. So Garrity knew enough, if he didn't
yet know all of it.

The girl stood up, with Stildyne steadying her; turned around,
reaching for the pull-handle of the door. She couldn't reach. There was
the stool she'd been sitting on, she could have climbed up on that; but
she couldn't see the handle of the door. She couldn't see at all.

It took Stildyne and Garrity together to wrestle the heavy panel
open in its tracks, to open the door. They were going to need as much
air as quickly as possible, an instinct proven by the stinking gust of
stale sour air that greeted them as the gap widened. Human waste.
Human despair. The sweet sickening smell of rotting meat. "We've
come to help," Stildyne called out, loud and strong. "You'll be freed.
Lights coming up. Guard your eyes."

He'd found the control panel by the loading door's tall panel, but he
got the wrong key by accident and the lights came on full brilliant all
at once. Maybe that was the only lights there were, off, full.

Somebody screamed, and once the screaming started it didn't stop. Some of it was terrified; some of it, Lek was boundlessly grateful to hear, was angry. The girl had Stildyne by the hand, and led him forward; Garrity had lowered his head to follow, which Lek understood. Garrity could see things out of his cyborg eye, more things, and in better detail. Lek didn't envy Garrity his augmented vision.

Inside, the warehouse was one open-faced pen after another, all opening out into the stables. Large stalls, generous stalls, barred to the ceiling, but all of them were full to capacity, or worse. Lek did his best to look, so that he could make an estimate for a report—number of souls, standing versus sitting versus stretched out on the ground. Nature and extent of injuries by visual survey. The girl simply led Stildyne on, and through the screaming Lek thought that he heard something far worse.

People were singing. Their voices were weak, but full of gratitude and love and in a Dolgorukij dialect that Lek didn't have to be told was archaic Birskovneyij. He already knew the words, because the song itself was traditional, and had been adopted and perverted by the heterodox sect—not the other way around.

Holy God, by tribulation you show your love, we thank thee, bless thee, love thee, grant us strength to witness to our faith. It was *Holy Mother*, not *Holy God*, of course. That was what the words were supposed to be.

He hadn't thought to warn his friend Garrity, and now it was too late. "She—she did this?" Garrity asked him, his fury making his voice tremble. Lek had to shake his head. It was far worse than that.

"No, to each other." Not all the cuts had been clean. How could they have been? These were a cult of religious fanatics, Old Believers, not educated at all in a modern sense. "Husband wife, parents children, brother sister. Until only one is left to bless the sacrifice in the eyes of Holy God. By themselves."

There hadn't been enough by way of even makeshift bandaging to go around. It had been hot, shut up in the prison, and by the stench it was obvious that sanitary arrangements were inadequate or overwhelmed or maybe entirely nonexistent. There were—opportunistic parasitical insects, Lek decided to call them. Otherwise he would have had to call them flies, and he didn't think he'd be able to endure it.

Someone was coming, running up behind them. The officer. Lek had seen horror on the officer's face before, but not like this. Koscuisko's experience of horror—at his own actions, of himself—stood them all in good stead now; Koscuisko had practice controlling it, containing it, working forward through it somehow. Koscuisko stepped right up to the barred face of the stall in which the Old Believers had been penned.

"My name is Andrej," Koscuisko said. "You are not meant to die, though your light is gone. You can still praise. Accept care, in the name of—" Would he say *Holy Mother*? Or would he say *Holy God*? Would he pretend to be a fellow-traveler, a God-fearer, to win their cooperation, or declare himself unequivocally the enemy of their schismatic creed?

No. He found a middle way. "Accept care. In the name of all Saints I ask this of you."

Nobody said anything. So nobody was telling him *no*. Koscuisko rested his forehead against the barred gate for a long moment. *You shouldn't do that*, Lek thought, suddenly alarmed. *You don't know where those bars have been*. Before he could say anything, though, Koscuisko straightened up and turned around, looking at Garrity.

"Keep Riggs out of here," Koscuisko said. "I make this a medical order. She's on her way with the first pallets. Robert." That would be over the com-link, now, Lek realized. "Send through to the people from Canopy Base, at Couveraine. Tell them there are Old Believers. Tell them there is no light in a world God has forsaken."

They'd know. That was a comfort. The people from Canopy Base were the Malcontent's people, whether or not they were all Malcontent themselves. People would come from home, from the Dolgorukij Combine. Maybe the Old Believers would refuse to go back—they were despised, reviled, discriminated against there, or they would not be in Gonebeyond for slavers to prey on them—but the Malcontent didn't care whether they were heretics. The Malcontent never had. The Saint would see them cared for in respect and reverence.

"Who stays with these people?" Koscuisko asked Stildyne. Who only just almost said *you tell me, your Excellency*, because Koscuisko had completely reverted to The Officer under the stress of these events. "I am outside putting together immediate care."

"Right behind you, Andrej," Chief said. He was under stress

himself; he seldom called Koscuisko by his personal name where anybody could hear him, now that they were self-same. "Lek, with me." Then he didn't move. He waited until Koscuisko was halfway to the outside door. Reaching into the cage Stildyne spoke. "I'm leaving this woman here," Stildyne said. "Taking your hand, sir. Hold on to each other. Now more than ever you've got to stay strong together."

Why did he want Lek to stay behind? In case he ran into difficulties, maybe. Maybe he didn't know whether any of these people spoke Standard. Had the girl been left for last because she did? Had that been a sliver of self-preservational instinct? Or had that been punishment? Lek repeated what Stildyne had said in his best formal Dolgorukij, just in case. Enough of it would get through.

"Take each others' hands, you, and you. We'll be back soon. Stay together. No one is left behind."

Stildyne had jogged to the far end of the stablelike warehouse, and was walking back more slowly, speaking loudly and calmly. "My name is Brachi. The slavers are gone. Help is coming. You will all be freed. Hospital will be here for you. Wait just a little longer."

It might mean nothing, but it was all they could do, until the freighter from Agavie arrived with the full field hospital Lek longed for, now, as he had scarcely longed for anything else in his entire life.

And they had yet to open up the second warehouse.

From his privileged position as a person too important to be placed in harm's way in any sense Bat Yorvik had watched as the well-rested, grimly determined, Hilton Shires had developed—or devolved?—day by day into the haggard white-faced clearly exhausted man who stood, mere days—no more than ten—since Bat had seen him at his first introduction. Then, as now, it had been for a briefing. Now, as then, they all sat together, but in a conference room in Couveraine proper, with full interaction with the Jurisdiction Fleet Ship *Ragnarok*, fresh off the Pavrock vector and on its way to Holding.

"It's selfish and it may be stupid," Shires said, staring at the flask of cavene that sat before him just to one side of his clenched fist. "But we are Langsariks, and this is our home, now. I feel responsible. Therefore I request your report, Captain ap Rhiannon, have you heard anything through your intelligence channels that we haven't heard?"

On the *Ragnarok* the Captain was taking the meeting in her office, rather than in the larger and more formal setting of the officer's mess. Bat recognized it. He'd sat for an informal meal with her there, when they'd been talking about Taisheki Station. The Ship's Engineer wasn't there. The officer from Canopy Base—Felsanjir—was there, and Specialist Ivers. First Officer was there. So was Ship's Intelligence, Two.

The Langsarik Coalition's spymaster general was dirtside Couveraine, harvesting resources. Bat didn't like the implications—a harvest implied clearing a tree of fruit or a field of grain, didn't it? to the detriment of the fruit and grain—but it was what people said. So he had to take the implications under advisement, nothing more. Nothing less.

"We're still hours away from planetfall," ap Rhiannon said. "Getting the field hospital on site is our current priority. The situation on the ground is apparently demanding, in terms of medical resources. There's a specific message from the advance party for Felsanjir, Koscuisko says to tell you that there are what he called Old Believers. He's asked me to tell you further, his words, there is no light in a world without God's presence."

Felsanjir had gone pale: her lips were almost grey. "What does that mean?" Specialist Ivers asked her. Felsanjir took a moment before she replied.

"It means an atrocity has occurred," she said. "A self-inflicted one, in a sense. One presumed there might be Combine nationals seeking refuge in Gonebeyond, but that they would be vulnerable—and yet such people would seem marketable goods to slavers, they are docile, they do not resist."

He could press Felsanjir on the issue, request details. Or, Bat reminded himself, he could query the Bench archive on the Dolgorukij Combine to see what an *old believer* was, later. Yes. That would be better. More efficient. Wouldn't slow the meeting down.

"We hear nothing about the freighter *Biruck*," the intelligence officer said cheerfully. She had a cheerful translator. Bat had no way of telling whether she was actually cheerful by nature or not, but he had to admit that he'd found her engaging, in the limited contact he'd had with her on board of the *Ragnarok*. "We have very vague rumors about a vector from Holding that is not Pavrock. I do not waste your time with potentially inaccurate information, but we pursue."

"And on our side, Mission Commander, Captain, we have nothing immediately promising," Felsanjir said, reluctantly. "There are other angles. I defer to Specialist Ivers for now, Mission Commander."

Ivers sat silent for a moment or two, as though collecting her thoughts, considering carefully what—and how much—she wanted to say. "We've probably heard the same rumors as Two has done," she said, finally. "Unfortunately I can't promise anything solid. There are significant incentives on offer for information, or outright surrender. Nothing more at this time, Shires, I'm sorry."

Silence. Bat waited, but nobody spoke, so he thought maybe he'd ask a question, while people were thinking. "Wondering whether I might tour Couveraine city," he said. So far he'd been straight from the launch-fields into the administrative areas, under heavy protection. "I'd like to see the battlegrounds. For context. If appropriate."

Shires sat down. "Deferring to you, Bench specialist," he said. "Your call, Dame Ivers? I think it's not a bad idea, really, so long as you think it's worth the risk. Haspirzak might not send us a replacement, and we want to make this work."

Haspirzak certainly wouldn't send another *him*. Because he was the only one of him there was. On the other hand, if he thought cynically about it, maybe he'd make a good martyr; then the Third Judge could have the credit for taking a significant risk to her prestige without the trouble of continuing the development of Bat's career going forward.

The moment he had the thought he rejected it as unworthy. Yes, it was his job to consider things from all angles, and to not dismiss any possibility without careful consideration. On the other hand, the Third Judge was just not coded that way. That was a Verlaine thing. The Second Judge's First Secretary had been a very deep thinker.

"It's not without risk, your Honor," Ivers said. "That said, I'm willing to accompany you, and stand surety. I don't think we'll be getting shot at. We'll get you fitted with body armor, just in case, but we should be all right. Nobody's going to know you're a Judge, after all. If those conditions are acceptable?"

If someone was going to shoot at him, surely it was better to get it out of the way before he'd become so deeply involved that bringing a replacement up to speed would delay the mission by an unacceptable period of time.

There was something else: he hadn't taken part in any actual fighting—he didn't mind that, he wasn't a soldier, and nobody had made him feel the least bit awkward about it—but he was going to be engaged in intensive negotiations with fighting men and women. He owed it to them, and to himself, to at least get a feet-on-the-ground idea of what they'd gone through, howsoever after-the-fact and incomplete.

"I like it, Bench specialist." Not just because he was a little bit bored. No. He didn't find even the remote prospect of being shot at the least bit boring. It was something that had to be done. "At your convenience."

And suddenly Shires slammed his fist down on the conference table, making the flasks of cavene jump, spilling ones that were still full. "I hate this," he said. "There's a freighter out there. They'll have taken all the prisoners they could pack into it with them. And we haven't found it. Hate this. Hate them. All right. Does anybody else have anything?"

Dame Ivers did. "Behind you all the way," she said, and looked around her, at Felsanjir, at Two on-screen from the *Ragnarok*. "We'll get our chance. Nothing further at this time, Mission Commander."

So they were all in it together, Dame Ivers, Canopy Base, the *Ragnarok*. Bat wasn't so much surprised as heartened. And as for Pefisct, a deserter from his ship in Haspirzak Judiciary? There was another Bench specialist in Haspirzak, and those people were dangerous.

"Anybody?" Shires said. "Captain ap Rhiannon? Felsanjir? Your Honor? Very good. Meeting adjourned. Same time tomorrow, unless something turns up."

"With me, your Honor," Ivers said. "Let's get this started right away." Yes. Before he had more time to overthink things and get nervous. Bat followed Ivers out to go get fitted with some body armor, and set his sights on walking the first battlefield he'd ever seen in his life.

Danyo Pefisct was in triage when he saw the courier come down to land at Holding's launch-field. He'd been watching for it, out towards the launch-fields, through the clinic's windows. Specialist Ivers would be there, and that so-called "Surgeon General" for Gonebeyond, Doctor Gascarone. Probably a team from Nurail intelligence, that woman, Felsanjir. There'd be a briefing. He was ready.

It was a beautiful hospital Witt had sent, as field hospitals went.

There was an extensive surgical suite, a large outpatient module, an intensive care unit, environmental medicine—all of the requisite components, and all absolutely top-notch. Except for quarantine.

Curiously enough, there seemed to be just that little bit less of a quarantine module than a medical team might expect; isolation technology in effect, yes, but the unit had clearly been designed more for number of patients than severity of individual cases.

It wasn't much. Subtle. Well up to the best standard, but it seemed that the purchasing agent had pulled the wrong code, and filled for a cluster of cases, and left the critically-ill accommodations to a handful of life-litters.

Those were generally a last resort. Patients didn't do well in life-litters unless they were unconscious and could be safely maintained under heavy sedation, because there were natural instinctive resistances to being closely pent in what was at best a claustrophobic environment.

So far as Danyo could tell nobody had made a note of that yet. He was satisfied that it was only his particular interest that had tipped *him* off.

"Staff meeting, Doctor," one of the technicians said. "All senior personnel. Hospital administrative module, please, sir." From Danyo's point of view, had been able to tell, the people Witt had sent with the hospital were completely mundane, totally innocuous, law-abiding professionals. Which made for excellent camouflage, as well as a good standard of patient care. Gonebeyond had every reason to be honestly grateful to Agavie for the gift, and to Danyo for bringing it.

Danyo winked reassuringly at his triage patient, one of the newer arrivals at Holding from her relatively well-nourished condition. Intelligence would be wanting to interview her, certainly; she'd have relatively fresh experiences to relate. "Aikens will take over," Danyo told her. "I leave you in his capable hands. I've got to go take a nap, er, a meeting."

She seemed too wary of him to laugh, which was a bore. All of these people were very boring. He could have had good sport with several of them, but not here and now, where he had to be on his very best behavior. People were watching.

It was a very short walk from triage to administration; Danyo didn't hurry, though he took care not to seem to dawdle. He didn't really mind triage. He heard the gossip this way, and according to the gossip he'd been granted a piece of luck.

Some of the slaves were Dolgorukij *Old Believers*, apparently. Danyo had never heard of Old Believers, but the advantage he gained from their being here was potentially significant; their presence meant he had a ready-made vector on site for any viral infection Koscuisko might develop. Witt's virus had been engineered off a Dolgorukij substrate.

He could even come up with some way to introduce traces of the virus into the Old Believer population itself, just as soon as he'd delivered it to Koscuisko. It would seem a truly spontaneous outbreak, a mutation, perhaps, resulting from the physical challenges the slaves had faced even before their mass self-mutilation.

The briefing room in the administration module was full of people, and all of the chairs had been taken. That worked in Danyo's favor. He was happy to find his way through the crowd of people to stand quite near to Koscuisko, almost directly behind him.

Koscuisko had a seat at the table, of course. On the grounds that Koscuisko was medical representative for the Nurail polity, Danyo supposed, rather than because he was simply assumed to have more right to it than the man who'd actually brought the Langsarik coalition this beautiful hospital. That was all right with Danyo.

Taking his toothpick out of his pocket Danyo folded his arms and brought his hand up to his mouth, discreetly. There wasn't really time to get back to quarters for personal hygiene after every meal. They were all too busy, and all too tired, and there was a lot of work yet to be done. The warehouses were cleared, both of them, their combined four hundred and thirty-eight souls all rehoused in temporary shelters where they could be fed and watered and washed and clothed while medical evaluation continued.

There in the middle of the far side of the table, Bench Intelligence Specialist Ivers stood up, looking around her, checking for her principals. There was Danyo's future boss Doctor Yogee Gascarone, with his hair standing straight up from his scalp, uncombed.

The woman from the Nurail spymaster's service; some few others, and then all the rest of them, admitted to the audience to witness the deliberations of the important people.

There was cavene, coming around in disposable rewrap flasks.

Danyo took one. Hot and steaming, here, in the middle of the desert—the air was that dry. People were accustomed to drinking their cavene hot. Even Koscuisko took a flask, Danyo noted.

He had a wonderful idea.

"Overview," Ivers said. "My name is Jils Ivers, here on behalf of the mission commander Hilton Shires. Two items. One, Couveraine." This would be of interest to the one or two of the senior staff who merited a place in the room. Most of the hospital's officers were there, standing. They were all tired. Tired was good. Tired meant vulnerable to an attack that might otherwise be easily contained by the body's immune system without anybody noticing it particularly until too late.

Danyo couldn't see much of Koscuisko's face from behind, but he could tell from Koscuisko's slumped shoulders and lowered head that he was as weary as any of them whether or not he was one of those supposedly more resilient Dolgorukij. Danyo had chosen his spot specifically so that he couldn't see Koscuisko's face, because if he couldn't see Koscuisko's eyes from behind Koscuisko wouldn't be seeing him.

Consulting a holo-reader set flatfile format in front of her, Ivers raised her head again, raising her voice as well. "Support services in Couveraine have been fully restored at a baseline level, with some continuing constraints. Casualties from coalition forces have been returned to owned medical resources. Couveraine's casualties— including those from its civilian population—are being accommodated in Couveraine's existing hospital system, including overflow wards. And two. Felsanjir."

Ivers sat down. Felsanjir stood up. "Ekaterina Felsanjir, speaking for intel, Langsarik Coalition. Information received revealed two locations where Couveraine held slaves for market; here at Holding, and in intermediate detention on board of the freighter named *Biruck* for immediate sale. Gentles, we do not know where that freighter is. We're convinced there's an unmapped vector, an escape route."

Raising his flask of hot cavene Danyo took a sip, palming his toothpick from between his teeth to hold it securely against the side of the flask in one hand, and release the catch. It was very hot cavene. Holding was so dry that it sent up a plume of condensation even in the warmth of the room. He blew on its steaming surface to cool it down, careful to divert any residual moist warmth in his breath over Koscuisko's shoulder.

They'd be wanting Koscuisko back at Couveraine, but Danyo was serenely certain that Couveraine was going to have to wait. Holding was still an active displaced population situation, and needed all its medical staff.

"We continue to develop information in Couveraine." Danyo noted that Felsanjir wasn't looking at Koscuisko. She was Dolgorukij too, wasn't she, with a name like Ekaterina? He wasn't sure he'd heard one way or another. "Locating the freighter, and the people responsible for it and for this—" she looked around her, now, to include all of Holding—"is our first priority, all available resources. Thank you."

Danyo watched, fascinated, as Koscuisko raised his flask of cavene in his left hand and sipped. Danyo didn't need to see the plume of steam that carried the newly-released viral cloud to know that it was there, admixed and mingled with Koscuisko's cavene and rising to the heavens on a cavene-scented aerosol.

He'd find some pretext to visit the area where that one particular group of freed slaves were being held together. Medical staff were coming and going there all the time, because none of the Old Believers could see, and they needed watching to protect them from accidents while they acclimatized to their newly blinded status. Whether or not one of the Agavie people was on duty was immaterial. All Danyo had to do was drop by for a word with one of Agavie's people, maybe move among the patients a little. Before he changed his clothes.

"Doctor Gascarone," Ives said, still seated, as Felsanjir sat down beside her. Gascarone stood up now. "Yogee Gascarone, for overall medical support. We have four hundred and twenty-six live souls in custody. About one in six of them present a requirement for active medical intervention. Not counting the Dolgorukij patients."

Gascarone was watching Koscuisko carefully, Danyo noted, quite unlike Felsanjir had done. Acknowledging the possibility that Koscuisko was sensitive about the plight of his fellow souls, Danyo supposed.

"And for the rest." Suddenly Gascarone looked very tired indeed. "We're talking short- to medium-term rest, hydration, nutrition, understandable psychological disturbances. Heat prostration, but the environmental systems apparently failed last. *Fisher Wolf* did get here before things went from critical to catastrophic."

Gascarone sipped his cavene, grimaced, and set it down. "One piece of good news. There's a Dolgorukij evacuation unit en route to take charge of the Old Believers, just cleared through Poe Station for Holding via Couveraine—grant of compassionate access. They've offered to take on some of our patient load."

Suddenly Danyo's blood ran cold, warm though the room was. No. No Combine medical evacuation ship could be permitted to arrive at Holding. If he'd known it was coming he'd have reserved his action, and now here he was, gone from the satisfaction of a job well done to a near-despairing panic within the space of two sentences.

How soon would they be here? Would they be here and gone before Koscuisko came down sick? That could work. Or they might arrive just as Koscuisko's condition became enough of a concern to force an immediate evacuation. Could he hope for either of those things?

Someone should ask the question. And Koscuisko did, leaning back in his chair suddenly, lacing his fingers together at the back of his neck and rolling his head from side to side as if to relieve the ache of tense muscles. "Do we have an arrival forecast?"

Unfortunately for Danyo, Gascarone shook his head. "I don't have that information. I did mention that the condition of the Old Believers was not good. Sorry. Moving on."

So what should he do? Should he leave it to Koscuisko to communicate the virus, and hope that the population would be evacuated before real symptoms began to manifest? Should he continue with his original plan?

It had all been Witt's idea. How could it be Danyo's fault if the plot failed? He'd done as he'd been asked, what he'd agreed to. If circumstances conspired against him he was blameless. Witt would have to try again, some other means, some other method. If Koscuisko died it was all moot anyway.

If Koscuisko died, Witt couldn't hold it against *him*; nor could Witt hold the threat of showing his record of Danyo and Koscuisko's Joslire over Danyo's head. They were in the hospital Witt had provided. They were staffed with some of the best resources Gonebeyond space had to offer. It would be Witt's virus engineers who had failed Witt, not Danyo Pefisct.

He would hold to his original plan. As long as he could expose those Old Believers right now, immediately, before Koscuisko had a chance to begin to get sick, his hands were clean. He couldn't be suspected. He was golden.

And whether or not Witt withdrew his patronage as punishment for the failure of the plot, the Langsarik Coalition would still be one experienced Inquisitor short at just the time that Danyo, finished with this ugliness at Holding, would become available to assume the intelligence-gathering position Koscuisko currently held, with all the privileges and protections Koscuisko enjoyed.

It would be as though the malice of the Third Judge had never touched him, and he would pick up his career as a professional torturer right where he'd left off.

The staff briefing room had cleared, finally. Yogee had outwaited the entire lot of them; now it was just him and Andrej Koscuisko. "You look tired," Yogee said. Koscuisko had his elbows on the table and his face in his hands. They were all tired, of course they were, but Koski was Dolgorukij and Yogee had expected a little more resilience out of him.

Koscuisko had been the primary physician on site at Holding, though, before the medical ships following had begun to land the main party. He'd had a good deal more than just religious fanatics to deal with, and while the wolf-pack had been firmly directed toward light duty for a little rest and recovery in place once the main fleet had arrived, they hadn't had that luxury with Koscuisko. So Yogee needed to know whether Koscuisko was going to drop down dead of terminal disgust.

"And you look like the oldest plow-horse was ever between the sheets at a service house as well, thank you." Oh, yes, there was a bit of temper, there. Yogee was glad to see it. "I want to know when the Combine ship will be here, Yodge. I want them all as far away from me as possible."

"Now you're just being petty." There was more than temper there; Yogee heard an unresolved aversion, almost strong enough to be called hate. Maybe not as deep and sharpened as Koscuisko's hatred for Pefisct, but it was there. "I'll try to get you an answer. What have you got against them, though? Apart from the idiocy of it all. The waste."

The look in Koscuisko's eyes when he raised his head was one of what might have been compassion, coming from anybody but a professional torturer. "They made her do that to herself because she could speak Standard. She was contaminated, you see. Nobody else had to turn their hand against themselves. It's no wonder she botched the job, but, Yogee, she refuses any treatment that might save the one eye."

So what, Yogee wanted to say. *They're ignorant stupid narrow-minded zealots, and she's one of them, clearly. Who cares?* Except of course that Koscuisko did, and Yogee did, too. "I suppose if one accidentally made it all better she'd just keep on trying to finish the job."

Koscuisko nodded wearily. And changed the subject. "What are you going to do with Pefisct, Yogee? Not the hospital, I like this hospital. But Pefisct."

They hadn't had any time to talk about much of anything, he and Koski. Yogee wasn't sure he had anything constructive to say to him, but in this instance what Koscuisko knew about Pefisct was probably important to find out. "I've got no complaints about him, as a general practitioner. We need all the doctors we can get, you know that, Doctor. Your man Janforth, he hasn't killed Pefisct yet? Maybe you should give Pefisct a chance to make things right with you, for whatever he's done. You're in Gonebeyond."

He was a ranting hypocrite for saying such things to Koscuisko. There were crimes that nothing would put right. Koscuisko had committed his share, and in very generous proportion, really. "How is it said?" Yogee shrugged. He was off balance. He might as well continue. "So long as a soul can behave like a decent person they will in time become a decent person, and it doesn't really matter anyway, as long as they can genuinely act the part?"

Koscuisko laughed. It was a good sound, because it had genuine amusement, if only for an instant. Almost friendly, really. Then Koscuisko sobered. "There are not enough years to any allotted span," Koscuisko said. "If you really must use Pefisct, I think you should take care to ensure that there are either no people in his company, or two. Never one. Never let him be alone with anybody, especially me, because I will vivisect him very, very slowly."

"Na, you'd just get bored, after a while." It was an old point of contention, Koski and patience. "Then you'd just let him bleed out, and then there'd be no more in it for you. You'd mope. You'd be tiresome. We'd all get tired of you being tiresome."

Something passed across Koscuisko's face that Yogee so much disliked that he ignored it. It passed quickly enough. Koscuisko sighed and stood up. "I will go be tiresome about duty rosters and supplemental feedings," he said. "I like it at Safehaven, Yodge. I begin to be comfortable there, and even feel useful. I will not vivisect Pefisct. I will not kill him at all, unless he earns it fairly, and in Gonebeyond."

Ah, but you're leaving yourself a considerable field of play, there, Yogee admonished Koscuisko, in his mind. *I've heard stories.* He didn't think Koscuisko would see the humor of it, though, not just now, anyway. "I'll see if I can't get an expected arrival on that Combine hospital ship," he said, instead. "Andrej. Don't run yourself into the ground. You're good, not superhuman."

Koscuisko just waved, on his way out. Yogee was alone, for a few minutes, to wonder whether he still actually liked Koski and cared about whether he lived or died. He didn't want to. But he was beginning to suspect that the connection formed in late-night student gambling and brawls and all the rest of it still had a hold on him.

Koscuisko didn't need to know that.

Then the next meeting started to fill up the room, and Yogee went away to review mortality statistics and pull a shift or two in clinic.

Stildyne jogged along the track that ran from the field hospital to the launch fields and *Fisher Wolf,* listening carefully to the sound of his own footfalls in the dim silence that preceded the dawn. He'd been in deserts where it was noisy at night, as the desert came to life when the sun went down and everybody who'd been sheltering during the day stirred themselves to find something to eat and drink. To drink, by eating; insects and small rodents to eat fruit and the juicy pulp of cistern plants, birds to eat the insects and the small rodents.

Holding wasn't that kind of a desert. There was the shifting of sand from time to time beyond the hard flat surface that vehicles had compacted; the beetles that seemed to represent all there was to Holding of animal life didn't make enough noise to matter. And the shifting of the sand behind the emptied equipment containers that lined the route was too regular to be anything but the effect of the temperature gradients as the air warmed rapidly.

They'd moved the thula back to the launch-field as soon as there'd been room after the freighter-tenders had landed the hospital. Stildyne had a good excuse for being out here and not on clinic duty: he wanted to check on Riggs, their cargo-handler, who was watching the ship and bunking down there in the hammock she liked to sling amongst her cartons and crates.

When they'd made planetfall, ahead of everybody, days ago, Koscuisko had told her to stay with the ship; she hadn't, and that had been a sound instinct on her part. That was one thing.

But Koscuisko had told her that to keep her clear of whatever it was they might find when they opened up those warehouse barns full of people who'd been abandoned here, locked up in their pens and left to their own devices, when their captors had fled.

She hadn't succeeded in not looking. That was her call, as her decision to come with them had been; what they'd found had been unpleasant, unwelcome, horrible enough for experienced Security troops often exposed to horror, but Riggs hadn't seen such things in her life.

She'd mostly kept to *Fisher Wolf* since then, providing security at the launch-field and freeing the others up to work the clinics, orderly duty, triage, outpatient care. That was another good call. She was useful in that role, she was out of the way.

Even so, he was going to have to haul her back to the hospital soon, so she could see what things looked like when they were better. Otherwise the shock would haunt her for life. He owed her that much; people needed to have that opportunity to confront things they were reluctant to revisit.

He was being followed, and that wasn't a particular surprise, but that didn't mean he had to make it easy. Turning off the road at a break between empty cargo containers, Stildyne sprinted as hard as he could in the opposite direction, back toward the hospital. It was a long way. He'd nearly been across the launch-field perimeter when he'd made his move.

He decided to stop sprinting, and threw himself into a few swift rolls to brake his momentum. One. Two. Anybody would be expecting three at least, but as he came up from two he jumped for the roof of a container turned crosswise to the track, using the momentum of the roll to gain altitude. He wasn't getting any younger, no. But a man still had to stay in condition. They led an active life on *Fisher Wolf*.

Flattened on his stomach with his head down atop the cargo container, body tensed to move, Stildyne held his breath, listening.

It was a stressful life, a warrant officer—later Chief Warrant—running Security for Ship's Inquisitors. A man spent more time around Secured Medical where the screaming took place than other people, and really didn't have anybody else on board of a ship to talk to about it even if he'd wanted to. Which Stildyne never had. A certain degree of nonconsensual sexual access had always been the norm.

For reasons Stildyne didn't quite understand—and had made a conscious decision to avoid spending too much time pondering—none of the bond-involuntaries Koscuisko had sent away into Gonebeyond space these two-three years ago had taken their natural resentments out on him, not physically.

He answered personal questions when they came up, and in return they were sparing of the personal questions. He submitted to being flamboyantly exploited as their interface between *Fisher Wolf* and everybody else. Maybe they were a team, a solid working group, with him in it. He'd been a member of a kind of team when he'd been a boy, running the streets in Supicor; he hadn't remembered how good the feeling was, and he hoped it would continue.

He hadn't come to *Ragnarok* out of nowhere. Now his past confronted him, someone Stildyne had known before, someone who was newborn in a sense—no longer under Bond, but he hadn't stuck around in Haspirzak Judiciary to learn how to be a free man again, how to govern himself without the ingrained self-discipline that had been beaten into him to act as a curb on the expression of his resentments.

That wasn't Janforth's fault. As a choice—to stick around in Haspirzak, or to run as fast and as far away from Jurisdiction as he could get—it was value-neutral. There were important ways in which the wolf-pack were still learning how to not be under governor, after all. Hirsel went off from dead calm to dead fury without warning, from time to time. Lek sang. Godsalt raised his voice; Robert was halfway through his fast-meal before anybody else in the room had more than sat down.

The wolf-pack were resilient as bond-involuntaries had to be, and had the self-preservational strategies they'd had to develop in order to survive their punishment already available to them. But the most important thing was that the wolf-pack had had each other. Dealing with Koscuisko had forced the development of an especially strong team.

Janforth didn't have a team.

Stildyne knew *Fisher Wolf* needed to start developing redundancies in its crew, because life was uncertain and people moved on. There was a general unspoken hope that Janforth could integrate into the wolf-pack. Before that could happen, Janforth had to make up his mind what he was going to do about the history he and Stildyne shared.

Stildyne was a tall man, but so were bond-involuntaries, by and large. They got more intensive physical training than most because they were responsible for the personal security of Inquisitors when they were on remote assignment, and also because frequent opportunities to hit things—even each other—helped them manage their stress. Janforth had a good chance of taking him down. He'd been watching Stildyne. Stildyne knew.

He'd gotten the sense that Janforth was genuinely trying to stay clear, but he didn't think the effort had been entirely successful. There was the pressure of the situation they were in to sap a man's determination, even though it wasn't their personal safety under threat. It was hard to take, people captured for sale as slaves, old people, young people, ferociously self-punitive Dolgorukij religious fanatics.

If it hadn't been for how hard they'd all been working, how difficult it was to get some real sleep, how much pressure Janforth was under, Stildyne would never have heard him coming; and as it was he only barely caught the whisper of fabric against fabric behind him in time to gather himself up into a defensive crouch as Janforth came up over the lip of the storage container and stood there, looking at him.

"Now what?" Stildyne said. And waited.

"You used me like a handful of suds." And there it was. Vividly spoken, too. All of the hatred Stildyne had justly earned were in those words. "And these people, they don't seem to see you as dirty."

Janforth had been thinking about this. Stildyne had, too. "It's not for thinking I'm clean," he said. "Just that the stain's frayed to faded, over time. People don't seem to notice it as much as I'd thought they would."

He wouldn't bother pointing out that there wasn't much pure unalloyed cleanliness in peoples' personal histories in Gonebeyond, at least not in the company Stildyne and the wolf-pack kept. Desperate people did desperate things. There was less of an appetite to be outraged, by and large, and maybe he was just getting the benefit of the doubt by default, though he hadn't earned it.

It seemed to Stildyne that Janforth took it in, compared it against his thoughts about things, rejected it as a bad fit. "For other people, maybe. But what about those wolves? What about you and *them*?"

Stildyne stood silent, thoughtful, for a long moment. "It's not for me to say." Which was true. He wasn't hiding anything from Andrej, not anymore. He wasn't about to deny anything he'd done, but he wasn't setting it to music for a public concert, either. That would be even more of a violation of basic human dignity than helping himself to them had been in the first place.

"Why are you even still alive?" Janforth asked, wonderingly. Contemptuously. Unbelievingly; but also honestly.

"I've just been wondering about that myself." He owed Janforth answers as much as he owed the others, and with more reason, in a sense. After all, as far as the wolf-pack went, he'd been losing his appetite, more or less, even before Koscuisko had come on board. "I kept waiting for something, actually. Nothing's happened. Yet. So we're done. Maybe. Anything else?"

"I'm not done," Janforth said venomously. "I'm not finished. And I have to work with your officer."

Wait, was that a threat? If it was—should he pretend to be frightened, give Janforth a comforting feeling that he had something to hold over him? Maybe not. It would make Janforth feel that he'd been patronized if he ever did tell Andrej all about it, because he'd be able to tell that Andrej already knew, in outline at least. That wouldn't help. That would make things worse.

"I'll pick a fight, if you want one," Stildyne said. "Say some things about your mother, maybe. The wolf-pack will cover for us, nobody'll know. I don't think they'll step in, unless someone was about to get killed. But I'm fighting back, have no doubt of that."

He was careful not to say which one of them might be about to get killed. Janforth was fresh out of surgery. He hadn't had a chance to really grasp being free. Stildyne would have opportunities to fight dirty on a psychological level, which would give him an unfair advantage, which would mean maybe he wouldn't be the one who would get killed, if it came down to it.

"Not so easy as that." Something was going on with Janforth; Stildyne waited for Janforth to struggle through it. "Listen. I don't believe I'm telling you this. I need help. I can get it from *Fisher Wolf*. I just don't know how I can stand *Fisher Wolf* with you on it."

You're telling me because you're a survivor. You know what you need to do to live through this. That's why. "Tell you something true," Stildyne said. "I'm not always on *Fisher Wolf*. Sometimes I stay back at Safehaven. I'm not giving it up on your account, though. I have a job on *Fisher Wolf* same as anybody. Maybe I don't need it as much, any more, but I still need it." And maybe they needed him, too.

Janforth probably knew there was a particular relationship between Stildyne and Koscuisko, whether or not anybody but Dolgorukij—and the crew of the *Fisher Wolf*—knew what it was to be "self-same." Bond-involuntaries were almost preternaturally good at picking up on interpersonal relationships, because that was another survival skill.

So, Stildyne thought, *maybe Janforth did know about being self-same.* Bond-involuntaries could be deeply, passionately friends with one another. Lek and Garrity, for one. That was maybe about the same thing, if not of the same intensity. It was another survival skill, if a risky one; complicated by the ever-present danger of sudden death. As had been the case with Koscuisko and Joslire Curran, so far as Stildyne understood it.

"Never come up behind me," Janforth said. As a demand it came out a little pleadingly, but a person—Stildyne told himself—would have to know to be listening for it, to hear it there. "Never touch me. Yes maybe I shouldn't have come. But I'm here now. And I mean to live."

Stildyne considered carefully, so Janforth would know Stildyne had heard him in depth. Then he nodded. "*Fisher Wolf* will do everything in its power to make that work," he said. "With or without me on it. I'm confident I can promise you that."

Within the space of a few words on the top of a cargo container, the sun had crowned on the horizon. Already the air was appreciably warmer. It was time for them to get under cover, and Stildyne hadn't been out to see Riggs. He wanted to leave Janforth with the last word, but if Janforth didn't have one—

"Right," Janforth said. "Me back to clinic duty. Try to make sure I see you first, Chief."

That was a very fair deal, all in all. Nodding his head, Stildyne turned around and let himself down from the lip of the roof of the cargo container to the ground, to finish his jog out to the launch-field and suggest to Riggs that she should really come in and take mid-meal in the canteen sometime soon.

CHAPTER SIX

Things Go Wrong

Lek Kerenko sneezed, then grimaced with annoyance. That was *another* sterile mask to change. They'd only been on Holding for a few days, but that had been enough to set up some respiratory allergies, and now that he was inventorying in stores and supplies—that he was trying to inventory, that was to say—any residual sand or dust that had come in with the cargo, and there was sufficient of it clearly enough, was in the air and irritating his eyes.

Time away from clinic should have been a vacation, almost. Every time one of the Old Believers was escorted to clinic—they wouldn't come on their own, since even minor annoyances were gifts from God for Old Believers, to be borne patiently if not joyfully—every time he checked wound management or changed bandages he couldn't help reliving the horror of that first sight, the prison cage, the stink of wounds festering untreated in the heat.

Still Lek wasn't enjoying the respite as much as he'd have liked. They'd lost five of the Old Believers already, even though Dolgorukij nationals by and large had robust immune self-defense systems. It was all of a piece. Since he'd been exposed to some new allergen on Holding he was having a reaction. Once he'd developed a reasonable tolerance it wouldn't bother him again. Things would start to smooth out on the allergy front soon.

There wasn't anything particularly pernicious in the atmosphere at

123

Holding, or continuous environmental monitoring would have picked it up. It was just his luck to be hitting something that was novel enough that his body was taking distinct exception to it. There was the off chance that he had a minor respiratory event going on, of course, but he knew how to maintain all patient safety protocols; so that wasn't a problem.

The problem was that his joints ached, his plumbing was in a highly susceptible condition, and his face felt like it was about to explode right off of his skull. If things didn't clear up within the next shift he'd go to Infirmary for a dose of don't-have-allergies, but a field hospital had limited supplies by definition and a susceptible population to protect from allergies of their own.

Lek focused on his task as distraction from his headache, and concentrated on working through any inconveniences till he could get on the other side of them.

Because he was the senior medical officer on the ground it fell to Yogee to review the admissions and discharges report. A man was responsible for knowing what was going on in his own hospital, and he was just that many hours away from taking the daily briefing on remote with the Bench specialist now returned to the *Ragnarok* and Hilton Shires, the Langsarik Coalition's battle commander, back at Couveraine.

He swigged his jifka. Whoever those Agavie people were they pushed a good product, and Yogee wasn't too proud to take a bribe as long as it was sufficiently clean-shaven and presentable—open and public, that was to say. He wasn't a businessman, still less an economist. The hospital had food and water. That was all he cared about, for the present.

Unfortunately food and water weren't everything. The Old Believers were the most flamboyant examples, but they weren't the only ones who'd suffered wounding. There were even one or two other self-mutilations on the part of people taking logical steps to free themselves by destroying their own commercial value.

Those people were lucky they'd been abandoned before decisions had been made about their fate. Slavers had been known to make examples of what happened to people who destroyed other peoples' property, even when that property was a hand or a foot or a tongue or a pair of eyes.

Those other incidental self-mutilations had come out of a misguided self-protective interest, a way to win freedom even at cost, a sort of chewing off the limb to escape from a trap. The Old Believers were in a different category altogether. They didn't care what happened to them.

They sat unprotestingly to have their wounds examined and dressed; they politely received a warm beverage and a plate of food, or a bread-fold for ease of management. They ate patiently and quietly with their beverage gone cold in one hand and their bread-fold held carefully in the other with its napkin-wrapper turned back as they'd been given them, no more, no less, until someone came to clear their meal away.

Many of them were sick, yes. Several of them had died, only to be expected, really. The instrument they'd used was a crude cruel one made out of a bit of metal lathe sharpened into a point like a stylus that would have been found and confiscated if the slavers hadn't left, and none of them had had any clear idea of how to put an eye out with a sharp stick. There were cleaner ways and dirtier ways.

The job they'd done on one another had been clumsy, if sincere, so there was more damage than just the apparatus of the eye to consider and wound contamination on top of it all. So they were sick.

And they were dying, because not all the medical support under the clear bell of the blue skies could force people to stand up and fight for their own lives if they'd already made up their minds to go away. Koscuisko was just in denial, when he'd logged those deaths as due to a respiratory ailment. The respiratory ailment had merely been the immediate cause, not the underlying determinant. Pefisct hadn't logged any respiratory ailments, had he?

Yet there ought to be some. There always was when two populations came together, and here there were multiple populations on either side. Yogee pushed a flatfile flimsy around on the table in the administrative staff meeting room, impatiently. Yes, here it was, as he'd remembered. Pefisct had logged respiratory complaints in walk-in clinic, with three admitted on wards for documentation for a few shifts and then discharged.

No Old Believers. There wouldn't be. The Old Believers didn't come in to walk-in clinic. They just sat in the common-room of the dormitory building in which they were housed, row upon row of them, and from time to time they'd sing. By the time the hospital staff realized there was a problem on top of all the obvious problems they were either straight to critical care or dead.

Koscuisko had recorded their deaths himself because they were his countrymen, perhaps; but Koscuisko had made his detestation very clear to Yogee, so that wouldn't explain it. Not really.

"Gascarone for Doctor Koscuisko," Yogee told the still air of the conference room. Maybe it had just been Koscuisko's turn on morbidity report, but the cause of death was determined at the statistical analysis point, at the point of death. Koscuisko wasn't the only physician who had contact with the Old Believers. Yogee suspected that Koscuisko was stretching that roster as far as possible so that the frustration, and the horror, could be spread well out on the grounds of maintaining staff morale.

"Koscuisko is here," the talk-alert said. "What do you want, Yogee?"

Even in this place the cross-tempered tone of Koscuisko's voice made Yogee smile despite himself in fond remembrance. Koscuisko, trying to get his reading done when his eyes hurt from playing relki in a smoke-filled back room all night. Koscuisko, grappling with the final touches on a research case and a hangover at the same time.

Koscuisko, sitting at his study-set with a piece of white paper in his hand, thick heavy paper, non-standard size, on which someone had written with a pen in their hand. Therefore, from his home, parochial and backward for all its economic clout and political influence. Showing off. So rich they could communicate in ink on paper with words that were laid down by hand.

"I want to know where you are and why your shift-report is late," Yogee said reprovingly, scrambling all the while through his cluster of documents-cubes to find the one in which the latest shift-change reports were collected and plug it into a frame display. Right. Nothing from Koscuisko. "What do you have to say for yourself? Why are your patients dying of respiratory ailments?"

Not Koscuisko's patients, no, just people dying on his shift. When Koscuisko replied he sounded a little distracted, to Yogee. "I'd like to know that myself." Slowly Yogee's smile faded, as he listened to Koscuisko talk. "I'd ask Pefisct to have a closer look at the patient death profiles, except that I already did. I have yet to hear."

Not surprising, really, Yogee had to admit to himself. But

professionals didn't let personal animus interfere with patient welfare, and Koscuisko was still talking. Almost to himself, Yogee thought. "Old Believers keep strictly to themselves, wherever they are. Why would they be carrying a respiratory ailment around? They're isolated by choice, never mind being penned up with one another. Not so much as a single Telcheck or an Arakcheek or even an Aznir Dolgorukij among the entire lot of them, you're Birskovneyij or you're not an Old Believer."

So Koscuisko's point was that they shouldn't have respiratory ailments. But that also meant they would reasonably react much more violently to anything they did encounter, and there were countless chances for a little random exposure to an adaptable virus in a slaver's prison camp. Their wounds weren't clean. Even a very low-grade endemic ailment might take lethal advantage of people whose immune systems were as challenged as those of the Old Believers. Koscuisko wasn't stupid. He'd have thought of all that.

"Shirking clinic duty, more likely, Koski. D'you want me to have a look?" From the point of view of a man whose only specialization had been in epidemiology, that was to say. "You know what, just leave it with me. I suspect you're going to be called away soon. I hope your bivvy's packed."

People like Koscuisko didn't have bivvies. They had satchels. They carried a flask of something nice to drink and lefrols to smoke and fistfuls of cash. If he could find any sort of plausible pretext he could just search Koscuisko's bivvy on the way out and pretend none of those latter items had been there, *oh, but the mice are at it again.*

"I'm sure," Koscuisko said, absentmindedly. "Away, here." Distracted by analysis, if Yogee remembered that tone of voice. Koski could be like a professional rodent-hunter in his focus: let some abstract problem, whether of medicine or drink or relki or women, catch his attention, and he would be out of the world entirely for days. Had once been.

Yogee had to remind himself of the years that had passed, the very little time he and Koscuisko had had to become reacquainted, and the fact that the question of whether Yogee really even wanted to be was unresolved. All of what he remembered of his friend Koski was part of the package that had made an effective Inquisitor, especially the part about instilling terror of transgressing the Law.

There was also the question of whether Koscuisko was chasing a real issue, or simply working through his discomfort and dislike of patients dying when he didn't like them and asking himself relentlessly whether he had in some way failed to do his duty, a lapse resulting from unseen but pernicious influence of strictly personal emotions.

Well. If they needed a surgeon in a hurry, Yogee knew where they could find one at Safehaven. If Koscuisko missed clinic duty Yogee would send people to find him, and haul him back to his duty station. If there was something going on he'd get Pefisct on it; Pefisct had his quals in virology, after all.

But he'd hold off until Koscuisko had had a decent chance to resolve his concerns under his own power. There need be no requirement to bring the two men into any closer contact than they'd been at yesterday's briefing, and Koscuisko hadn't noticed Pefisct standing right behind him, had he? So Koscuisko's hatred receptors were not working on full power. If Koscuisko was tired enough there need be no major problems between the two of them.

He couldn't ride Koscuisko for not being in clinic if he was deficient in his own tasks by the time he was due to present status to the Langsarik Coalition at Couveraine, Yogee reminded himself; and clicked into cube to look at how they were doing at top-level in pharmacy stores, and whether his supplies people were expecting him to try to come up with some more beds.

When Andrej came into ambulatory report station to pull his duty shift he saw someone he knew in the cube-queue waiting, and he didn't like it. Lek Kerenko. They'd seated him in potentially infectious, so he was in an isolation clamshell: a seat like those in *Fisher Wolf's* wheelhouse, but equipped with quarantine-in-place—a sterile field that set up an invisible but effective barrier between any communicable anything and the rest of the people here.

It protected Lek, as well, from exposure to a novel virus while his body was in a stressed and weakened condition. Lek's initial statistics weren't critical. They just weren't very good.

Andrej tagged Lek's care for himself, without even the slightest twinge of guilt. He knew Lek. He could collect better information from the interplay between Lek's presentation and Andrej's unique insight on what it really meant when a man like Lek Kerenko said "I don't feel well." And there weren't many cases with a higher priority, since this was an ambulatory walk-in clinic, incidental ailments. So he got to pull Lek off into an examining room before too much time had elapsed, to see what was going on.

"Allergies," Lek said. He was still at rest in the quarantine shell, in its half-recumbent orientation now that Andrej had made a few adjustments. Andrej could reach through the sterile field to touch Lek's throat, gently pull the lower lid down to expose the pink cradle of Lek's eyes; the surface seemed dryer than usual, and there was the very most modest and well-behaved fever, enough to make Lek miserable without exceeding normal parameters. "Who was it came down with sneezes at the Matredonat? Was it Chief? I can't remember."

It had been several years, now, since Lek and the rest of the Security 5.1 team to which Lek had been assigned had accompanied Andrej home on leave, first to a personal estate in the grain-lands where he kept his new wife and son, then into the ancestral stronghold of the Koscuisko familial corporation in the mountains at Chelatring Side. Andrej couldn't remember if the hay in season had given anybody the sneezes.

Allergies could mimic the effects of a low-grade inflammation: and almost all of Lek's statistics were perfectly unobjectionable, blood pressure, breathable gas indices, capillary function. Heart rate. Perspiration. Sinus congestion, yes, and the kinds of respiratory system annoyances that could point in more than one direction.

Andrej decided to err on the side of caution. The Old Believers were Dolgorukij; they'd died of complications associated with having put out their eyes with a fearfully primitive weapon in an environment completely lacking in allowance for baseline hygiene beyond the primitive waste-vat in the back corner of each crowded stable-cell.

Lek hadn't put out his eyes and bandaged the raw wounds with a strip of dirty cloth and waited for days for someone to find him, no, he hadn't. Still. He and Lek both had done the first examination and amelioration survey on the Old Believers. There were other prisoners who'd been wounded, injured, tortured with brutal discipline. But none of the others had been Dolgorukij, and proportionately fewer of the others had died.

"I don't know that you have allergies, my dear." Because he and Lek were Dolgorukij, and he was fond of Lek and indebted to him, Andrej didn't try to sweeten his suspicions with ambiguous language. "I mean to check on that, of course. You and I are both somewhat depleted in our energies. I will take no chances." Lek knew about the Old Believers, too.

Andrej had asked Pefisct for some analysis of those deaths, but he'd done it by means of text transmission because he couldn't think about the man without feeling almost overcome with rage. That meant Pefisct might plausibly deny he'd ever seen Andrej's request. Andrej had heard nothing back, which meant that Andrej was going to have to go back to Yogee.

He'd rejected Yogee's offer to involve himself, before the scope of his inquiry had defeated him. Yogee wouldn't make it easy for him to ask for help now, but Andrej was confident that Yogee would take the problem on as his own on the medical merits of the inquiry.

Andrej wanted to know exactly why the Old Believers were dying—and what, exactly, they were dying of. His own attempts to consider the question had yielded no satisfactory answers.

"I can do—ah—I can do inventory reconciliation on my back," Lek said, hopefully. And maybe he could; the quarantine shell had adjustable screen-readers, after all, but then Lek coughed—dry, unproductive—without apparent pause to consider how the reflex undercut his proposal. "Oh. Sorry. But I can."

Andrej shook his head. "I'm sure you can, but you may not. I am putting you on infirmary report." Nothing in the clamshell's gross-format reports had anything alarming to say about droplets in Lek's cough than to note that the event had taken place and that a capture analysis would be run by standard operating procedure.

As long as Lek was at rest in the quarantine shell he was a risk neither to himself nor anybody else. Probably just allergies, after all. They were in the middle of a desert; there was a relatively high concentration of particulate matter in the air. "Shall I ask Garrity to bring music for you, from *Fisher Wolf*?"

Since the arrival of the field hospital they were all staying in the common dormitories, with everybody else. Yes, there was more room—and greater comfort—on *Fisher Wolf*, but they couldn't fit the entire staff on board. So someone would have to go fetch back Lek's music in cube for him.

Andrej was just grateful he didn't have to share a sleeping-room with either Pefisct or Yogee. He might have found himself sleeping beneath the examination levels or the meal-hall tables, had that happened.

"All right, I'll sleep. Just catch up on my fantasy life, maybe." Something Lek could do anywhere. It was a finely-honed survival skill for bond-involuntaries and doctors in field hospitals alike. "That Ekaterina Felsanjir, Cousin Ekaterina maybe, what, do you think I have a chance?"

Andrej agreed with Lek that Felsanjir was almost certainly a Malcontent agent, to be called "cousin" in intimate circumstances. As to the meat of the matter, however, Andrej dared not speculate.

"Go to sleep, Lek," he said. "Dream of what might be obtainable. I will see you again in a few hours."

Nor did Lek seem much inclined to argue further. He turned up the heat within the module without more than a nod of acquiescence, turning a little to one side, closing his eyes. Coughing a little, just a little, and just once. It didn't look like an allergy to Andrej. He needed more information to set his mind at rest.

Keying the module for a darkened field and a generous dose of an inhalable drowser Andrej put his thoughts in order—finish his shift, put in a status report for Yogee, maybe sneak a request for laboratory analysis through to the *Ragnarok* to see if they would entertain it—and called for Kerenko to be transferred to wards for observation.

Then he located his next patient in queue and got back to work.

Things were not going as planned for Danyo Pefisct. In a perfect world, a world in which one could easily or at least successfully complete one side of a contract at minimal cost and risk to oneself, he would have dosed Koscuisko. Koscuisko would promptly have obligingly gotten very sick after the short incubation period characteristic of exposure to a new and possibly dangerous mutation of a previously tame virus.

There being no autoimmune suppressants in stores for Koscuisko's ethnicity, and no assurances available that the in-house labs would be able to manufacture an as-yet-poorly defined counteragent in time to save Koscuisko's life with any degree of certainty, Koscuisko would have been shipped out on a fast courier within hours of the diagnosis.

Which would naturally have fallen to the virologist to make. Clean, straightforward, and Danyo would be left alone to do his job as a general practitioner, winning acknowledgement from senior staff and gratitude from patients by simply being there and doing less over-all harm than good.

It wasn't happening. It had been a good three days since he'd gently blown a plume of virus Koscuisko's way on the steam from a cup of hot cavene. Koscuisko didn't seem to be getting sick. Koscuisko was making trouble, because he apparently didn't have anything better to do than worry about a group of crazies who'd put their own—or each others'—eyes out, just because they were Dolgorukij.

Danyo's successful bit of covering his tracks had only resulted in catching Koscuisko's attention just when Danyo needed him to fall down and start dying, and as luck would have it there was another Dolgorukij here in the hospital who just happened to be a man Koscuisko was fond of.

"Try not to do too much with your right hand for the next few days," he told his patient, an older man of some generic ethnicity—*all right*, he told himself impatiently, *a category one hominid, system of origin Fontailloe Judiciary, Etzac national, characteristic semi-detached ear-lobes*—who'd been one of the last of the prisoners taken and warehoused before the slavers had abandoned the camp.

Which was exactly what Danyo would have done in their place. They'd have been able to predict the arrival of a Langsarik Coalition party in the near future, after all, any reasonable person could have done that, especially with the Langsariks next door—figuratively speaking—at Couveraine.

Shaking his head Danyo forced himself to concentrate. "And, I know you're probably tired of hearing this, but go slow, get plenty of rest, be sure to take in plenty to eat and drink, you've got recovery to do."

If it had been him he'd have set the secures on auto-unlock and instructed a few sensible captives on where to find the stores of food and how to work the water-pumps before he left, but he was a doctor, after all. He was a humane man. As it was, that girl had only been loose by accident. What had she done with her opportunity? Sat down and blinded herself.

"I can run the recyclers one-handed," the man said confidently, but with a bit of a question in his voice. Danyo thought about it. There would naturally be safeties in place, if Holding's cycler lines were anything like every other trash management system that Danyo had ever seen. So he nodded.

"Lending a hand," he said, approvingly. "Well done. Much appreciated, just see the schedule on the way out to log disposition and departure, yes?

"Oh, just one thing, Doctor," the patient said, reaching awkwardly into a pocket on the front of his work-smock with his left hand. "I found this in the hand-pick stream just before I came here. The man who was there to monitor the line said he thought it was yours."

Holding some small object out to Danyo in the palm of his hand the man waited, while Danyo stared. He shouldn't have tossed that toothpick into the trash. He'd thought it would go in harmless anonymity into its cycler bin to be destroyed, returned to its component parts, unrecognizable, untraceable. The trash management systems had betrayed him.

Their sensors clearly hadn't known what to make of a common toothpick, confused perhaps by the compartment inside that Danyo fervently hoped he was the only one who knew about. He hadn't thought ahead and he should have: it wasn't an ordinary toothpick, in a place as poor as Gonebeyond, but a component of a gentleman's personal grooming-kit. Naturally someone seeing it would retrieve it. Stupid, stupid, stupid.

He took the pick. "Nice," he said, bringing it up to eye-level to get a closer look. It was the exactly wrong toothpick. It was unquestionably covered in now-spent virus, dead, no longer dangerous, but with its genetic remains all too easy to recover and analyze. "What made that person think of me, I wonder?"

"Said he'd seen it on you," the patient said, gratified, clearly feeling he'd done Danyo a favor. "That you knew each other. Nice thing like that, I knew you'd be missing it. Things do stray when there's so much going on all around, important things. You're welcome. And thank you, Doctor."

Sure you don't want it? Danyo could ask. He decided against it, because there was only one person that line-monitor could possibly be. Janforth. Pulling an admin shift in his spare time, they were all doing two and three shifts end-to-end. That dirty little sneak. He was the only person here on Holding who could possibly have claimed to have seen Danyo with the toothpick, and the bitter irony of it all was that it was genuinely not his.

It was an exquisitely precise copy of the one in his grooming-set, yes, but if an intelligence analyst looked closely enough Danyo was sure they'd find some special features that were very interesting indeed. "I'll put it to good use, yes," Danyo said. His first move had to be to pretend it wasn't his, it only looked like the one Janforth would have seen when it had been Janforth's turn on valet duty. At least there was good reason now for Danyo's fingerprints to be all over it.

He could drop it into a flask of sterile wash to clean away as many of the traces of the virus as possible—because the pick had been pulled out of the trash, of course. Then, little as he wanted to, he was going to have to use it and be seen using it, as public proof that he had no idea it was anything but a toothpick.

If he could plausibly make that work. So little pressure was required to spring the catch on its virus-cache once Danyo had broken the seal, to spread the virus to Koscuisko three days ago. Who wasn't sick yet. Or was Koscuisko sick? Had Danyo just not heard about it yet? Danyo hadn't seen him, but he wouldn't necessarily do that with Koscuisko's attitude being what it was. Maybe Koscuisko *was* noticing symptoms. A man could hope.

Danyo decided he needed better cover than his program of passive noninvolvement. Koscuisko had asked, had demanded, an analysis of the deaths of the Old Believers. Danyo had ignored the request. He was a busy man. Now, however, that Lek Kerenko person was ill of a respiratory complaint, and two more of those wretched fanatics were dead.

His curiosity had been piqued now, he would say. The notifications on the shift reports had aroused his sense of urgency, he could say. Koscuisko had been low on his set of priorities as long as the indicators seemed clear enough to Danyo—who was the virologist, after all—and he'd had no reason to suspect anything apart from the obvious in the deaths of those Dolgorukij.

If he was absolutely forced to, he'd confess that Koscuisko's attitude annoyed him, but the moment he had the very slightest reason for concern—Lek Kerenko—he'd taken prompt measures. That would be a blue mark on his professional medical evaluation, which he was sure there were even in Gonebeyond, yes, but if it worked to divert suspicion he'd do it.

If there was any suspicion. There didn't have to be. Koscuisko might not get sick at all, and it would be Witt's fault, not Danyo's, for providing a useless instrument. Lek Kerenko might have a perfectly innocuous garden-variety case of the lung-rasps. There might be overwhelming evidence that those Old Believers hadn't been exposed to anything except their own ignorance and cruelty.

Or maybe he'd just find a box to hide in, somewhere in an unmonitored clinic area, one going back empty to the freighter *Nikojek* on a resupply run; and tell *Nikojek's* captain, when he got there, that something had gone wrong and he needed the captain's courier ship and a pilot for Couveraine immediately.

Once *en route* he would have time to consider his alternatives, including whether or not to actually proceed to Couveraine. That seemed like a simpler solution to the difficulties of the situation he was in.

It was a risk to leave the area before he'd finished his shift. There were patients waiting. But a man had to see to the performance of some natural functions, or get a bread-fold in case he'd missed his meal, or any number of things that might call him away suddenly for a few minutes.

Doing his best imitation of a man in increasingly urgent need of a toilet Danyo slipped out of clinic to pick up a few small and readily negotiated essentials from his quarters on his way to get away from Holding, before that damned Janforth could make even more trouble for him.

Medith Riggs had walked back from the hospital mess to the launch-fields not exactly dawdling but not in too much of a hurry to get back either. They'd been dirtside at Holding for ten days now—had it really been ten days?—and she was ready not to be at Holding any longer.

She'd been warned. She wasn't sorry she'd come out with *Fisher Wolf* to help unload the forward aid station module and then help pitch the forward clinic. But Stildyne had been right. She'd seen horrible things. Now she couldn't exactly wish she'd never come, because she never had to do it for the first time in her life ever again.

They'd given her a scrap of coarse green fabric to tie around her upper left arm that gave her the right to be walking patrol on the launch-field. Seven couriers; four freighter-tenders for the deep space freighter *Nikojek*. The Malcontent's thula *Fisher Wolf*. *Fisher Wolf* needed particular protection. People were always just passing by, just wondering if they could poke their heads in for a quick look around.

She was part of the relief party at Holding and she was doing something that needed to be done. Every day she walked to the hospital mess facility, took a meal, and stayed around to pull a clean-and-prep shift. Then she came back to run two shifts on launch-field security, with a few hours' sleep in between. There weren't any codes in the *Cargo Handler's Handbook* for that statement of work. So far as honing her cargo management skills went, she was swinging her rump in her hammock all day, doing nothing more strenuous than eating someone else's food and taking the occasional stroll.

And yet she kept on coming back to the problem. She'd seen things. So she knew why she'd been warned, now, and she had a feeling of desolate dread that what she'd seen hadn't even been the worst thing that the *Fisher Wolf*'s crew had, in the course of their careers. She appreciated that Stildyne had shown her respect in making his presentation to her once and then not trying to talk her out of her decision on the grounds of youth and inexperience, but—at the same time—she was wrestling with a certain amount of anger at him because he hadn't refused outright to bring her on.

All in all she had a lot to chew on, but also a job to do. Three times around the perimeter a shift, visual check for any signs of tampering or potential mechanical problems. Through the launch-field's park where most of the hospital's transport craft were arrayed corner-to-corner on the diagonal. She always took a check on *Fisher Wolf* first because she had a responsibility, and this time she was doubly glad she did. Because the passenger loading ramp was open. And someone was in the wheelhouse talking, either to himself or to some party on comms.

She ascended the loading ramp into the body of the ship with a firm and deliberate tread to warn any intruder off. There was no cause to expect trouble; nobody could shift *Fisher Wolf* on their own, so the ship really wasn't in danger of being stolen, after all. She'd hardly seen the wolf-pack since the hospital had arrived, though. Busy. They all had medical qualifications that the hospital was very glad to exploit, apparently.

It wasn't anyone from the wolf-pack in the wheelhouse. She recognized the voice as she got closer to it all the same: Andrej Koscuisko, who had more to do at the hospital than any of the rest of them, so what was he doing *here*? Who was he talking to? Why? And how had he gotten in?

She'd left *Fisher Wolf* closed up tight, voice command access only, and the comm boards were supposed to be locked. *Fisher Wolf* had recognized Koscuisko's voice: all right, so that was obvious. She'd have to have a word with Chief about whether even Andrej Koscuisko ought to be able to come and go at will. Yes, he had history with all of these people; yes, they let him get away with a lot, not as though he apparently noticed. Operating on habit. It just wasn't prudent practice for anybody but its own crew to have unlimited access.

"Yes, your Excellency," someone was saying. "The assays are running well. Another few hours and we'll have some information for you, tell me again why we're doing it for you, sir?" Male voice. One she didn't recognize, but it was transparently obvious that Koscuisko did.

"Because frankly it is not my field." There was the confident familiarity of command. He was talking to the *Ragnarok*, Medith guessed, to someone who'd once been in his direct line of report. There wasn't any of the hesitation, the diffidence, Koscuisko could display when he was talking to *Fisher Wolf*'s crew. It was interesting to listen to, so she kept listening.

"And I feel foolish, to tell you the truth. But the population of Old Believers has been isolated, so if Lek Kerenko—do you remember Lek?—if he's sick because of his contact with the Old Believers there should be no trace of any specifically Nurail genetic drift in the virus. There were no Nurail captives in the slave pens. I have asked."

"There are Nurail with the hospital, your Excellency?" It was clearly as natural and normal and habitual as it could be for whomever to call Koscuisko by his rank. She could tell. She would be willing to stand here all day and just listen, because they were talking about Lek; but she had work to do. She cleared her throat, loudly.

"Sorry, Doctor," she said, pitching her voice to carry from one end of the wheelhouse to the other. Not too difficult, that, it wasn't an exceptionally spacious wheelhouse, though exceptionally well equipped. "Didn't hear you come on."

Hadn't heard him at all, of course. Because she hadn't been here. Koscuisko looked back over his shoulder at her, obviously startled; but spoke to the person on the other end of his convo. It wasn't as if he was ignoring her presence, however; no, he waved her in to join him at Robert's comm-station.

Robert would want to know who'd been toggling his transmits in his absence, when he returned to *Fisher Wolf*. She'd have to tell him it was Koscuisko, or risk letting aspersions arise pertaining to her performance of her guard duty. He'd say something like "Himself? Well, that's all right, then," and decline absolutely to acknowledge any further aggravation. People could be like that when they loved each other.

"Yes, Nurail," Koscuisko was saying. "So for it to get to Lek, with the degree of separation that exists in our world-families between the Old Believers and Sarvaw, it would have had to get to our Old Believers, and then make its adjustments within one generation of the virus, and then pass to Lek. So either I am confronting a virus that has integrated a chance contact with Nurail and then reinfected the Old Believers within days, or there is something else going on. Either way I am not comfortable."

Koscuisko glanced at her with his eyebrows upraised into the *I'm sure you see my point* position, but whether he was directing the message to her—or psychically, to the *Ragnarok*—she wasn't sure. Except that Koscuisko had no reason to accuse her of psychic ability. He was looking at her as he continued, so maybe she was just a point of random intercept.

"One would almost imagine that the virus that has stricken the Old Believers has been somehow artificially communicated, and is targeted so carefully to Dolgorukij who are in frequent contact with Nurail that one could even imagine that it had been aimed at just such a population by someone with familiarity of Nurail subclinical respiratory infections in mind. I hope to hear from you that such cannot be the case, Mister Renring, or else I will have to speak to Doctor Gascarone."

There was a moment of silence from the other end and Medith didn't blame who . . . Renring? A bit. Koscuisko could get complex. It wasn't his ethnicity, either; Lek Kerenko was fully capable of getting from one end to the other of a complex sentence in less than ten words. Maybe Koscuisko was just tired, and thinking in his birth-language, and not managing the interface as seamlessly as usual.

"Getting the stats, your Excellency," Renring said, finally. "Seven in a set, and then Kerenko? Should I get one from you for index? I can plug the data in, but going down to generational regression, that could take maybe a day. Doctor Mahaffie will authorize the run, no worries."

"Um." Koscuisko sounded a little embarrassed to Medith, not that she'd ever met an embarrassed Dolgorukij autocrat. "I wish it were so on my end. We have a virologist, but I am not, I'm afraid, anywhere on his list of priorities, and I have somehow neglected to mention my intention to ask for your help to Doctor Gascarone. I make you complicit in violating my chain of command, so we will politely forget this part of the conversation, yes?"

Was that a laugh she heard? "So far as that goes, your Excellency, Doctor Mahaffie is still blaming delinquent status reports on you, and so far as we know Fleet still thinks you're our Chief Medical Officer. So there's no violation of chain of command, sir, so long as a person is willing to squint a bit, and that's what got us all here in the first place, isn't it? With respect. Er, sorry, your Excellency, on task, away here."

"Koscuisko away." Koscuisko cut the feed, then turned back to face her again. "I explain," he said. Medith wasn't very hopeful about that.

Koscuisko didn't always come across with an explanation in good form, and she sometimes thought she heard an underlying conviction in his voice that *because I wish it* was in his possibly unconscious mind all that was required at any given decision point. "Pefisct is our virologist, Pefisct is corrupt in my view, I want my answers more quickly than I am getting them. I have probably forfeited his cooperative goodwill, because I may have told him how much I would like to skin him alive."

Koscuisko was standing up as he spoke; a little stiffly, Medith thought. The medical staff worked harder than anybody else here. There were fewer of them, and they had to stretch even further as the degree of their specializations narrowed. There was only the one of Koscuisko, for instance, and they all did general clinic hours. Maybe Koscuisko was being unfair to this Dr. Pefisct. She didn't think she knew which one he was, but maybe *he* was just tired, too.

"Oh, and I apologize, for being present in your absence." He yawned; actually yawned. "I wasn't sure the ship would let me on. It grants me credence because we are of the same race, one suspects. It is the only place I could port data to the *Ragnarok* and not attract unwanted attention, but I remove myself now, thanking you for not throwing me out."

And not a trace of *because I wish it*. That was just him being really tired, Medith told herself. She wondered whether she didn't like him better rested and self-assured. He reminded her of Stildyne's lover Cousin Stanoczk, from time to time, and she liked Cousin Stanoczk.

"Your results are coming here, or going to the hospital?" It was something he'd want to know, she thought. If the information he was looking for came back to *Fisher Wolf* how would he know when to come looking for it?

He nodded. "I will ask Robert to draw a path. He will know how to go. Good-greeting, Riggs."

Yes, well, that would work. It was Robert's job, after all. She made sure her default secures were back in place once more, and followed Koscuisko out of *Fisher Wolf* to seal the thula up and get on with her patrol.

It was such a tight fit that Danyo was having a hard time getting enough air, with his knees cramped up against his chest and the wall of the crate less than three fingers in front of his face. All part of the camouflage.

He was not Danyo Pefisct, a man with a certain need to get away from Holding to the freighter that Witt had placed him on, where Captain Morrisk would see how fast she could get him across the vector to some safe haven where he could contact Witt for assistance. He was a crate full of depleted metal cartridges now emptied of atmospheric gasses for patients with respiratory challenges, on its way back to *Nikojek* to be refilled from the reservoir tanks and sent back down again.

The weight was an approximate match, once he'd emptied the crate of most of its containers. If anybody found them neatly stacked in a not-yet-fully-stocked cabinet they were welcome to simply assume the empties were being informally collected pending a full crateload.

He didn't have to travel from the hospital to the launch-field, risking exposure all the way. He could ride in comfort: that had been the plan, and it was working out, more or less. Since he was a crate full of thick-walled empties no danger could be done if the crate knocked around a bit, and it had. At least he was loaded now, stowed. He'd checked the shipping schedules. The kind of crate he was went up to *Nikojek* every two shifts, priority medical supply. Twice a day.

It was quiet now. He was alone. He was still more or less upright in his crate, and since he was alone he could afford a little light panting. The convolutions he'd had to go through to fit in squeezed his lungs down to a much reduced capacity and restricted his ability to expand his ribs, but it wouldn't be for long. *Nikojek*, and escape. He'd have his cabin back, since Gascarone wouldn't be there to claim it as senior medical officer. There was plenty of room to breathe in his cabin.

He hoped Gascarone hadn't drunk up all of his cortac brandy.

CHAPTER SEVEN

Things Get Worse

Jils Ivers had borrowed Captain ap Rhiannon's shallop from the *Ragnarok* to return to Couveraine, so she could take a quick index on what progress the Langsarik Coalition was making in processing captured resources. The Malcontent detachment from Canopy Base was deployed as Tamsen Gar's main presence dirtside.

It bothered Hilton Shires less to have Malcontents at the harvest than Nurail, because there was a fundamental philosophical difference between the two polities when it came to the question of pushing people around. At least Koscuisko wasn't here: though he would be, soon.

As a battle commander, Hilton Shires didn't let his personal feelings stand between him and information that might save lives or stop slavers, nor did he display any desire to disclaim his responsibility for his role in Koscuisko's deployment.

As a senior Langsarik officer, however, a representative of the Langsarik fleet, Provost Marshal at Langsarik Station, Shires was jealous of the honor of the Langsarik polity. Where was a reconciliation of those two considerations to be found? Because if Shires had adjusted his personal feelings in light of his command imperatives she certainly hadn't heard anything about it. Not a hint.

The Judge that Haspirzak Judiciary had sent into Gonebeyond— Bat Yorvik—would be studying the problem presented by multiple stake-holders with diverse values, looking for ways in which commonalities could be derived on which to base an understanding. That was his job. She wished him joy of it, cynically.

She'd become a cynic, as a Bench intelligence specialist, in the service of the rule of Law and the Judicial order. For now, Yorvik—sitting at the table in Shires' conference room—wasn't raising his voice on any particular topic, unless it was to ask questions carefully phrased to elicit information and discussion.

He wasn't doing much of that, either. He spent most of his time listening. Carefully listening. It wasn't the first time Jils had looked at Bat Yorvik and seen the makings of a Judge who would accomplish great things.

The hospital that Agavie had sent for a bald-faced bribe had included a very respectable communications suite in its administrative package. Tamsen Gar's people had been all over it as soon as it had been deployed, needless to say; it had been clean, no snoops, no spotters, no data kidnappings. No voice recordings for retransmission of planning and information.

There was, however, a full visual display—of Dr. Gascarone, and some of his direct reports. Jils searched the screen for Dr. Pefisct and didn't see him. She didn't see Andrej Koscuisko either, and hoped he wasn't off having a quiet talk with Pefisct about watercolors or needlework.

Jils wondered if the donated hospital itself had been a true arm's-length removed from Witt's personal empire. That Witt was in there somewhere was clear from the fact that Pefisct was here in Gonebeyond with the hospital.

She'd have to put Garol on it. Bench Intelligence Specialist Garol Vogel didn't like Dolgorukij, though he'd apparently liked the pastry enough to learn how to cook an impressive range of Dolgorukij baked goods. He wouldn't like Witt any the more for Witt's well-attested fascination with Dolgorukij everything and one unique Dolgorukij in particular. It would add sauce to the search, for Garol.

Not as though Garol didn't have enough to do in Gonebeyond. "Not like those religious types, what does the report say, Old Believers?" the Nurail spymaster Tamsen Gar was saying. She'd found Gar back on Couveraine when she'd returned from Holding, but he hadn't yet tied her in on what might have happened during her absence. That had been a disappointment on several levels.

Gar's tone of voice was its own kind of cynical as he talked on. "Reasonable, sensible people. Flexible. Oddly enough almost all of them never comfortable with slaving, just waiting for their chance to transfer to a cleaner line of work." Amused, yes, but not contemptuous. Couveraine's people were agreeable to transferring their allegiance, as long as they could feel confident that their families wouldn't be targeted for retribution. That was a promising element in the next concern Gan raised.

"Once we can show them that we have the resources to come to a successful conclusion we may reasonably hope for even better results. We think that we know where freighter *Biruck* has gone to, sorry, Dame Ivers, this information has just been delivered. *Ragnarok* has got a previously unidentified vector, vicinity Holding—that would be Danais, we think. To develop information from some of the senior people on Couveraine, though, for that we could use a little extra help, Doctor Gascarone. Can you accommodate?"

Gascarone didn't seem completely sure. Jils couldn't read his exact reservations. "Ah, possibly difficult. It's not *that*." That what? Jils wondered. Maybe just the obvious, the *we need Koscuisko in surgery and in clinic, not all the way away at Couveraine wasted on a single source of information and that one not even a medical problem really.*

"Then what, Doctor?" Shires asked. Mildly. Having already concluded that Gascarone had a particular issue in mind, Jils guessed. "And, ah, excuse me for asking, but where is Doctor Koscuisko, we should have him here for the briefing. So he knows the situation." It was good leadership on Shires' part, not just saying *go there and do that* but *go there because of these specific issues and do that in order to address these specific requirements.*

"We've had a troubling uptick in mortality that seems to be concentrated amongst those Old Believers, but one of *Fisher Wolf's* crew has come down with a virus and he's Dolgorukij too. It's making Koscuisko unhappy."

Jils frowned. She wasn't on first-name terms with the *Fisher Wolf's* crew. They didn't have a social relationship. But she had good reason to know from her experience with the thula that there had been only the one Dolgorukij—Sarvaw—on Koscuisko's team of bond-involuntaries, and he was the thula's default pilot. What he'd done with

Fisher Wolf at Taisheki Station had been a thing of genuine beauty. She would hate the waste, if anything happened to Lek Kerenko.

"If it turns out we have a situation we may want to put Holding on quarantine lockdown." Gascarone seemed clearly reluctant to take so drastic a step, and aware of the fact that it was his call all the same. "But I expected him to be here, frankly. One moment. Doctor Gascarone for Doctor Koscuisko, we need you in a meeting."

"You've got a virologist on staff, according to the personnel manifest," Gar said. Pointed out. Surfaced for consideration. "Koscuisko isn't it."

No. What Koscuisko was, was a good battle surgeon, a superlative neurosurgeon because Jils had asked what it took to pull a governor successfully five times in a row and now six, as she'd been given to understand. A perfectly adequate general practitioner according to Safehaven's chief medical officer, and a man whose peculiar psychology married to all of what else Koscuisko was made him one of few whose harvest of information when it was necessary to extract it by force was more consistently complete and correct than any other Ship's Inquisitor in Fleet's inventory.

Except that he was no longer in Fleet's inventory, of course. And if the Third Judge at Haspirzak Judiciary had her way there would be no other such men in any Fleet inventory, ever again.

Dr. Gascarone frowned. "Yogee Gascarone for Doctor Koscuisko," he repeated. "Your immediate presence required. Respond, please." Gascarone waited. There was silence. Still silence. More silence. "Mission Commander, request tabling of the balance of this briefing, I want to go find him and shake him till his teeth rattle. On your behalf, of course."

Gascarone was worried. There was considerably more passion in his voice than Jils had heard from him throughout, and a stronger hint of an accent to his Standard—*preysance* for *presence*; *Ewer*, for *your*.

Old Believers the focal point for the unexpected increase in mortality rates. Lek Kerenko in Infirmary for observation. Andrej Koscuisko not responding to talk-alert, so Koscuisko wasn't anywhere the talk-alert thought he ought to be, or Koscuisko was asleep, or Koscuisko was engaged in intimacies and didn't care to be interrupted. Or something.

"Give us an update on his availability when you can," Shires said to

Gascarone, standing up to nod politely to Yorvik in acknowledgement. "Briefing is suspended, thank you, your Honor, thank you all."

A distracted nod from Dr. Gascarone, and transmission from Holding cut out just as Gascarone pushed himself to his feet and turned toward the door. "And Pefisct, where's Pefisct, left clinic has he, without authorization—"

Shires left.

Tamsen Gar sat, one hand stretched out before him on the surface of the table, flexing his fingers from right to left. Not frowning. But thinking. Jils had a sense that he was actually pleasantly diverted, in an obscure sense; something unexpected had happened. Bat Yorvik sat listening. So Jils sat still and waited, listening to Gar's silence, and wondering what if anything he was going to say.

"Someone spent a lot of money to get that virologist close to Koscuisko," Gar said finally. "And Pefisct has got plenty of juicy questionables on his tally-sheet. I call it a suspected assassination attempt, and close the vector to all traffic till Pefisct's found. Agreed?"

Virologist, and a suspected virus. Danyo's timely arrival at Couveraine with a hospital. It was a long way to go, an expensive approach, if it was nothing more than a complicated assassination setup, and people at the tops of criminal cartels—like successful businessmen everywhere—kept a careful eye on unnecessary extravagances. Jils nodded. "Agreed," she said. "Any questions, your Honor?"

"Yes," Yorvik said, while Gar looked up at him from beneath his black eyebrows as if he'd been expecting something to happen that just did. "But this is a clearly very complicated situation, and my questions will clearly require a lengthy investment of your time and attention. Which I don't want to ask for, just now. I'll wait."

"Right you are," Gar said. "Your Honor. Bench specialist. We're done for now? Good-greeting."

And he was gone. Yorvik shook his head. "He seems to me to be a peculiar man," he said. "I'd have thought an intelligence chief would take pains not to seem unusual, in any sense. To create a false sense of complacency and confidence." That was true, perhaps more so than Yorvik realized. One of the most effective weapons a Bench intelligence specialist had was an innocuous demeanor and an unremarkable personal presence.

"These Nurail." As it happened she knew things about Gar that she was probably not expected to know, but since she was almost certain that he knew things about her that would surprise her, she didn't mind. Sauce for the verdure was sauce for the breadloaf, after all. "Nothing reasonable or sensible about any of them. They get away with it by being dangerous. Cover for me? I suddenly want to go sightseeing on a desert nearby."

"We're both just sitting here talking, and hoping to hear from Gascarone," Yorvik said obligingly. "Until I'm sitting here by myself, of course, writing up an analysis brief. Good-greeting, Bench specialist."

She had to smile. But she made it out the door before Yorvik could see it, and wonder if she was laughing at him; and went straight down to requisition the immediate use of the fastest courier she could rationalize removing from Couveraine's resources, and get on vector before Gar had a chance to put a stop on traffic to Holding.

As mission-assigned staff without more than rudimentary field-expedient medical skills Brachi Stildyne was on hospital security, pro tem, not because the hospital faced external dangers or internal sabotage—though of course there was always the potential—but because four hundred and twenty-three people were a lot to keep track of, even if they did occasionally take themselves out of circulation by dying. They'd started with a base inventory of four hundred and thirty-eight. He hoped the Old Believers would stop dying soon. It was depressing for everybody.

As a sort of supply management issue, Traffic Control had its desk in stores-and-receipts where Stildyne could collect all the transmits—outpatient clinic, patients in transit from patient intake to observation, people in transit from critical care to the mortuary hut pending disposition of remains—and make sure that all of the running tallies the hospital generated added up and agreed with one another.

The task took concentration. In his career as a Security warrant officer he'd gotten good at knowing where thirty or forty people were at any one time—the Security for whom he was responsible, *all* of the Security formally treeing up to Chief Medical, not just the bond-involuntaries; many of the officers and staff in Ship's Infirmary; and the officer of the day; and so on.

But there were easily eight hundred souls on Holding between freed prisoners and medical staff and all the administrative support people that were needed to make the entire enterprise go. He knew it could have been even more complicated. They could have had a full rehab facility on site. They needed one. Maybe one was coming.

He heard the talk-alert's chime at his station followed so quickly by an urgent demand that Stildyne's ears didn't quite make sense of the words at first. "Gascarone, Stildyne, if you know where Koscuisko is, tell me right away but get started there first." Gascarone was talking fast and apparently moving faster, crossing from one limit-of-coverage to the next in the time it took him to get from *Stildyne* to *started.*

"Yes," Stildyne said, to let Gascarone know he'd gotten the message. He had to think, to refocus his attention from the many to the one: Andrej Koscuisko. What time was it? Not in clinic, then. Not in his room. In the hospital's pathology lab, possibly, not much more than a large closet really but—as Koscuisko had said—they were lucky to have a path lab.

Stildyne looked around to catch someone's eye, to pass coverage of the Traffic Control function off during his unplanned absence; exchanged a crisp nod with one of Agavie's people—a technician named Zho—and started out of stores-and-receipts for the place between critical care and the mortuary hut where the pathology lab had been set up as a sort of an outgrowth from the less-well-trafficked corridor, like a wart in the walls.

"I'm checking the path lab," Stildyne said, grimly. "He's been working his mortality problem. Stildyne for Doctor Koscuisko."

Gascarone would already have called an all-trans on talk-alert. Stildyne was confident of that. But he could no more keep from doing exactly the same thing himself than he could have taken a leisurely route. Maybe Koscuisko had simply been in the toilet when Gascarone had sent a hail. Maybe he'd been outside the range of the talk-alerts entirely, smoking a lefrol. Either of those things would explain it.

Maybe Koscuisko had decided to just ignore Gascarone, but he wouldn't have ignored Stildyne, so Stildyne tried again. "Stildyne for Doctor Koscuisko." There was no reason he should run, no reason he should focus with such intensity on alternatives that would explain Koscuisko's silence. Except that Koscuisko was the most Dolgorukij kind of Dolgorukij in the entire Dolgorukij Combine, and also hadn't been happy with Lek being sick for more reasons than just friendship and affection.

"Gascarone for Stildyne," the talk-alert said. "Meet you there." Stildyne broke for the outside: he could cut straight across to the path lab over open ground more directly than through the corridors of the hospital, which also had people in them, among the other obstacles they presented. If something was wrong he wanted to be the first to know.

If nothing was wrong he wanted to let Koscuisko know that Gascarone was coming. If Koscuisko wasn't off in his own little world in the serene privacy of a pathology lab he'd . . . he'd . . . he'd send someone to *Fisher Wolf* while he ordered up some clinic sweeps and had someone check the mess areas and run the perimeter smelling for lefrol smoke.

Stildyne used the mortuary hut's external access doors to get back into the hospital, starting from the far end of the corridor, working inward toward the path lab. Did he smell lefrol smoke? No. Wishful thinking. Koscuisko wouldn't be smoking in a lab anyway. The door to the path lab was firmly closed, of course it was, but not secured. That meant there was someone inside, because otherwise the door would auto-secure if the lab was empty. That didn't make Stildyne feel any better.

It was bright and cheerful inside, small though it was, full of the merry noise of alerts and alarms from test runs and completion codes. Stildyne didn't see anybody, he'd never been in here, where was he supposed to look?

There. Behind the central island, the work bench with its equipment in array. It was the fact that one of the low-backed analyst's tall-chairs was not squared to the work bench but shoved off into the corner, up against the rear angle of the second rank of test equipment, that drew his eye.

And there on the floor between the island and the back wall there were feet, sticking out from the cuffed trousers of a white Infirmary over-all, feet wearing cloth-wrapped boots just like everybody else's footgear but which Stildyne was nonetheless immediately convinced that he recognized.

"Napping on duty, Andrej?" he said, but his heart wasn't in it because Koscuisko would have woken up by now if he was going to.

Stildyne went sideways between the end of the island and the small space between it and the back wall as quickly as he could.

Koscuisko lay there awkwardly twisted, half on his back, half on his side, his face turned toward the door and his color emphatically not good. Hair clumped with sweat. Frowning, lips slightly parted, as though he wasn't getting enough air, a feeble cough the only sign of a reaction to Stildyne's presence but Stildyne welcomed it because it meant that Koscuisko was still breathing. If he wasn't careful, Stildyne told himself, he'd believe he could sense the heat of Koscuisko's fever, and what did Koscuisko have in his hand?

There wasn't enough room on the floor between the island and the back wall for Stildyne to get close enough to Koscuisko's head to check for a pulse. If he rested his weight against the surface of the central island he could just barely reach the crumpled flatfile flimsy in Koscuisko's hand. It meant a stretch to the limits of his flexibility. When Gascarone came crashing into the room the sudden noise started Stildyne so much he almost lost his balance, and he had to release the flimsy because he was afraid he'd started a tear.

"Other side," Stildyne said. Gascarone was tall but slender, and fit into the cramped space more efficiently. He still had to struggle to get down to Koscuisko-level on the floor. How were they going to extricate an unconscious man?

"Doctor Gascarone for emergency response," Gascarone said, on his knees on the floor. "Life-litter to path lab priority one." Gascarone was doing the emergency checks, standard procedure, unconscious patient. Stildyne could recognize it, airway, wounds, internal bleeding, compound fractures. He waited. "The body-wrack," Gascarone said, but Stildyne had been expecting that.

He'd checked on Kerenko an hour or two ago and found him worse instead of better, supplemental air, intravenous drip. Not dead yet, though. It was strange, wasn't it, that Lek and Koscuisko were exposed to the Old Believers within moments of each other and Koscuisko had had more subsequent contact, but it had been Lek who'd sickened first?

"What's he got in his fist?" Stildyne asked helpfully, because Gascarone was busy loosening clothing to cool things down a bit. Oh, and for the resuscitation spider, if they needed it. "Careful, I almost tore it, I'm afraid."

Gascarone pulled Koscuisko's fingers away, and swore, waving the flatfile flimsy at Stildyne. Koscuisko had written something down. Some of it had been smudged; because Koscuisko was sweating, Stildyne guessed. "If that's even Standard I'll stand in wonder," Gascarone said. "Oh. Good."

The life-litter was here. Stildyne hoped they wouldn't close the lid. In his previous experience with Koscuisko on a raging drunk he'd grown familiar with the fact that sometimes hints of things got through to Koscuisko's disordered mind even when a chief of Security had every reason to believe Koscuisko safely insensible. In his psychotic state Koscuisko would misinterpret things, in his dreams. A respirator mask could be bad, very bad, because Koscuisko had a genius for improvisation with just such otherwise innocuous things during a field-expedient Inquiry. And Koscuisko had to live.

Retreating into the outer corridor to let the med-team work Stildyne flattened the flimsy Koscuisko had been holding against the light-colored surface of the wall. It was in Standard, as near as he could make out. Not Gascarone's fault if he'd mistaken it; but Stildyne had experience reading Koscuisko's hand-script that Gascarone—that nobody else living—could touch.

So close, and yet so far away, Stildyne told himself bitterly. Something that looked like "virus." Something that looked like "sau" or "srou." Two or three other words scrawled across the flimsy, none of which Stildyne could grasp, but they had to mean something.

The technicians were carrying Koscuisko's limp body out of the room to fit into the life-litter. Gascarone came following after; they deployed the top of the casket-like litter down along one side in its "open" position, Stildyne was glad to see. "Standard, but I can't get anything, not yet," Stildyne said. "I'll ask the others as well. Maybe run a pattern analysis."

Gascarone just nodded on his way past, his mind clearly elsewhere. Gascarone didn't know what *self-same* meant, in a Dolgorukij context. So Gascarone had no way of knowing how Tikhon had taken the death of his friend, his more-than-friend, his self-same shield companion and counterpart. Stildyne decided against going any further.

He went back into the lab, instead, to see if he could recognize anything on the analysis grids that would give him a hint about what Koscuisko had been doing here, exactly, when he'd laid down on the floor. Because he might have collapsed, but if he'd known it was coming, he'd have stretched out on the floor before he fell. Maybe it hadn't been more complicated than that the floor was cooler, and he'd had a fever coming on.

Why hadn't Koscuisko called for help? Infirmary said that Lek was confused, when he'd been conscious. Maybe Koscuisko had meant to engage the talk-alert when he'd lain down. Maybe Koscuisko had forgotten that he could engage the talk-alert. It didn't matter. There was something Stildyne needed to do.

"Security Chief Stildyne to Grey Wolf One." He heard the chirp; the talk-alert was there, all right. "Gentlemen, at your convenience. Officer down."

He didn't want to get any more specific. The wolf-pack would know where to find him. One quick but thorough scan of every report he could see running—just in case some solution jumped out at him and knocked him flat—and he'd be away after Gascarone, doing his best all the while not to think about the joke it would be if Andrej Koscuisko—Uncle Andrej, Black Andrej Koscuisko, Ship's Inquisitor—were to be assassinated by a fever, after all that he had done in the world.

Medith was stacking sterile serving trays in the wash-pantry—kitted up head to foot as though she'd been a med tech on restricted wards—when she heard the all-talk trolling for recipients in the clear. *Security Chief Stildyne for Grey Wolf One. At your convenience, gentlemen. Officer down.*

She recognized the voice. She hadn't heard the crew of the *Fisher Wolf* called "grey" wolves before—though maybe Pyotr was picking up a little dust around the hairline—but if Stildyne said it, it couldn't be anybody else. That meant she knew who the "officer" was. That meant it was particularly bad news, because even though she'd seen them push back politely and only once there was no mistaking the deep bonds of mutual affection still alive and active between them.

As she moved from stack to stack, and stack from counter to counter, she realized there was something else that "officer down" might mean. She'd caught Koscuisko on *Fisher Wolf* just yesterday, not four shifts ago. Had Koscuisko heard back from the *Ragnarok*? *I'll tell Robert*, he'd said. Had he done that?

She decided it could be either very important or not at all. If it turned out to be very important, and she didn't just go ask, she'd lose her berth on *Fisher Wolf* forever; and also maybe a little bit approximately never forgive herself for being afraid to risk a little embarrassment—even maybe losing her berth anyway—instead of sharing what might be key information.

So "Shades, I need to take one-two," she called out to the work-team leader on her way out to the discards closet to turn her clean-line overalls for sanitation and get out. Go where? Go to *Fisher Wolf* and ask it? Plus side, saving embarrassment, not becoming involved except to the extent of telling *Ragnarok* to find Robert, yeah.

Minus side, travel time to launch-field and she didn't know for a fact that *Fisher Wolf* would let her access anything in the wheelhouse when she got there. Anybody could say "urgent message, lifesaving mission, maybe." No self-respecting ship would fall for that without a much more convincing argument.

So. Find Stildyne and-or the wolves and report directly. That meant finding them, and she didn't want to ask in the clear for a number of very good reasons the most obvious of which was that if it was "officer down" she doubted they'd even hear her, not on all-talk in the clear. People didn't have conversations on all-talk. She had to find them in the flesh.

She had an idea where to look; and she had a green arm-band, designated administrative personnel. With luck that would get her through to places where she had no business being but where she'd find the crew of the *Fisher Wolf*, less Lek Kerenko.

He was still in critical. Garrity had told her when he'd come through the meal line. Actually he'd just shaken his head and said "no report," which was the complete conversation and delivery of important status and everything right there.

She put on her very best *mission critical coming through, thanks* expression and went out into more strictly controlled medical areas than she'd had occasion to visit before. She saw the traffic control monitoring status, stopped at one; said "Chief Stildyne?" and got waved through with a helpful pointing of a finger at the nav sign, *infectious quarantine critical no entry*. That didn't apply to Stildyne, Medith told herself, firmly. Any stray infection, any airborne contaminated particles, he'd just have to scowl at it and it'd shrivel down to nothing. No. Better. Not scowl at it. Smile at it.

They stopped her at the next control station, though, and wanted to know whether she was sure she was supposed to be there and maybe she'd like to just sit down and wait while they checked further up the line for clearance. What could she say? "Koscuisko was talking to the *Ragnarok*?"

As a reason she should be allowed into a medical control area it didn't sound very convincing, but if traffic control ran a trap on her at least they'd know she was there, inside. For some reason. They'd come find out what reason it was.

She was feeling too stressed to sit down and the chairs weren't very comfortable anyway. She didn't have to wait long, though, standing impatiently beside the chairs, staying out of the way. One of the wolves was coming down the corridor, and it was even Robert St. Clare. "Riggs," he said, not stopping. "With me."

He was moving too fast for her to ask him whether he'd heard about the *Ragnarok* if she didn't want to share the question with the world. Traffic control just saluted with a wave of the hand as she hurried past, so she was in. She'd been thinking how to say it on her way here, she was prepared when they stopped for an instant while securities in place at the third-level entry barrier were processing.

"*Ragnarok's* running tests for Koscuisko," she said. "Privately, results to *Fisher Wolf.*" There, that should do it, but St. Clare just gave her the glance of a man whose mind was somewhere else, and nodded.

The secures cleared. Robert pushed through while the barrier door was still only half-open. She followed, he might not have heard her, he might have questions, she didn't know if she'd communicated. She'd have to try again.

Now they were in the narrowest corridor yet, walls strung with telltale lights all glowing blue. She could hear voices, so it was easier to follow Robert because now she at least knew where he was going. Past an actual Security post, two souls with sidearms watching the tell-tales rather than Medith—looking for a containment breach alarm. Maybe uncomfortable.

Around the corner to the right, and straight into a confrontation on the verge of becoming a war. There was an actual Security gate, cross-barred and alarmed. There was the hospital commander, Dr. Gascarone—standing in front of the security gate with his feet set at an angle that said *you're not getting through* and his arms folded in the *except through me and I bite* position.

Then there was Chief Stildyne, facing him, his shoulders speaking their own kind of language even from behind, things like *I'm coming through you one way or another* over a baseline note of *you and what army? Because I've brought mine.*

"If he's going to die I have to be there," Stildyne was saying. "And I mean, I *have* to be there, Doctor Gascarone. There's something you might not understand about Andrej and me."

St. Clare had taken his place in a combat alert formation behind Stildyne. They'd left him a space in the line. Everybody else was already here; even the new guy, Janforth, Medith noted, standing in for Lek Kerenko. Medith kept well back, thinking *I shouldn't be here what am I doing here how soon can I run away which is the only rational thing to do right here right now?*

"Look, you're friends, comrades, you mean the world to one another all of you, but the last thing he'd want is to take any of you with him and there's no telling how much worse this thing could get. So. No."

Medith was impressed, while she was unnerved. Facing down the wolf-pack with Stildyne in the lead had to take real guts, especially for a doctor, especially for a doctor with no army of his own standing between Stildyne and the security gate. "Self-same," Stildyne said, gently, which was more frightening than anything Medith could imagine right here right now. "It's a sworn compact, dedicated, more than married, stand aside and open the door, I'll be with him."

Robert coughed. In the place they were, if the situation being as Medith had decoded it was that Koscuisko was specifically sick of the same thing that had Lek Kerenko still in critical care, Robert's cough caught everyone's attention with maximum utility. *Kudos Robert*, Medith though. *Well coughed.* "Riggs says Koscuisko's got tests on with the *Ragnarok*," Robert said. "We should have a quick listen, Chief, might give you leverage with Gascarone."

Yes. That was why she'd come. That was why she was here trying not to make herself the focus of the deadly determination being generated by *Fisher Wolf's* wolf-pack, trying not to grab Gascarone and flee before Stildyne cut him into pieces with his naked voice. Gascarone shifted his sharp grim stare from Robert's face to Medith, as Security angled themselves to one side and the other so Gascarone—and Stildyne—could see her. "Leverage, bedad?" Gascarone repeated, angrily, but in control. "Talk to me."

Which she couldn't really do, because she'd already said more or less everything she knew. "I found Doctor Koscuisko on *Fisher Wolf* yesterday. He was in the wheelhouse talking to someone on the *Ragnarok*, someone Renring, I think."

She was more relieved than she'd almost ever been when the wolf-pack reacted to the name: it was clearly one they knew. From the *Ragnarok*. She was ahead already.

"And I'm really really sorry, but I didn't understand a lot of the discussion. Summary. It was about infection going from Old Believers to Lek, but with something Nurail involved? Somehow? And Koscuisko didn't believe the Old Believers had been carrying it when they were brought to Holding in the first place. He'd sent data. Renring was running tests."

There was too much of it. She couldn't possibly get it all out in time. She had to speed it up. "He was going to report through *Fisher Wolf* because Koscuisko was going around Doctor Pefisct. Or he was going to message Robert about it. This was yesterday, probably about shift-change, I don't know anything more, sorry."

Gascarone exploded. "*Son* of a bitch," he swore, and pushed Stildyne so hard that even Stildyne staggered. "Son of a *bitch*." Not Stildyne. Koscuisko. That was clear. "And not to tell me, go run your little problems on your own you bastard, you, Riggs, he had a direct link? Yes? We're going to *Fisher Wolf* and we're going there right now."

"Except me," Stildyne said, calmly. "I'm going in through there. Right now. Do I have to set off a percussion tap? Here? Inside a hospital? There'd be a lot of debris."

Gascarone stood for a moment, shifting his weight from side to side as though he was arguing with himself, his lips moving as if he was providing his own dialog. He apparently had one last unresolved question on his mind. "Married, you said?"

Stildyne nodded his head with gravity and assurance. "Friends before birth," he said. "Comrades to the death, no credible information available for what happens after that. Self-same in this world. Romantic friendship. Everything but the sex, so, yeah—pair-bonded, married."

"You go in, you don't come out until he's clean," Gascarone said, brushing wrinkles out of Stildyne's blouse where Gascarone had pushed him. "All right, go. Cleared for entry. *Fisher Wolf*, Riggs, and Robert you said, hell, you can all come, so long as we can go right now."

They didn't need her. And she hadn't checked out of her shift, which meant absence without leave in form and in function. She would just have to take the demerit, because she was going with the wolves out to the launch-field and be there when Gascarone turned around from the comm boards and said something like *See? All better now.*

If what Gascarone said instead turned out to be *too late, we've just lost Kerenko and there's nothing to be done for Koscuisko now*, then at least she'd know she'd done everything she could to facilitate a good outcome.

Danyo lay comfortably in a semi-inclined position on the vid-chair in his suite, breathing an enriched gas mix from the discreet little tube that clung of its own electrostatic accord to his cheek, listening to the hellish ache in his chest and legs and shoulders beginning finally to subside.

He hadn't realized how much it was going to hurt. He'd never imagined what torture it could be to sit crouched in a small box for hours, and it had been less than a day since he'd hidden himself away to make his escape. Less than a day.

He'd shut people up in boxes for extended periods of time during that interesting period between an intake interview and a determination of what to investigate and with what degree of rigor. He clearly hadn't realized what it was really like, or he'd have appreciated it more, maybe ordered it more frequently. It was spoiled for him now. He couldn't so much as think about it without shuddering.

"Call my office," Danyo said, closing his eyes in weariness. His office: the drop-box where he was to have left a welcome message for Witt, package en route, particulars to follow. Not to be, more was the pity, but Danyo was lucky to have gotten away when he had. Witt was simply going to have to come up with another plan.

He was getting his voice back; not that he'd been screaming—though he'd had to yell, loud and long, before he'd gotten anybody's attention once the transport craft had reached *Nikojek*. He'd brought a whistle. He hadn't been able to reach it, for the cramps in his legs. They would have found him soon enough; as a crate he was to be unloaded, refilled, returned within a three-shift window. What he would have had to endure if he'd had to wait—how long? Three shifts?—had he not been able to make himself heard, didn't bear contemplation.

No, it had been all of three hours struggling to breathe through his half-opened mouth because he hadn't been able to draw in sufficient volume of air through his nose, it was too much work, his ribs declined the effort, he'd been choking.

He sipped his drink, with its dose of topical soother—the stuff the clinic used when a breathing tube had to be placed, the gel coating infused with anesthetic. He ignored the taste. He needed the soother more than the fine flavor of the brandy.

He hadn't heard any reply. Had he slipped out of consciousness, for a moment? The captain's words were growing louder, more distinct. "Dangerous virus strain of the common body-wrack," she was saying. "We're locked from here to the vector, nothing going out, limited traffic incoming. Something's gotten into the hospital population, some sort of—what? Mutation? Ah, antigenic drift? Dirtside is on top-level quarantine. I'm sorry, your Excellency."

The virus. Witt's virus. Danyo had planned on the deaths of any Old Believers being attributed to the infection of their wounds, and for the anomalous elements of case presentation to be lost in the noise and debris as the hospital struggled with other problems.

Witt would have had something done up that wouldn't call attention to itself when Koscuisko got it, apart from the planned claim for the virulence of Koscuisko's own immune response to a slightly shifted strain. Yes, Danyo could well imagine that it would have had a bit of Nurail in it, since it was targeted for Koscuisko and Koscuisko had been living at Safehaven these two years and more.

People from all over had been called in by the Langsarik Coalition to provide medical support, first at Couveraine, and now at Holding. Too many people with no prior contact with endemic subclinical Nurail strains of the body-wrack.

Danyo was afraid to ask for a body count. Captain Morrisk only knew that Danyo needed a way to send messages to his "office;" that had been the extent of her knowledge—hadn't it been? She wouldn't have been told about Witt's plans for Koscuisko. She had no need to know. It was always best practice to ensure that each link in the chain knew only what they had to know to understand their mission.

"I'll be a ghost, then," Danyo said. "No one to know I'm here, so make sure people are warned." It was a significant hitch in his plans to get away. But it could be turned to his advantage. Witt didn't need to know that Danyo had been careless in his disposal of the toothpick. The failure of the plan could not be laid at his door, not with a heightened infection rate and the entire vector under quarantine.

If Koscuisko survived—as he'd been meant to, from the beginning—they'd try again, maybe take an entirely different approach that Danyo wouldn't have to be involved in. If Koscuisko died, well, Witt couldn't blame *him*, and Danyo wouldn't have that hanging over him any longer. That was all.

Morrisk was waiting for him to finish his thought. "Contacting the office will be too risky until the quarantine is lifted, there could be an increased level of scrutiny on outbound communications traffic. To guard against any panic spreading. Naturally."

In fact that worked in his favor too, Danyo decided. Witt didn't need to know Danyo had sat out the quarantine on *Nikojek* at all. Let Witt assume Danyo had been on site for the duration.

He'd have to think carefully about it. That falsehood was too easily discovered, and Witt would naturally wonder why Danyo had let a misunderstanding go uncorrected. In Witt's line of work a suspicious nature was a survival trait. Danyo couldn't afford to raise any questions in Witt's mind.

He'd have time to consider the problem from all angles, though, here in the comfort and safety of his suite on *Nikojek*, for as long as it took for Agavie's gift—the field hospital dirtside—to grapple with whatever was going on and get things back under control, again.

He could afford to relax a little while longer with his drink, and think about something a little nicer for his meal than he'd been able to command on Holding.

"So it's not the Old Believers." Jils Ivers was just off vector. She'd been met with a priority request from the *Ragnarok* that came with a tie-in at Holding with Dr. Gascarone. Gascarone was pale and apparently furious, the corona of brilliant red hair that framed his face looking as though it could be actually on fire from the depth of his passion. His accent was more pronounced every time she met with him.

"The virus was deliberately introduced, but only after the arrival of the hospital from Agavie. We'd already quarantined the Old Believers. *Ragnarok* is on priority production of anti-inflammatories and ACE inhibitors to control the immune response. Of our two patients within the hospital itself Lek Kerenko is responding well to course of treatment but Doctor Koscuisko has the stubbornest immune response I've ever seen, though he'll survive, oh, yes, he will survive, because I've promised myself I'm going to kill him."

She was on viewscreen herself from the wheelhouse of her courier, or she'd be rubbing her forehead ruefully. She could see the *Ragnarok's* Chief Medical Officer—Gille Mahaffie—rub at his chin as if something itched suddenly: wiping the grin off his face, maybe. Mahaffie knew Andrej Koscuisko.

Jils herself had been watching Koscuisko move through Jurisdiction for years, since First Secretary Sindha Verlaine at Fontailloe Judiciary—now deceased—had asked her to keep an eye on him, thirteen years ago, when he'd first figured in a disruption of standard operating procedure at Fleet Orientation Station Medical.

Koscuisko was not of himself a chaotic man; no, in a manner somewhat similar to ap Rhiannon, he'd always been able to explain a rational basis for his actions. Koscuisko's scope for creating chaos was broader than ap Rhiannon's, however, and he'd only grown more effective an agent of disorder over time. He didn't set out to sow anarchy, Jils was sure. He simply made up his mind and pursued his objectives in a forthright and efficient manner.

"I have authorization from the Langsarik Coalition mission commander to quarantine the vector, Doctor Gascarone," she said, rather than something unhelpful like *if you want to kill Koscuisko you're going to need to get in line.* "Any progress on identifying the exact avenue of introduction?"

Gascarone might have spat on the floor, he was that disgusted. Jils was glad to see that he restrained himself, even in the grip of his passion. "There is. There's circumstantial evidence."

Gascarone's ethnicity spoke a language that could be transliterated into Standard script, but the exact weight of the pronunciation of the vowels shaded a little toward the next vowel Standard. *Lake*, for *Lek*,

Kerainko. Evidence almost *aye-vidence.* Close enough to an unaccented Standard to pass under previous occasions she'd spoken with him, but he hadn't been particularly angry then.

Gascarone apparently regained a degree of calm, however, because his language refocused on the Standard index line. "Pointing to Doctor Pefisct, I'm sorry to say, because he's disappeared. We think we know where he is, so no further action against Pefisct has been taken pending your arrival, Bench specialist. Also not really my area. I deal with the effect. The cause, that's the job of you lot, no disrespect."

There was a lot to think about, then. It was still an odd sort of an assassination attempt. If Witt was behind Agavie, if Pefisct's role as disease vector was a Witt mandate, then it almost couldn't have been an assassination; unless Witt's obsession with Koscuisko had led Witt to a desire to have Koscuisko stuffed and mounted as a final trophy.

A kidnapping attempt, then, ashoal on the discovery of Dolgorukij Old Believers amongst the slaver's prisoners. Witt was going to be as angry as Gascarone was. There were probably avenues for further examination to be found.

While Jils was forming her next question—*more information, please*—the sharp-muzzled prick-eared visage of the *Ragnarok's* intelligence officer popped up unexpectedly into frame at the left-hand portion of *Ragnarok's* on-screen tile, possibly saying something. The effect was a little startling, but Jils realized what had happened—Two stood, rather than sat, in chairs. She had perhaps just climbed up into one. Jils waited. She knew she could count on Two for pertinent information.

"This person has not been located at Holding," Two—Two's translator—said cheerfully. "There was a supply ship to freighter *Nikojek.* Therefore Pefisct is on *Nikojek.* There are many interesting things in *Nikojek's* personal logs that we do not admit to having discovered without clearance from a Bench specialist."

Jils was looking forward to hearing all about it. She didn't want to keep Gascarone from his hospital; one more question, and he could go back to plotting Koscuisko's demise for whatever reasons he might have out of what would predictably be more than several. "Before you go, Doctor Gascarone," she said, so that he'd know he was going to get out of this meeting soon. "Do we have an uncontained outbreak? What's your mortality assessment?"

"Ehh," Gascarone said. "I have a few more staff on sick report than is quite convenient. But nobody's dying any more. That's what really matters. And no. I think officially we can call it contained, with measures in place, of course. We'll be ready if something jumps the fence. Are we done here, then? I have someone to go murder. Koscuisko will want Pefisct, and for crimes committed here and now, so he's all right under the Covenant. But I have first crack."

Gascarone sat for long enough for somebody to tell him *no*, and nobody did. Pushing himself up out of his chair he keyed his end conference, clearly enough, because the screen went dark and the feed from the *Ragnarok* reformatted so that Jils could see all of the officers in ap Rhiannon's office. Yes, Two. There was also the *Ragnarok*'s sole remaining Lieutenant, Seascape, along with the First Officer and the Captain herself.

"Your recommendations, Captain ap Rhiannon?" Jils asked. She wasn't just being polite. The *Ragnarok* had been here, had had a chance to digest developments as they surfaced, and Two had clearly dodged around in *Nikojek*'s on-board systems.

That could still mean that Witt, or someone in Witt's organization, had received a notification, regardless of how good Two—and the *Ragnarok*'s intelligence resources, they'd never been completely mapped in its career as an experimental test bed—actually was. Two would have harvested anything that caught her eye, though, and Two was interested in everything.

"Two's information indicates that *Nikojek* is implicated in the abrupt abandonment of Holding. We've passed all pertinent details direct up to the Coalition, of course. I suggest it's time to send a boarding party, before systems are physically purged. Our intrusion seems to have escaped detection thus far, but we don't want to gamble on losing any information in background."

And they would certainly notice when the *Ragnarok* locked *Nikojek*'s comms, so there'd be the risk of mechanical destruction of potentially valuable information. There wasn't an encryption code in known Space that wouldn't eventually yield its secures—over time— so taking a sledgehammer to a console board, crude as it was, remained the most reliable way of destroying evidence.

"I'll proceed to *Ragnarok* on standard approach, your Excellency. Requesting docking facilities. That'll give you enough time to field a welcome party?" To avoid arousing any suspicions in *Nikojek*'s mind, if *Nikojek* was watching. She was just returning the Captain's shallop to the *Ragnarok*; the Wolnadi fighters *Ragnarok* would deploy against *Nikojek* would merely be escorting her in, at least at first notice. *Nothing to see here.*

Once *Ragnarok* had *Nikojek*, once Two had data streams ported back to Couveraine, then Jils would sit down with a nice hot cup of shocattli—and she'd brought some with her—and have a look at information coming into *Ragnarok* on the traces they were unearthing of the freighter *Biruck*.

Slowly, camp by camp, market by market, an augmented coalition—Bench intelligence specialists, Jurisdiction Fleet, Judiciaries, Nurail spymasters, Dolgorukij Malcontents—would put an end to the slave trade, and no one would be able to claim the freedom of Gonebeyond to trade in such commodities any longer.

CHAPTER EIGHT

First and Final Acts

When Lek Kerenko woke up, really woke up this time after several false starts, he was alone in a tiny room with no one for company but Garrity. So that was all right.

He felt like someone, four or five someones, had been beating his prone body with sticks all over to make felt, stopping from time to time to turn him front to back for even coverage. Garrity saw he was awake, apparently; because Garrity poured a glass of what turned out to be fruit-flavored glucose solution—generic citrus—and brought it over to him. "Better not gulp," Garrity said. "Sorry."

That was because it was relatively nasty stuff, and as much like fruit juice as the cold-meal mush that Robert ate with such relish was like good Sarvaw home cooking. For a moment Lek thought Garrity might try to steady Lek's hand, an alarming concept, Garrity being the reserved character he was. But no. Garrity merely assured himself that Lek could hold his own glass, and stepped away to let him at it.

"What's the sitch?" Lek asked. Voice very rusty. Throat sore. He remembered coughing, but not much more than that. There was a great deal more he wanted to ask, but there was no sense laying more stress on Garrity's store of conversation. Garrity had been sleeping in a chair, apparently. Where were they? Intermediate care unit. So he was all better, Lek realized.

"The body-wrack got you good." Garrity had a flask of cavene there, but it was apparently strong even by Garrity's standards because Garrity grimaced as he drank. "Officer didn't like that, went off on an oblique, snuck into *Ragnarok* on remote."

Lek waited, sipping fruit-flavored glucose solution. At least it was cold, and he was thirsty. Garrity had himself a proper jug of cavene, and poured himself another flask. "Then Anders went down, but harder and faster," Garrity said. *Anders?* Lek thought, startled. It was an interesting measure of how tired Garrity really was, and a little alarming. "There was raising of voices. Riggs had overhead him talking to Renring, remember Renring?"

This was a lot of talking, for Garrity. Lek was becoming a little concerned, but he didn't want to stop Garrity and suggest he not overstrain his vocal apparatus, because he wanted to hear the story. Garrity would only get annoyed at him anyway.

"You might not get all this first time through, Lek. That Pefisct person had a virus for Koscuisko. Get him so sick they'd have to evacuate, we think. He poisoned the Old Believers, too, to hide behind, but Koscuisko flagged it because there was Nurail in the juice. You got it from the Believers, but by that time there was Believers in the juice, too. Then Koscuisko went down. Chief threatened to blow up critical care quarantine. You're sorry you missed it. Fun."

Lek held out his flask for a refill. He'd only drunk half the flask, but he was a little alarmed at the reckless way Garrity was burning through the words. "I thought I was allergic to something," Lek said. So that Garrity would be forced to pace himself. "But I don't think I've ever been. I thought it was pretty severe, for allergies." To have laid him out, that was to say. "Officer's down, you said?"

"Dropped like the world-anchor. Chief found him on the floor. Immune systems in hyperbolic overdrive." Garrity handed Lek back his flask of glucose solution. Lek took a sip. Still hard to swallow, in two ways at least. Garrity sat back down in the chair, letting the blanket that had been half-draped over the back of the chair drop to the floor. He didn't pick it up. Was that it? Was that all?

"I was doing inventory reconciliation," Lek said. "I'd made a note. We seemed to be at baseline levels for standard cytokine protocols." In other words not prepared to handle more than a few cases of cytokine storm, and the records showed some issued already. To Old Believers, once Koscuisko had started to look more closely at the deaths to date—Lek could see who requisitioned, who authorized, who collected every immune system inhibitor base therapeutic quantity one each.

From what Garrity was telling him, Lek suspected he'd absorbed some of that himself. They'd had enough yet for Koscuisko, though, hadn't they?

"I hope he doesn't wake up as sore as I am." There. That put the question without too much melodrama, *tell me Koscuisko's not dead, he'll be all right won't he,* and so forth. Garrity relaxed in his chair, putting his head back, closing his eyes.

"Worse, maybe. *Ragnarok* sent us some tailored doses and a lot of inhibitor, on drone-drop. They're going to make him sit in Intermediate Quarantine for another two days, Gascarone's really angry."

About Koscuisko going off on a tangent. Well, Gascarone would learn; everybody else in Koscuisko's life had. Koscuisko could be brilliant when he was off on a tangent. Some of the ways in which his brilliance manifested itself were simply better off not noticed too clearly, that was all.

After a few long moments' silence Garrity spoke. "Feel like getting dressed? You're cleared to go back to ship and sleep there, so long as I keep you quiet. Hydrated. Your choice."

If it was his choice, he wanted to go home. *Fisher Wolf.* "Standing up," Lek said. He wasn't going to want to walk, but he expected they could borrow a mover so long as they brought it right back. Garrity handed him his trousers. His underwear was already perfectly adequate; someone had been changing it out as he slept, Lek decided, because he couldn't smell himself, and people running fevers did start to stink once it had passed and a man's natural fragrance had a chance to reassert itself. "Everybody else okay?"

"Certain degree of complaining." The usual only-semi-serious stuff about people lying down on the job, taking unauthorized breaks, not keeping their end up, Lek supposed. It was only what Lek himself would do in their place. Lek sat down to fasten his footgear, cloth half-boots, their reduced bulk easier to fit under hospital sterile costume. When he stood up again Garrity was a little closer to him than he'd been before, holding his overblouse.

But he didn't give Lek his overblouse. He put his hand on Lek's shoulder and just stood there for a moment, not speaking, not moving. Lek was startled. Garrity had never failed to offer comfort when it had been needed: bond-involuntaries were a team, they did whatever it took to keep each other going. For his own part, however, what Garrity mostly preferred was to be left alone, so this voluntary and apparently spontaneous gesture could only mean that he'd been worried past his capacity to keep it to himself.

It was great. At the same time it was a little alarming. So he patted Garrity's arm, gently, *yeah, thanks, all better now.* And he got the gesture in before Garrity was out of time to keep his gates open, so when Garrity stepped back it was without a trace of embarrassment.

"All right, let's go," Garrity said. "Riggs'll publish status change to the rest. The fruit juice will be fruit juice, but we'll have to water it down to stretch."

Sleeping in the chair. There when Lek woke up, really woke up, for the first time. Voluntarily offered physical contact outside of maximum stress situations. His friend. Because Garrity was his friend Lek did not try to give Garrity a hug, but simply followed him out of the room to find a ride out to the launch-field and an invalid's berth on *Fisher Wolf*.

"Re-gray-shun analysis confirms virus activated as recently as arrival of Agavie freighter *Nikojek*," Stildyne read, putting his own version of a spin on Yogee's dialect. Andrej thought he might have succeeded in smiling but he wasn't sure. He hadn't had so bad a headache in years.

Stildyne looked up. "You were actually the first to be exposed, but marginally. Then the Old Believers, though a complete analysis of all cases hasn't been finalized. I think that's what he said. Then Lek. Janforth saw a toothpick he thought he recognized down on the hand-select line in trash management, says Pefisct would normally have raised a stink about misplacing it and hadn't."

"I'm feeble, Brachi. I'm weak, I'm not myself, and therefore you kindly decline to tell me how many times I've already asked this, Lek is recovered? Everybody, they're all right?"

Stildyne rolled his eyes, which was actually a significant accomplishment for a man whose skull was shaped like Brachi's was— narrow occipital orbit, narrowly visible eyes. "No new cases among the

Believers. Only Lek, of course, and one or two occurrences in general population, but we're on top of it now. Lek's returned to *Fisher Wolf* for bed rest and recuperation, not as though I believe that'll go, his hazard. And I'm fine. Perfectly fine. You'll be fine too. Now."

A man couldn't help himself. Stildyne had been here every time Andrej had grasped a moment's consciousness, every time he'd remembered hearing voices in dreams, every time he'd opened his eyes. It was the immune reaction itself that forced him to keep asking, Andrej told himself—psychoactive component, paranoia.

He'd experienced it himself, the body's natural defenses communicating a panic situation up through the brainstem and into the mid-brain with urgent persuasiveness. *You are in danger of your life, the enemy is at the gate, the shield-walls are failing and the front line is thinning out because people you love are dying one by one and you've got to get out of here or you will be breathing your last.*

It was an artifact, a no-longer-useful component of the mind-body connection. The pain of a burnt finger was a message to move the finger. The drumbeat warnings of the fevered mind served no purpose, because the only way out of one's own body was exactly that which one's body was desperate to avoid.

"And yet I am to be in prison here for two days yet," Andrej pointed out, very reasonably, no, he was not grumbling, he was not. "All because Yogee is annoyed. I had my first misgivings to him already confided." To be fair, they'd been his second misgivings. His first he'd communicated to Danyo Pefisct when he'd asked for assurance that it had not been a virus that had killed the Old Believers. "He and I knew each other once. He should not have been surprised. A man is not to be punished for showing initiative."

Perhaps too severe a statement, when in the student days they'd shared a certain number of incidents resulting from initiative misdirected into socially less acceptable avenues. The fact remained that he'd contacted the *Ragnarok* before the scope of the problem had begun to broaden.

"You can't stay awake for more than an hour, Andrej," Stildyne said. It was true, but very tedious of Stildyne to insist on it. "And look, he's authorized you to receive this, so you can start thinking about it. Peace offering. You should accept."

Flatfile docket. Andrej took it in hand, but had to do a certain amount of squinting and adjusting his arm's length before he could bring it into focus. Not a holograph document, he was glad to see; decently printed. Draft for review. Areas of interest, Danyo Pefisct.

It was an interrogatory.

A summary, and not in standard Judicial format of course; but the larger meaning was clear. The Coalition wanted some explanations from Danyo Pefisct. They wanted Andrej to ask him a few questions. "And I thank Yogee very much." Yes. Good news. Something to look forward to. A treat, even.

There was an obvious problem, though. Gonebeyond needed doctors. From all Andrej had heard, reluctant though he was to credit it, Pefisct was an able general practitioner, and that was what Gonebeyond needed most. Yet not under any circumstances—Andrej was utterly sure—could Pefisct be allowed in direct patient care, unless he was carefully watched at all times.

Here on Holding their resources had been apparently adequate; for the rest, Andrej had told Yogee everything he needed to know, and could only hope to be assigned the task should a signal correction of unacceptable behavior become required. But if Andrej executed the most informal of interrogations of Pefisct there were altogether-too-good odds that Pefisct would be unfit for duty at the end; for months, if not forever.

That would be irresponsible on his part. So he couldn't take advantage of the opportunity to revenge himself on Pefisct for Joslire's sake, no matter how passionately he wished to. He could take steps. He could have Stildyne with him, to keep him focused on what he needed to do—and what he needed to not-do, perhaps as important, in a sense.

Or he could have Janforth. Janforth, with Brachi; Janforth, in the place of the Malcontent's torturer's assistant Yalta. Janforth knew how to assist an Inquiry. Janforth would enjoy his own revenge, howsoever partial. Then all they would have to solve—Andrej, Yogee, Gonebeyond—was how to exploit Danyo's medical experience in clinic duty, without risk that he would bully or otherwise mistreat his patients.

Andrej gave the docket back to Stildyne, thinking hard. There was something at the edge of his mind, lurking on the borders of his consciousness; Janforth, and establishing a measure of control over

Pefisct's actions that could be relied upon to maintain correct behavior even if Pefisct should have the opportunity to amuse himself with vulnerable—defenseless—people. Janforth.

When Janforth had awakened from the surgery Andrej had performed, Andrej had offered the extracted governor to him, but Janforth had declined to so much as touch it—and Andrej couldn't blame him. Yet such things were expensive and highly specialized. Andrej had put it carefully away in a small box, and he'd extricated the Safe Janforth had been wearing, and made sure to keep them together.

So the governor didn't know it had been extracted. Once the Safe had been removed from close proximity, once the governor was active once again, it would think it was on the job. It would continue to be on the lookout for a specific profile of stress hormones that would signal it to invoke its power to punish, to deter, to remind, to enforce.

Andrej had removed governors. That didn't mean he had any business trying to implant one. But did that have to matter? If he showed an active governor to Pefisct, and performed the pretense of the implantation, would Pefisct be able to guess the difference?

Governors didn't start to torture and correct immediately upon implantation. It took time and conditioning for the governor to learn the stress state that was its trigger. It wouldn't respond to Pefisct's raw fear—not immediately. Here in Gonebeyond, far from any dancing-masters, how long would it take for a governor to learn when Pefisct had done something he knew he oughtn't, to learn when Pefisct should be punished?

More to the point, how long would Pefisct imagine that the process might take, how long would it take Pefisct to realize that there was no governor there, that there was nothing to prevent him from taking his old amusements?

It might be enough to work without implantation, on Pefisct's fear alone. But, oh, the alternative . . . Andrej had the map of the governor's linkage placement in his mind. He knew where he could get more details. Where there were Malcontents involved a man could get anything. There was reason to suspect that the Nurail spymaster might be able to oblige with the technical specifications. He had set micromachines to control intractable neurological pain.

If only he got the chance, he was confident that he could do it, he could take just the one modest step to one side and put the governor where it would invoke, and not quiet, the same agony. It would be fitting, just, poetic. The Nurail spymaster Tamsen Gar owed him. Didn't he?

He had two days to think about it, to enjoy the fantasy, at least. For now he was tired, and closed his eyes.

Danyo Pefisct had been betrayed by circumstance every step of the way—and he was very bitter about it. The confinement to which he had been consigned was the quarters he'd occupied on *Nikojek*, so he was better off than he would have been in a slave stables on Holding— but perhaps not all that much better.

It was prison rations. He had access to a toilet and a water-basin but nothing more than that. They'd let him drink his stores dry, except for the cortac brandy, they'd taken the cortac. And he was being watched lest despair drive him to attempt self-murder. He was not in despair. He was angry. He had good cause to be.

Haspirzak had treated him foully. He had a contract with Fleet for position and authority in return for the performance of professional services that only someone in custody of a Writ to Inquire could lawfully perform, and where were they going to get their mission-critical information, their background intelligence, their object lessons in the power of the Bench to ruin lives with a touch, without the Writ?

That Haspirzak had decided to forego the efficient and effective tools in an Inquisitor's hand was Haspirzak's decision. It didn't change the fact that he and Fleet had had a deal. Haspirzak had wronged him.

Witt had used him, well, he'd known that, that had been a contract of quid pro quo from the very beginning. Those parties. Oh, Witt's parties. But Witt had taken advantage of Danyo's vulnerable position to pursue his private interests, to indulge his personal desires, to have Andrej Koscuisko for his own forever and always.

It would have been good for Koscuisko. Danyo had no doubt that Witt would have kept Koscuisko in a style entirely comparable to that which Koscuisko would have enjoyed in the heart of the Dolgorukij Combine, if Koscuisko had ever gone back. Koscuisko would have been free from having to engage in negotiations and the making of business decisions and dealing with a large and probably querulous family.

Koscuisko would have been cherished, adored, respected, provided with all and everything he could ever possibly have wanted, approached as a demi-god by Witt himself, with only the small matter of the loss of a degree of personal freedom. As if Koscuisko had personal freedom in Gonebeyond. They worked him mercilessly in clinic.

Danyo had watched Koscuisko slave for the Surgeon General day and night when a man of his surgical talent should have been able to set his own hours and decide when he was good and ready to put in a few hours of clinic time. So it would all have worked out in Koscuisko's best interest, and if Koscuisko himself would not have been likely to see it quite that way—especially at first—Danyo would at least have gotten what *he* wanted, freedom in Gonebeyond, safety from Fleet prosecution for desertion, liberty to write his own ticket; because Gonebeyond needed him more than he needed Gonebeyond.

He'd demanded of the people who had invaded his privacy—*Ragnarok* security troops—that Bench specialist Ivers be notified of Danyo's imprisonment immediately. Ivers had offered him a job, hadn't she? Didn't Ivers owe him some consideration? And they'd nodded and assured him that Ivers had been contacted, and would get back to him as soon as possible. Nothing since. Danyo hadn't been surprised.

Witt's intelligence had failed Danyo and Witt alike. He could have made the plan work, at Couveraine. Why hadn't Witt known about Holding? How could Witt have failed to foresee that with determination—and Andrej Koscuisko—the Langsarik coalition was certain to discover the slave camp, once they knew it existed?

At Couveraine there would have been medical staff coming and going from all over Gonebeyond space. Anybody could have communicated a virus. No fingers would have been pointed at Danyo. Not like Holding. What had Witt been thinking of?

And to stoop to blackmail, showing Danyo that stomach-wrenching scene from Port Rudistal and Administrator Geltoi. Yes. Witt had certainly made his point with Danyo. Danyo wasn't too proud to admit that he'd made a mistake, tried to get rid of the virus prematurely, all things considered. He would have considered more carefully if he hadn't still been able to hear the noises Geltoi had made. Witt had overdone it. That was Witt's fault, but Witt wasn't likely to see it that way.

So here Danyo was. Koscuisko was apparently not dead. The

scheme had failed. There was unplanned collateral damage. Witt wasn't going to get what he wanted. Witt was entirely capable of sending Koscuisko a nice gift of that old material from Fleet Orientation Station Medical, out of sheer spite. Under other circumstances that would have merely been part of what Danyo liked about Witt, his nasty streak; but not when he himself—Danyo Pefisct—was on the wrong end of it.

He had no entertainment, no conversation, nothing to read, nothing to watch. They'd taken out any timekeepers or even time-markers. He assumed they fed him at regular intervals but he knew very well that playing with the intervals between meals was only standard operating procedure for managing prisoners being held for questioning. The environmental adjustments—the lights, the temperature—didn't respond to anything he tried, so just to be uncooperative he lay down to sleep only when the cabin was brightly lit and too warm.

It wasn't working all that well for him. He'd begun to find himself falling asleep sitting upright in the dark at the table they had not yet taken away, but he kept at it stubbornly.

People came in when he was asleep, under the influence of soporifics in his food or his drink or the air, doubtless. When he woke up he'd find that his bed had been stripped, and clean furnishings left for him to make it up again; or his water-tumbler would have been moved to the wrong side of the mirror in the lavatory. It was all standard stuff, and so petty.

Such games wouldn't work on seasoned practitioners, on Ship's Inquisitors. Danyo had learned all the tricks years ago, and he'd schooled his bond-involuntaries assigned carefully on faithful execution of his instructions in the years he'd exercised his Writ. They couldn't possibly believe they could get to him with silly pranks of that nature: it was merely annoying. That was all.

The lights were bright. The room was warm. Danyo lay down on the bed in his boots, legs crossed at the ankles, hands clasped over his chest. He hadn't made the bed up; that was what an officer's orderly was for, and whether or not he had an orderly he was an officer. Changing his own sheets was beneath him. He closed his eyes.

He woke abruptly to what seemed to be pitch darkness, but the room was immediately flooded with light of such painful brilliance that he thought he must have imagined the dark. Bright lights. Loud noises. Seized suddenly by rough hands that pulled him bodily off the bare mattress, tumbling to fall heavily down onto the floor; and a loud cheerful voice with an edge to it, bloodlust, an undernote of savagery.

"Wake up wake up, time for prayers, come along my darling, I have questions for you."

No sooner had his head hit the floor than he was taken up again, raised to his feet, pulled roughly through the open door of his bedroom into the outer cabin. Koscuisko. That was Koscuisko. He recognized the voice. If it wasn't Witt—and it couldn't be Witt—it was Andrej Koscuisko.

The people who'd taken Danyo in charge pushed him one way and another, roughly; Danyo felt the cut and burn of fabric pulling against his skin, tearing away. They were stripping him, and they did a thorough job of it, too. They didn't stop until he was completely naked, barefoot, shoved face-down across the surface of a heavy table—*that was new*, Danyo thought, dazed as he was—to pull his arms tightly together, and bind them at the elbows behind his back.

Then they stood him up again, clothed only in secures and bruises coming up. Koscuisko was sitting behind the table, the desk that had once graced Captain Morrisk's office, Danyo recognized it now; he was looking well, he was looking rested, he looked like he was having fun. "Good-greeting, Danyo," Koscuisko said. "My name is Andrej Koscuisko, and I hold the Writ to which you must answer. State your name, and the reason why I should not have you beaten to death for my amusement here and now."

Danyo was awake enough now to know exactly what was happening. "Covenant," he said. No, that was no good; his voice was shaky with shock and quavering with furious humiliation. Naked? Really? "Covenant. And you hold no Writ to which I must answer. Forget it, Koscuisko, save your breath."

"What do you say to *that*, your Excellency?" That was a woman's voice; Danyo started to turn his head toward the sound to see who was there, but one of the men now standing behind him slapped him across the side of his head and made him stagger. By then he thought he'd placed the voice anyway. That woman from Intelligence. Felsanjir. What was she doing here? And what was she doing, exactly?

"I say two things, Miss Crownéd, I mean to say Miss Felsanjir. The first is that I am careful not to touch him, having very carefully selected people who have no history with Danyo to resent. Thank you for Yalta, by the way." Which meant nothing to Danyo, and he didn't care. Koscuisko had yet to offer any real explanation. "I leave aside the impertinence offered to my Writ, which is on record as still active and in force. Of this fact I have been recently assured by one in a position to know. The second thing."

That was completely nonsensical, Danyo thought, suppressing a moment's panic. Koscuisko was in Gonebeyond, but as a deserter, because he wasn't on the *Ragnarok*. Danyo had heard all about it from Witt. *Ragnarok* had committed mutiny in form at least, in fact more likely, and Koscuisko had been on board the *Ragnarok* when it had. But Bench Intelligence Specialists were involved, or at least one of them: was Koscuisko actually pursuing a Bench investigation?

One of the significant privileges granted with the Writ to Inquire was immunity from criminal liability for any act short of mutiny. Desertion was a form of mutiny. Danyo had unquestionably deserted. Mutiny was punishable at the Tenth Level, Command Termination.

"The second thing is that we speak of the strictly current offenses he has committed, the willful release of a dangerous virus into a fragile population and in a hospital, the death of fifteen people, the attempted murder of my mother's eldest son which is to say myself. The Covenant does not grant immunity for wrongs committed *within* Gonebeyond space, is it not so?"

"H'm," she said, and presumably went back to whatever it was she was doing. Maybe nothing. Maybe she was only here to keep an eye on Koscuisko, who seemed as fey as ever he had seemed in the stray snippets that had been all even Witt had been able to obtain—because Witt had spent his entertainment budget on those two vids he had not shared with Danyo before, perhaps, the Tenth Level, and the damning evidence from Fossum.

"Danyo, tell me," Koscuisko said cheerfully. "Where is the freighter *Biruck*?"

They'd changed the temperature in the room again. It had been warm when he'd lain down. He was cold, now. He was naked. It was surprisingly distressing, especially with a woman present to look at his unclothed body and sneer. "What? Freighter?" Then he remembered. *Biruck*. Slave ship. "I don't have the first idea, why would I?"

"He says he doesn't know," Koscuisko said, to the woman in the room somewhere behind Danyo. "Isn't that nice? I shall send flowers to those who care about him, if we can find any. Why would you know, you ask, that is an easy question. You know because it was you who warned the slavers at Holding that the Langsarik Coalition would be coming for them. You who put *Biruck* on alert. So. Where is the freighter *Biruck*?"

"No such thing," Danyo said, scornfully. But his brain was working hard on the problem. He was to have sent word to Witt through a channel that Captain Morrisk had ready and waiting. Captain Morrisk knew how to get a message to Witt. Therefore she could send other messages.

Therefore Witt had neglected to mention that along with getting Danyo close to Koscuisko and providing an infective agent to force an emergency evacuation, Witt was using the hospital to plant a spy in the Langsarik Coalition's headquarters. Danyo could respect that, but things *were* awkward. "I never heard the name until Ivers and Felsanjir briefed us all, I don't know where it is, I have no connection with it. I'll get dressed now, thanks."

Except that of course that wasn't going to happen. "Well, you're lying," Koscuisko said, closing a flatfile docket he'd had open on the desk in front of him with a slap. "At the same time Miss Felsanjir is right, of course. We should be careful to avoid the appearance of impropriety, and therefore these gentlemen merely take you to surgical prep. I will ask you again post-operatively, at which time you will either tell me a truth that you definitely know to be the truth, or you will be so very sorry. —Oh."

It was as though Koscuisko suddenly remembered something he was supposed to tell Danyo, but Danyo knew spontaneous speech when he heard it and this was not. "Oh, that's right," Koscuisko repeated, reaching into his overblouse for an inside pocket. He was wearing civilian dress, not hospital whites. Danyo recognized the cut of the garment from ones he'd known Witt to wear, a nicely tailored overblouse with a collar the width of two fingers set upright at the neck.

Witt's were embellished with lace, lots and lots of lace, on his collar and cuffs and cascading down off one shoulder over his upper arm. Koscuisko's was relatively unadorned. "You remember Janforth, of course?" Koscuisko asked. "He's not here. There is no sense in taking an unnecessary risk with *his* future. He's brought us both a nice gift, though. Would you care to see it?"

Koscuisko had a small flat hinged container that he put down on the table so that Danyo could look. Koscuisko opened the box: sterile specimen container, why? There was a little bundle of grey threads in one side, grey threads with a glittering green gem-like eye. It was alive. What was it?

"He came to us on Safe, of course, since his governor was still in place. I asked him what he wanted to do with it, because these things cannot be had for any price, they tell me. He said he'd like for you to have it. Wasn't that generous of him?—less the Safe, perhaps, until I know I can trust you to behave. It may be a little rough for you at first. I can do the basic surgery, but for calibrations to your particular chemistry, we will just have to take our chances, you and I."

Governor.

For a long moment Danyo could only stare in horrified fascination. Was that what one looked like? He'd never actually looked at a governor, how could he have, they were held in strict security, individually identified, individually tracked. No. It wasn't possible. This was a fake. Koscuisko had made one up out of wires and a bit of a light-chip to try to frighten him.

It was working. Koscuisko had pulled governors on Safe before; Witt had told him all about it, and it would have been an unbelievable story if not for the fact that the survival of the six bond-involuntary troops Koscuisko had sent into Gonebeyond was apparently a well-attested fact amongst people in the intelligence communities.

Danyo had contacts. He'd heard the story through other channels as well. Koscuisko had removed the governors from five bond-involuntary troops. The sixth had had emergency surgery some years ago, and it hadn't killed him, so how hard could it really be? Except that the governor in question had apparently been dying and taking the troop with him, and Koscuisko not available, so it had been a desperate gamble that had paid off.

And if it really wasn't impossibly difficult to remove a governor, if Koscuisko had apparently done it five times and what had he done with *those* governors, then who was to say that Koscuisko couldn't reverse the process? Koscuisko had been Ship's Inquisitor, yes. But also the *Ragnarok*'s rated neurosurgeon, and an apparently very good one.

Danyo had seen what governors could do to people. Koscuisko meant to plug it in and let it figure things out for itself, a governor that had already had the years of experience with Janforth learning exactly when to warn and when to correct and when to torture. It was a governor Danyo himself had fine-tuned, in a sense, working with Janforth, honing Janforth's discipline to peak performance.

The chemical signature of fear, even of a specific fear of having done something wrong, was not so unique from soul to soul that the governor could not identify it in Danyo as it had in Janforth. He would be as helpless as any day-new bond-involuntary, because he knew how easily it could be set off.

He would not even have the baseline protection of a conditioned set of behaviors in which to take refuge, confident that so long as he could only keep his actions within established parameters he would not be punished. Koscuisko would be able to do anything he liked, anything at all, and Danyo knew that he could not let that happen, no matter what he had to do to avoid it.

"You can't do that to me," he said, shaking off the restraining hands on his arms and shoulders with a gesture that he knew to be only symbolic. They let him; perhaps because they were interested in what he was going to say, not because he could actually break free from them. "Listen, Koscuisko, you make one error, even the slightest, and I'll never be able to tell you anything. You'll lose valuable information. I can't tell you what you want to know if I'm dead, Felsanjir, surely you can see the logic in that?"

It could be a trick. Dirty trick, stinking trick, she'd take Danyo's side, pretend to protect him, pretend to intervene. So obvious. So trite. So overdone. And he had no choice but to let it work, because Koscuisko had Janforth's governor, Koscuisko had the neurosurgical qualifications to implant it, and Koscuisko controlled the Safe that would be Danyo's only protection against unimaginable agony.

He'd seen it working on bond-involuntaries throughout all of his career, he'd used it, because the Bench expected bond-involuntaries to suffer and it was Danyo's plain duty to execute the judgment of the Bench up to a point, the point at which constant honing wore down the edge past hope of sharpening it up ever again—or the point at which his own Chief of Security said something to First Officer about it, and the Captain had a few tiresome words.

"There is a point in what he says," Felsanjir said. Danyo couldn't see her face, but he could watch Koscuisko, and Koscuisko was not pleased. "There are ways that generate good report, from prisoners with a sound idea of the situation. Perhaps—"

"But I have never had so good an opportunity," Koscuisko interrupted, sounding aggrieved, a little resentful at her interference. "Do not deprive me of my experiment, he cannot tell us all that very much more than *Nikojek* will, surely I have earned your indulgence."

"Why take the chance, Koscuisko?" Danyo put it as a question, not a challenge. He had to be very clear: he had no defense and no protection. His only chance was to be completely honest. The stakes were too high for him to contemplate trying to manipulate either Koscuisko or Felsanjir. "Take the governor to Captain Morrisk, see what she can tell you. Me, I'll tell you everything I can. I may know things about the Witt organization that *Nikojek* doesn't, and I'm willing to take my chances with them, far more willing than to give anybody any excuse to use that governor."

All true. All completely true. He didn't know how much he could tell them about Witt. He *did* know from experience that a prisoner not infrequently possessed important information in complete ignorance of the degree of its usefulness. Koscuisko would know that too. And Felsanjir. They all knew. So they all knew he was right.

Silence. Danyo kept his eyes fixed on the box on the table, the box with the governor. Then Felsanjir spoke, calmly, almost gently. "Doctor Koscuisko." To remind Koscuisko that he *was* a doctor, maybe, and no longer Ship's Inquisitor with a team of bond-involuntary Security slaves who would do just as they were told when they were told. "We have been working together for more than a year, at Canopy Base. You've had opportunities to observe. Do you trust my sense of when I hear the truth?"

Koscuisko didn't answer, seeming to be struggling with himself. So Felsanjir asked again. "Do you trust me?"

Koscuisko didn't want to admit that he did. Koscuisko wanted what Koscuisko wanted. But Koscuisko knew when he was not going to win. Not when he was beaten, because Koscuisko hadn't been; but because Koscuisko could admit the sense of Danyo's argument, of Felsanjir's willingness to take over. Koscuisko would want to get back to Safehaven. He had a job there. Danyo's best chance lay in the hope that

Koscuisko hated him enough to be quit of his company, if he was not to have revenge.

"Miss Felsanjir, I am not at all happy. I have been looking forward to this for days." Finally Koscuisko closed up the box where the governor lay, and put it away in the inner pocket of his blouse once more. "I will leave it with you to conduct that which is your task. I strongly urge full measures against self-harm. You do not, if I may say so and not give offense, do not truly understand what this thing can do, if you have not seen it. This man and I, we both know."

Saved. "No offense is taken, your Excellency," Felsanjir said. "Thank you, sir." Saved. Danyo closed his eyes, overwhelmed by the magnitude of the horror he had faced, the narrowness of his escape. He was standing in a pool of fast-cooling urine and he hadn't even realized he'd lost control of his own waste. He hardly noticed the humiliation. Koscuisko would not be allowed to operate.

At the door to Danyo's cabin on his way out Koscuisko paused to look back over his shoulder at Danyo, who knew that he was weeping out of sheer relief. "Well, I'm sorry, Danyo," Koscuisko said. "I should have liked to use Janforth's generous gift. You will remember, I hope, how much I should like a second chance, and that I will be saving this for you."

That went without saying. Koscuisko knew it, too. "No cause," Danyo managed, finally. "I swear."

He was newborn into a life in which he could afford no contemptuous speech, no sneering thoughts, no subterfuge. And as little as he liked it he could not go back. His world had ended when he'd seen Janforth's governor.

He would spend the rest of his life on the best behavior he could achieve, because Koscuisko would always be there, Koscuisko had a governor, and no price in all of Creation was too much to pay for protection against what Andrej Koscuisko would do if ever Felsanjir—Jils Ivers—Doctor Gascarone decided it was time to look the other way.

The Old Believers were among the first to leave Holding. The entire social services apparatus of the Dolgorukij Combine had apparently been activated on their behalf, on receipt of Andrej's message to Felsanjir; he hoped the rescue party was at least mostly Malcontent. Not only because social services were foundational to the Saint's kerygma. But also because Old Believers were heterodox outcasts from the mainstream mercies of the Holy Mother and the Malcontent was friend and shelter to all such disdained and denigrated souls.

The representative Haspirzak Judiciary had sent to Gonebeyond had come down to Holding from Couveraine direct; he was to be housed on the *Ragnarok*—having apparently been the *Ragnarok*'s guest before—but he'd come here first, to see some of what a slave camp meant in a larger sense.

He was a very young man, in Andrej's estimation, but he was a Judge nonetheless, and Andrej himself had been much the same age in Standard terms when he'd graduated from Mayon Medical College. What Bat Yorvik was going to make of these arcane Dolgorukij rituals Andrej could not guess. He had work to do. He had to concentrate.

The ship to bear the Old Believers to a safe haven of their own stood ready for passenger load and departure at the launch-field, but the Old Believers had refused transport from their temporary housing to the ship: they'd insisted on walking. Yes, the hospital commander— that was Yogee, of course—could have called for a Security team and forced the issue. Yogee hadn't done that. If they meant to walk they'd walk, and get no trouble from Yogee Gascarone.

So they came out of their lodging-place *as exiles on foot leaving the temptations of the Great Enemy behind*, and walked. They were escorted by groundcars on either side of the remaining forty-plus of them on the road, because not only were they recently blinded but they refused all but the most primitive of available aids—walking-sticks.

Andrej stood in the middle of the road just clear of the launch-lane where their ship awaited them, hoping they wouldn't run right over him through not knowing he was a barrier. Once he opened his mouth they'd know he was there, though that didn't mean they'd stop. He was dust and excrement beneath their feet.

In the scriptures of the Old Believers—oral scriptures alone, existing in print only where some apostate had written fragments of them down—Andrej himself was a soon-to-be-shed hair on the head of the Great Enemy. Andrej was heterodox, and only they possessed the true orthodoxy.

The part he knew was in the Saga, though. So he folded his arms across his chest—that was what the Saga said—and called out in High

Aznir. He didn't speak Birskovneyij. He was relying on the linguistic structures common to all daughters of the ancestral language of the Blood; that, and the resonance of the songs they shared in common.

Where are you going, misguided ones, spurning the comforts of the Creator, turning your backs on the Holy Mother? He'd researched this. He had notes in his pocket, but since it was chanted or sung—and since the phrases were part of the Dolgorukij cultural heritage, even rejected by the Church as they were—he was mostly confident of his lines. He *thought* he was confident.

There was silence. They just kept walking. Except that one reached for another, five by five in array, and suddenly they sang out at once in an archaic harmony whose sheer vocal power was staggering.

You will not keep us. Holy God defies your corruption. We will worship in purity. Do not prevent us, or you defy God. He knew what the words were, if he could not quite grasp them.

It stopped as abruptly as it had started, the reverberation of their massed voices lost beneath the desert skies of Holding in an instant. Andrej swallowed hard. This might be more difficult than he'd expected, and he had only himself to blame. Nobody had forced him to come stand in the road and chant at them. It had seemed the least thing he could do.

There are clear skies, warm sun, the fruit of field and forest, and you go to darkness and despair upon a friendless barren ground.

He was in for it now. He knew what came next. *No true light shines on a world without God. There is no comfort where there is not God. True light makes bright the darkness, soft the rock, pleasant beyond words plain reeds and silent water.*

A man could feel overwhelmed by such courage, such conviction. A man could crave the company of such saints. But Andrej couldn't put what he'd seen out of his mind. He would never forgive these people for punishing that girl for having learned some Standard, godless speech.

Can nothing reconcile you to live in peace and fellowship? This land is good, these people worship with goodwill and in holy fear. He didn't mean it. He hadn't realized how angry he actually was; he'd drowned his fury in the terrible witness of their wounds. He could have saved enough of the sight in one of her eyes. Nothing more than distinguishing light from dark, but under Jurisdiction there were therapeutic approaches—or cyborg augmentation—that would have given her back the vision she'd scorned. He could curse them all for that.

We do not curse you, slave of the Great Enemy, but we will not stay.

There were several variants, at this point in the Saga—in the versions of the Saga that still preserved narratives of the Old Believers at all. There was the one where the man Andrej was representing, the land-pledge Volgerd Hecht, was overwhelmed with shame and remorse, fell to his knees, was granted a vision of the Divine, and followed after the departing Old Believers humbly to serve them for the rest of his days, earning the blessings—but not inclusion in the ranks—of their holy community thereby.

There were the ones in which Hecht knelt down in humility and blessed them on their way, to a greater or lesser extent. There were almost as many variants as there were even people who'd read the story in the first place; Andrej went with the one that was in his heart.

Go, then, and be separate, as you have chosen. No hand of any of my blood will be outstretched to grant you aid, as you have spat upon it now.

There was no kneeling in humility in that variant. Andrej spat on the ground at his feet, and left the road. Maybe it was a little harsh, and not completely true; if that young woman broke ranks with the others and asked for help, he wouldn't hesitate. But that wasn't happening. So he couldn't care. They were welcome to load and leave without him to bear witness to their self-exile. Judge Bat Yorvik was waiting to have a word with him.

Andrej put away his rage against the cruelty of fanatics and went to join the Judge's party, to attend a meeting on the *Ragnarok*.

Jils Ivers stood before the Captain's Bar in the *Ragnarok*'s senior officers' mess. The last time she'd been here in person, the room had been full to capacity and Hilton Shires had given Bat Yorvik the entry briefing on the Langsarik Coalition's campaign against the Couveraine slavers. Koscuisko hadn't been on board for that, but Felsanjir had particularly wanted him to be here now, in his capacity as an expert witness.

What they were going to ask Yorvik to do would have been unheard of, three short years ago, and would set formal precedent for years to come: a first concrete step in establishing a recognized judicial relationship between an as-yet-undefined polity in Gonebeyond space, and Haspirzak Judiciary. Haspirzak did not speak for all of Jurisdiction space. The Third Judge was only one of nine. And yet it was a first step.

Jils wished that she could claim that she—and Bench specialists Garol Vogel and Irenja Rafenkel—had planned it this way, but in fact they were making it up as they went along: the Bench intelligence specialist's greatest strength was adjusting on the fly, taking advantage of circumstances.

Bat Yorvik was seated alone at the Captain's table above the Bar. He'd changed his overblouse to acknowledge the solemnity of the occasion: a Bench judge's traveling dress, the deep rich dark green of the fabric as much a signal of rank and identity as the exact shade of black worn by a senior officer on a Jurisdiction Fleet cruiser-killer class battlewagon.

Like Captain Jennet ap Rhiannon, who stood to one side of the table in a formal attitude of command-wait: above the Bar, because she was the captain of the *Ragnarok*; standing, not sitting, because she was not a Judicial officer, and court was in Session.

Technically speaking, perhaps Andrej Koscuisko was still a Bench officer, but he wasn't wearing uniform. There was another officer performing the duties of Ship's Surgeon, and no Ship's Inquisitor on the *Ragnarok* at all. Koscuisko's civilian dress was a little dusty, after the ritual he'd just conducted with the Old Believers dirtside at the launch-field at Holding; Jils had given her own overblouse a brisk shake-and-brush and knew that she'd only managed to get most, not all, of the fine-ground sand beaten out.

They had a screen-engage with Hilton Shires, though Shires was still at Couveraine. Shires was seated, as befit his status as arguably the single seniormost civil representative present. It was of critical importance to do this first thing right—by the statutes and administrative codes that Haspirzak could formally accept as binding. That meant being very clear from the very start who stood up for whom, in Proceedings.

"Good-greeting, gentles," Bat Yorvik said. He had a flatfile docket spread open in front of him. "My name is Bat Yorvik, seconded in an advisory role from Haspirzak Judiciary—Third Judge Nantik Parline, Presiding—to offer judicial support to the Langsarik Coalition and other polities of Gonebeyond space on a nonbinding, as-requested basis only."

He pulled his official seal—his Judicial chop—out from underneath his overblouse, placing it near at hand before he continued. "I see here present in this room the captain of the Jurisdiction Fleet Ship *Ragnarok*, Jennet ap Rhiannon. Bench Intelligence Specialist Jils Ivers. Ekaterina Felsanjir of the Langsarik Coalition intelligence service, with authority delegated by the Coalition Mission Commander Hilton Shires, who attends on remote from Couveraine. Mission Commander, has Ekaterina Felsanjir your delegated authority to speak to the issue at hand?"

Yorvik waited. It had to come from Shires, and it had to be said out loud. "I affirm so," Shires said. "Ekaterina Felsanjir, working on behalf and by the direction of the intelligence service of the Langsarik Coalition, has my proxy to petition for your action in this instance, your Honor."

"Thank you," Yorvik said politely. "I see also Doctor Andrej Koscuisko, standing by to provide additional information as it may become desirable. Now." The information was in the flatfile docket. But that didn't matter. These were legal processes and procedures that formed the foundation for a common judicial system for all souls under Jurisdiction—and might come to serve the same purpose for Gonebeyond.

The ritual Koscuisko had performed with the Old Believers had been lifted out of the saga of Dasidar and Dyraine, Koscuisko had told her, the ancestral story on which all of Dolgorukij culture was defined and defended. She didn't know how old the Saga was. But it was a near-certainty in her mind that the rituals and procedures of the Jurisdiction Bench were at least as old—or older.

Yorvik wouldn't actually read the docket. Would he? Judges were judged, by their peers, by their followers, by their superiors, on their ability to summarize a brief, to extract the pertinent points, and put the argument in such concise and persuasive terms that careers could be made, and lost, on a single well-chosen or misplaced phrase.

"The Langsarik Coalition has been prosecuting a campaign to end trade in prohibited merchandise within its markets located within its area of reasonable oversight. An element of this prohibited activity is trade in enslaved souls, where such slavery is not permitted under existing Bench exceptions, referenced here for the purposes of analogy only."

Not saying that the slave trade was illegal under Bench legal codes. Not claiming that the Bench's mandate ran to Gonebeyond. There was no Law as the Bench understood it in Gonebeyond at all.

After a considered pause Yorvik continued. "An integral part of this campaign is the identification and elimination of suppliers, including organizations responsible for unlawful detention and enslavement of members of Gonebeyond's population. During the recent activity at Couveraine and Holding credible and trustworthy information has been presented indicating a parent company's responsibility for the conduct of said prohibited activity, this parent located in, and substantially operating illegally from, Haspirzak and other Judiciaries."

Witt had an organization of remarkable scope and complexity. He had by no means invented the practice of separating his interests and dividing them amongst trusted lieutenants; he'd been more than usually successful, or lucky, in his selection of reliable subordinates. Until now.

"I have before me a request for extradition of a person of interest materially implicated in this matter. Felsanjir, if you would present your case."

She was one of the interrogation team leaders from the massive debriefing of Dolgorukij terrorists at the now-neutralized Canopy Base. Malcontents had an entirely different approach to developing human intelligence over the long term, by forming in-depth trust relationships. It was a very productive approach; and for the short term—for immediate requirements for vital information—there was, among other instruments in their inventory, Andrej Koscuisko.

"Thank you, your Honor. A person of interest has acknowledged the attempted kidnapping of a Gonebeyond resident, an attempt which resulted in several directly related deaths. Under questioning this confederate made credible by-name identification of a resident of Haspirzak Judiciary already subject to investigation by several Bench intelligence specialists, one of whom is here and can corroborate. Inasmuch as that person is materially involved with crimes committed in Gonebeyond space, the Langsarik Coalition requests extradition of the named party for questioning and potential prosecution."

Yorvik nodded. Jils was impressed. The Malcontent clearly had some decent legal professionals not only available, but available at a moment's notice, to write a statement and coach its representative in a persuasive delivery. "I have reviewed the particulars of your findings and allegations," Yorvik said. "How far do you defend these representations as complete and correct in substance?"

"We have availed ourselves of the expertise of a recognized former Judicial officer with a uniquely qualifying skill-set to issue a professional assessment of the reliability of the evidence presented, your Honor. His assessment has been endorsed by all parties here present. On that basis we assert the validity of our claim."

Or, in other words, Andrej Koscuisko had given the records the once-over, if he had not taken the interrogations himself. Jils didn't know which. She had no interest in finding out. Yorvik glanced from Felsanjir to Koscuisko, with an inquiring look on his face; Koscuisko came to attention—he could do that so beautifully, when he put his mind to it—and bowed.

He didn't speak. That was prudent. Felsanjir was stretching things just a little as it was. Fortunately Jils knew that Haspirzak had no issue with Koscuisko's presence in Gonebeyond as an independent agent.

"Specialist Ivers. Can you provide any feedback on the likely response from Haspirzak Judiciary on receipt of the requested warrant?"

"I can, your Honor." She'd been in touch with Rafenkel, at Haspirzak Proper—covering for Jils, in Jils' absence. Jils' expected-to-be-extended absence. Rafenkel had briefed the Judge. "Haspirzak states its willingness to take this request under careful and serious consideration." In this case, yes. Yorvik could make no assumptions in his official capacity; but Jils was sure of him, regardless.

"And Mission Commander Shires. Do you take responsibility for the safe transport of, and due process for, the named individual?"

"Yes," Shires said. "I do." No more. No less.

Yorvik took a deep breath. He was making history. They all were. "After consideration of the evidence presented I agree that probable cause exists to connect this named individual with the active conduct of an illegal slave trade in Gonebeyond, in Haspirzak Judiciary, and in other Jurisdictions not explicitly named. I approve this request for extradition on behalf of the Langsarik Coalition in Gonebeyond space, and set my seal thereunto."

Yorvik picked up his chop, and set his seal on the flatfile flimsies that comprised the docket. Another deep breath; and done. "Thank you, gentles. Hearing is concluded by Bench Judge Bat Yorvik."

"Thank you, your Honor," Jils said. Witt was hers: but even more important than that, a Bench judge had issued an extradition order on behalf of the Langsarik Coalition, and Haspirzak Judiciary would honor it.

It was the first solid undeniable incontrovertible act of a formal legal relationship, an endorsement, a recognition of Gonebeyond as its own independent political state-in-formation in the eyes of the Jurisdiction.

So Witt had perhaps done them all more good than harm: but would be brought to account fully for all the harm he'd done, regardless.

EPILOGUE

Chancellor Witt rose up in the late morning out of his great soft bed in which there was room for a man and his wife and the nurse and the baby in the best traditional Aznir style with a frown of dissatisfaction on his face and a lingering sense of unease in his heart.

Pulling his sleep-shirt off over his head—fine linen, priced by the threads per knuckle in the old Aznir fashion, with the traditional three geese or seven ducks for the woman who set the threads on the loom—he hung his garment on the hook in his dressing room and stepped into the shower, preset to his preference, a soft well-laundered rug of thick-piled toweling awaiting him when he was done.

The bathroom was warmed as if by a fire on the hearth, though he had no hearth and no fire. There were limits. Even in the court of the Autocrat herself wood was burned in moderation, for the sauna, for the preparation of traditional roast game, for festal hearths, or to warm the bathing-rooms of the highest of all Aznir and her guests.

He dried and dressed himself, a sober workmanlike morning costume differentiated from that worn by any domestic worker or skilled craftsman by the quality of the fabric and the embroidery that adorned the yoke of the shirt and its cuffs. Fast-meal was waiting. He didn't wear an overblouse to eat his morning meal, so he was still technically undressed, in the formal Dolgorukij sense. And all the while he rehearsed in his mind the several causes of his perturbation.

Things had seemed to be going well for Agavie's bulk commodities business. Then they hadn't. He hadn't heard a report back from Pefisct,

191

when he had made such careful arrangements to get him next to Andrej Koscuisko first thing before he could lose the carefully prepared container for the virus or simply lose his nerve. Witt didn't expect Pefisct to let him down, but why was there no news?

Captain Morrisk was a trusted operative, if so junior that she had no idea of the actual scope of her employer's business interests. He made a note to himself to issue a gently worded inquiry to the senior officer in her supervisory chain, one that would clearly communicate that a rebuke if necessary would be for him and not his subordinates.

Rarely were a man's servants, his retainers, at fault for their failures. A proper householder looked first to see that he'd issued instructions that had been clearly understood, and next to be sure that the successful performance of the task was within his staff's ability to perform to expectation.

Then there was Couveraine. Witt had expected to lose his position in that market. It was a normal hazard of doing business. Exactly where the initial Langsarik compromise of Holding had taken place was uncertain, however; the Biramie cartel should have had more by way of advance warning.

As it was they had to leave valuable merchandise behind. All of the risk and the expense of acquiring it by thirty-two and sixty-four souls at a time was gone to waste, without so much as salvage costs in return. There would have to be a complete investigation of where a data breach had taken place, and how. He could not be too careful of maintaining a good network in Gonebeyond space.

His fastmeal was waiting for him, prepared fresh from the moment the alert had sounded in the executive kitchen as he'd stepped into his shower. Steaming hot rhyti with red-root sugar and Aznir dairy cream. Bread, eggs, meat, pastries—Witt lifted the snowy white linen cloth away from the platter of his fastmeal pastries to make his choice with pleasant anticipation.

There would be sloeplum knots so tender they almost fell apart when one so much as looked at them. Airy sweet raised dough dumplings filled with a smooth silky black paste of ground poppy-seeds with just enough of the grain left to them to amuse the tongue while delighting the palate. Perhaps a bit of cake with a fruit topping, translucent slices of rich crimson tree-fruit curled into an artful flower with stem and leaves of green ground nuts. What new delights awaited him today?

Yes, all those things, and a jam-pocket with petals dripping with a white sugar glaze that had been too generously, too clumsily, applied. Witt frowned. The plate was wrong. All of the same pastries in basic form, and Witt would have found them very satisfactory three months ago; but that had been before a genius—no, *the* genius—had come to Haspirzak Proper, a man whose artistry rested unwaveringly on the foundations of Dolgorukij pastry cooking and transcended it at one and the same time.

These were the work of the skilled and able pastry-chefs in Witt's kitchen, yes, and perfectly respectable in their own way. But only that. They could not be compared to that of the man Witt had hired away from the Magnard Hotel at such cost in coin and favors, and Witt was spoiled now.

He signaled for his steward, who would be waiting in his office opposite the main doors to Witt's suite seeing to accounts and calendars while he waited to be called. When the fast-meal service was cleared away they would discuss the day's events and who was coming to dinner, and sometimes engage Witt's valet—Aznir Dolgorukij, as the steward himself was, from families who had served autocrats as long as the autocrats had ruled—on whether he should properly wear cloth embroidered boots or plain black leather ones.

This question was of a magnitude that would not wait. "Alcho, is there an issue with pastry-master Jachil, this morning? A message for me, perhaps?" If it was a question of money, then it was a question of prestige. But also of fast-meal pastry and the reputation of his dinner table, business and pleasure combined.

"Some persons rather, your Excellency," Alcho replied, over the talk-alert. His voice sounded a little strained. "They request to be admitted. You have had the Bench specialist Dame Ivers to dinner, and there are two others. They request the indulgence of a private meeting."

Yes, he *was* an Excellency, just not in Haspirzak. He was Chancellor Witt, and in major enclaves outside the Dolgorukij Combine itself people holding such civil ranks were frequently afforded the courtesy title. Witt nodded in the general direction of his butter-dish. "Yes, of course. Bring rhyti, and a tray of my best Camperdown in shirku juice."

The Camperdown he had in stock was one of the nicest of the

sparkling white wines in his cellars. Mixed with fresh-squeezed shirku citrus juice—a particularly sweet and floral cultivar, the rage of the moment in elite society circles—Camperdown and shirku juice made a festive fast-meal beverage and a satisfying display of wealth. Sixteen eights of the common form of the beverage available through normal mercantile channels could be bought for the same price as a single bottle of true Sheharij Camperdown wine.

That he could afford to use it in a breakfast beverage was a sure sign that he had plenty more to spare. Witt had been reliably informed that guests whom the Dolgorukij Combine's Autocrat wished to especially honor were greeted with just such a drink, in place of a more prosaic fruit juice with their fast-meals.

He could hear the outer doors open. Alcho opened the door to the room in which Witt took his fast-meals; standing aside, Alcho held the door for Witt's unexpected visitors, one two and three. There seemed to be more people behind them, but Alcho had said nothing as he left the room, closing the door behind him. Of a tray of lovingly chilled drinks in tall fluted crystal glasses there was no sign.

"Good-greeting, Chancellor Witt," Dame Ivers said. She presented herself this morning in a sober sort of uniform, a standard Jurisdiction Fleet pattern, but unique in color—an otherwise drab greyish hue made notable by the fact that no other uniform under Jurisdiction was that shade. "Thank you for seeing us. You remember Specialist Vogel, I presume?"

Why would I? Witt thought. Another Bench specialist, clearly enough, because the uniform was the same; but if otherwise Vogel could be any man of ordinary height and calm expression, any apparently middle-aged man with a hint of melancholy in his eyes and an iron-gray moustache and floury fingers.

Wait. The man beside Ivers had perfectly clean hands, at a glance, and yet Witt clearly remembered an image: one that provided the key. Jachil. That was pastry-master Jachil. That was the man who'd made traditional Dolgorukij pastries the rage of Haspirzak Proper, but more than that, a Bench specialist? The man Witt had enticed into his household, into the heart of his house—his kitchens, a man who'd had what amounted to the run of the place for months, a Bench specialist?

"Ah," Witt said, and stopped. The single word seemed hardly adequate to express his confusion. "I see. Good-greeting, Specialist

Vogel." And who was the third person here, a younger man, slim and blond and elegant of appearance in a sort of muted version of a Dolgorukij aristocrat's daily dress, the person who looked as though he might easily have been Andrej Koscuisko's thirteenth cousin on his mother's side?

Here was the servant with Camperdown in shirku juice. But Witt didn't recognize the man who carried in the tray; should he be concerned? "And to you, Chancellor," Vogel replied, with a polite bow. "We've come with some documentation for your review. Let me introduce to you Chancellor Witt."

Vogel had got that phrase wrong, somehow, surely. There should have been an inflection, there, and a name; *let me introduce to you this person named thus-and-such, Chancellor Witt.* Because *he* was Chancellor Witt. "What is of this the meaning?" Witt asked, using his best imitation of Dolgorukij syntax in order to make an elaborate show of confusion. To cover over his genuine confusion.

A Bench specialist in his kitchens was a clear sign that he might have some significant compromises in his operations, but he was very careful about sanitation on all levels. And he had connections, a network, valuable relationships with influential people in Haspirzak and elsewhere.

Nor would any of his business dealings rise to the level of a Bench concern, surely. The Bench had more important things to do than pursue violators of mere commercial codes, regardless of size of the enterprise. And it would take years of legal maneuvering to get anywhere near him if the Bench tried. He had people within the chambers of the Third Judge herself, though not as many as he would have liked.

The young man had not bowed. He hadn't spoken, He was watching Witt carefully, as if he was drinking in every gesture, every expression, every shift of position. Mirroring them. Reflecting them. Was it his imagination—Witt wondered, in bewilderment—or had that young man been disappearing right in front of him, since the moment he'd walked in?

He was a professional actor, Witt realized, a skilled craftsman and a quick study. Suddenly Witt knew exactly what the young man was doing here. He wasn't Chancellor Witt. But he was going to be.

"There is a security detail waiting for us outside this room," Dame

Ivers said. "You are to go with them to Canopy Base in Gonebeyond space and place yourself in the hands of the judicial center there in accordance with this extradition order, to face charges of being a material accessory to wrongful death directly related to an attempted kidnapping in coordination with former Ship's Inquisitor Danyo Pefisct. To start. Here is the extradition order."

She didn't hand it to him. She would have guessed he would refuse to accept it. She lay it down on the fastmeal table in front of him, instead, and indicated its endorsements with a gesture. Third Judge Nantik Parline, Presiding, Haspirzak Judiciary.

"In your absence, and pursuant to a longstanding Bench investigation, this man will act in your stead and in your name. He is in law your proxy by direction; *my* direction. That he is not you in fact will be of less interest to your social acquaintances than you might think."

Could she be right? Would his history of adjusting his appearance be enough to conceal the truth from people who didn't know him well, and among those who did know him well enough, how many would care enough to raise a question?

"And for the rest, in the eyes of your extensive business associates— if a man looks like Chancellor Witt playing Andrej Koscuisko, and he is in your place as Chancellor Witt playing Andrej Koscuisko, knowing everything that Chancellor Witt knows, doing business as Chancellor Witt, he will be the functional equivalent of Chancellor Witt, and no further notice taken. Until it is too late."

No, that wasn't right. It couldn't be. He had a large establishment. People would notice. And yet Ivers could give them good reasons not to notice: escape from charges of complicity in criminal conspiracy; or simple economics, perhaps. His people had always been able to guess he had private interests. They might even conclude that his change for a slightly different man with a certain degree of forgetfulness signified a business coup, and was none of their business.

"Who is to look after my people?" Witt protested. "And I have many legitimate business concerns." It was clearly too late to profess absolute innocence, after having hosted a Bench intelligence specialist in his kitchen. This was all down to Danyo Pefisct: and the obvious fact that Witt had been compromised, even almost perhaps fatally, with respect to the slave markets of Couveraine and the slave camp at Holding. "My business partners will believe innocent people are to blame. There will be a bloodbath."

"Trust in me to distinguish and take appropriate action," Ivers replied, unmoved. "You have a large presence in some areas, but believe me that we have access to related networks which may be as influential. It's time for you to leave now."

The door opened, and what could only be a security detail came through. He didn't recognize the uniforms they wore; not Bench security, not Fleet, something Gonebeyond perhaps except that Gonebeyond had no security force so they were perhaps from the Canopy Base that Ivers had mentioned. He remembered now. A formidable business competitor had been headquartered at somewhere called Canopy Base, until quite recently. What else was going on in Gonebeyond space that he didn't know?

Did Ivers know why Koscuisko was to have been kidnapped? If they were getting information from Pefisct did they assume, as Pefisct had done, that he'd meant to collect Koscuisko for his own? That was an agreeable fantasy, yes, but only that. Witt was first and foremost a businessman. If Ivers didn't know how much money Witt's customer was willing to pay to have Koscuisko delivered into Bench custody at Cintaro Judiciary—to be put on public trial for crimes against humanity—Witt would hold that information in reserve until the time was right.

He wasn't surprised to see the walking cage, the security hood, they'd brought for him to wear. No one would see Chancellor Witt leave his house, board a ship, disappear. He suffered them to buckle a restraint belt around his waist, drop the heavy fabric shroud over his head, pull his wrists through the holes in the front of the garment to shackle them.

He didn't bother to resist, not physically. He knew something they didn't know, about Cintaro. He would know how to turn that knowledge to good use, and despite Ivers' claims people would be coming to his aid. Already there was hope.

As Security escorted him through the doors and away, he only barely heard Ivers behind him. "Thank you, Chancellor Witt," she said. "We'll leave you to your fast-meal, now, sir."

Witt was grateful to Ivers. A man could take omens from the universe just when things were at their worst: he was a prisoner, he was being removed with swift efficiency from his place where he could reach for assistance, his future was far more uncertain than he could ever have imagined.

But nobody, nobody, would have Pastry-Master Jachil in their kitchens, ever again. And for now Witt would hold to that tiny bit of irony for hope, because it was all he had.

Andrej was ready to go home.

Fisher Wolf stood ready to receive him on the launch field. It was black starry night on Holding, and the chill in the desert air at this altitude was bracing. In the near distance Andrej could see the lights of the field hospital shining cheerfully in the night; the hospital would be closing, soon, as the last of the freed prisoners were evacuated, if not to settlements that had been destroyed by the slavers, then to new communities within more familiar settings. They had no further need of him.

"Don't think I won't be keeping my eye on you, Koscuisko," Yogee said, beside him. Yogee had his arms folded high across his chest so he could tuck his fingers close beneath his armpits to keep them warm. Andrej remembered that about Yogee, and it made him smile. "I'll be speaking to Safehaven about whether you're keeping your clinic hours up to requirement. So you'd better just watch yourself."

They were carrying no cargo away with them, so Riggs had said good-bye and gone off with the Langsariks back to Langsarik Station, where Hilton Shires apparently had a job for her. The temporary hospital at Couveraine had been packed out as well, since Couveraine City's existing facilities were equal to the task of supporting the city's civil population and its occupation force.

The Langsarik Coalition hadn't yet decided about Couveraine, from what Andrej had heard. It had warehouse facilities and functioning launch-fields, as well as an experienced support staff. There was no sense in wasting a perfectly good market hub, so long as a Port Authority could be established to administer and keep an eye out for prohibited activity. Slaving. Traffic in stolen goods.

"You are the last man in known Space to sit in judgment on my clinic hours, Yodge," Andrej said. They hadn't discussed the great divide that was between them, Andrej's role as Ship's Inquisitor. Andrej wasn't sure there was any point. It had been a long time ago. Yogee wasn't likely to have softened in his disapproval and Andrej wasn't apologizing to Yogee for things that had never been Yogee's business, so there it was. "If you make trouble for me I will not sponsor you into our gaming nights."

They played cards. He, and Stildyne, and senior officers at Safehaven—the provost marshal "Beauty" Sangriege, the spymaster, the port authority generally. There was liquor involved. Yogee might find himself surprised at how much more equal were the terms on which Andrej had learned to compete, though to be fair they did not play relki so often as other things.

Yogee stood silent, looking up at the stars. He took his time answering. "You take Janforth with you, I see," he said, and nothing whatever about games of cards. Stubbornly maintaining his distance, perhaps, or simply at a loss for sufficiently dismissive terms in which to respond.

Andrej smiled. If Yogee didn't want to become friends again it was Yogee's choice. Andrej couldn't hold it against him. He admired Yogee's willful stubbornness. "The gentlemen have been in Janforth's place. They have the best idea of how to smooth the way."

There could well be more bond-involuntary refugees coming into Safehaven. Someone would be wanting to write a reception protocol. He would talk to Dr. Ailson—the chief medical officer, Safehaven Medical Center—about the idea. He'd suggest that Yogee Gascarone be tasked with the coordination. That would be a good joke on Yogee.

He realized that he hadn't quite finished his point. "And *Fisher Wolf* should have crew members to rotate. It may be a good match. I have no say in it, one way or another."

"How does that feel to you, though, Koski?" Yogee asked. "I mean. I've wondered. I don't know how they stand you." It wasn't an attack, but an honest question. It deserved an honest answer.

"I am not their officer any longer. I enjoy meeting them, after all of these years, I am surprised by who they are themselves, and significantly delighted. I think that one at least of them and I are friends, but I try not to presume." He could say that about Robert with a degree of confidence. For the rest, it was not necessary for them to be his friends for him to love them. "I do my best to mind my manners, and be on my best behavior. I do not always succeed."

Maybe not so reserved as that. They didn't have to re-establish the intimacy once forced on all of them, Andrej included, by prior circumstance. They could continue to be comfortable with each other whether or not they were all friends. Hope for him and Yogee, then.

"Well, if I come to Safehaven, maybe I'll take you up on your offer. I can share scandalous stories about your student days. I might enjoy that."

As a threat it wasn't a very serious one. Yes. Hope. "I'll see you later, then. At Safehaven. Good-greeting, Yogee, I should be leaving, now." He could see Stildyne at the foot of *Fisher Wolf*'s passenger loading ramp, waiting for him. He wondered how things were between Brachi and Janforth, but he wasn't going to be the one to introduce the topic.

"Safe travels," Yogee said, and hopped into his waiting mover to trundle back to the field hospital, where he could warm up.

When Bat Yorvik arrived at Langsarik Station he was met on the tarmac by the Langsarik Coalition mission commander, now returned to his normal position as the provost marshal. There was still a Langsarik Coalition, of course, but it was spearheaded pro tem by the semi-retired flag captain of the Langsarik fleet—a formidable woman named Walton Agenis, who according to Bat's intel briefing from Haspirzak was Hilton Shires' aunt. And keeping company with Garol Vogel. Bat hoped to meet her; but right at this moment he wanted some answers.

"Good-greeting, your Honor," Shires said cheerfully. He'd brought a mover, and a man to drive it. Bat looked around; it was a pretty place, warm breezes, green vines climbing the sides of the blast walls. That was evidence of the sophistication of the ships Langsarik Station received: the blast walls were not, apparently, called upon too often to buffer the thermal shock generated by older, less efficient couriers than the one that had ferried Bat here from Couveraine. "Permit me to explain this diversion of your flight plan."

That was exactly the explanation Bat had in mind. "Thank you, Provost Marshal, I *am* interested in that topic." He'd expected to travel to Osmer, to which a substantial party of freed prisoners from Holding had been repatriated. Visiting the victimized systems had seemed to be a natural starting point in familiarizing himself with all the worlds in Gonebeyond; and in this way, his itinerary could be clearly seen to favor not the strongest or largest of Gonebeyond Space's polities but precisely those places most in need of a framework for agreements and partnerships with each other.

"And we won't detain you. We've been in touch with Haspirzak for their advice on an acceptable neutral location for your base of operations, during your stay here with us in Gonebeyond. Your travel to Osmer brought you naturally off vector at Langsarik Station, so a short stopover seemed a natural opportunity for you to transfer to your own ship. Judicial independence. Freedom of movement."

Bat had little by way of personal belongings with him, and those had already been offloaded to the groundcar Shires had brought with him. At a gesture of invitation from Shires, Bat stepped into the open groundcar and seated himself. "Do I have one?" he asked. "A ship, I mean."

His interactions with Shires had been positive thus far, and the Langsariks were unquestionably among the more organized and coherent of settlements in Gonebeyond space as far as Haspirzak knew. It came as no particular surprise to hear that Shires had been thinking about the vital importance of Judicial neutrality. Up until now Bat had been basically the guest of the Langsarik coalition. That need only be a problem if it went on too long, to the exclusion of other communities all of which deserved his full attention.

"Haspirzak has sent you out a ship on loan, for the duration. Much as the Malcontents out of the Dolgorukij Combine have loaned out the thula *Fisher Wolf* to prosecute its interests in Gonebeyond. Sweet machine, I don't mind telling you."

Pursuit of Dolgorukij terrorists mostly, as Bat understood. It all went back to the amnesty that Bench intelligence specialist Garol Vogel had brokered between the Langsarik "pirates" and the Bench, the one that had been forced into failure by those same Dolgorukij terrorists. The Angel of Destruction, to speak the name of which—Bat had been told—was as to spit.

"Sort of a chambers-in-transit, then," Bat mused aloud. "Without any chambers attached, of course." He was here to observe and learn. Nothing more. Except that of course he'd agreed to entertain an extradition request on behalf of the Langsarik Coalition that had been honored by the Third Judge. He'd approved it, too, in full knowledge of the wider implications: the first peer-to-peer exchange between Haspirzak and Gonebeyond space.

Now they needed a reciprocal transaction to continue building on that foundation—a similar request from Haspirzak. A much more delicate matter. They would have to choose the right occasion very carefully, but it would come in time. "I'd like to see this ship."

"And here it is, your Honor." It hadn't been a very long drive, but there was a mistake; the groundcar had taken him to *Fisher Wolf*. At least it looked like the Malcontent's thula; there was the *Fisher Wolf's* cargo handler—Riggs?—coming down the cargo loading ramp to direct the stowing of some crates on board. There appeared to be a full load of them, on the tarmac. He didn't see any other crew he recognized, but it wasn't as if he'd gotten familiar with any of them in the first place.

And yet it carried the ship's identification chevrons and striping of Haspirzak Judiciary. Shires looked upon the ship with a certain amount of satisfaction, strangely wistful in some way. "Your ship, your Honor," Shires said. "The Haspirzak thula. Also named *Haspirzak*. The Third Judge has requested we provide home-port accommodation for purposes of cabin refresh and supply. She expects you'll be using it more than she's done, recently."

The Haspirzak thula? For him? Bat stared at the beautiful thing, the Third Judge's own elite courier. Could there be more definite, more deliberate, a gesture from the Third Judge of her commitment to forging a relationship with Gonebeyond space, than to place the finest courier she had at his disposal?

"I like it a great deal," Bat said. It was an understatement. "Does the cargo handler come with?"

"Your crew is provided by Haspirzak, on rotation, since it's Haspirzak's thula. But Riggs has prior experience with the unique characteristics of the only other thula in Gonebeyond space. So she's in a position to be of material assistance, should you and she come to a mutually agreeable arrangement in terms of scheduling and salary. Oh. And Haspirzak's opened a line of credit for you. Through some banking people at Euberlin, details to be briefed by your ship's crew."

Shires sounded rather pleased with himself, really. "Well, I'll be on my way, then?" He meant to be more definite about it; it came out a question regardless. He had a lot to think about.

"If you can spare us a few hours, your Honor, it will be just about enough time for third-meal before your cargo has been stowed.

Haspirzak has sent some supplies out for you, we understand. I would consider it a privilege and a pleasure to entertain you to some dumplings, should it not violate judicial rules of neutrality. My wife makes—really nice dumplings."

It was going to take him some time to work through the broader implications of this new development in his mind. The Haspirzak thula. For his use. Judge Bat Yorvik. Gonebeyond space. Presiding?

It wasn't Chambers at Haspirzak, the Gelisar Gardens, all soaring towers and deluxe accommodations. That was all right. He'd never been a child of privilege.

"Dumplings sound wonderful," he said. "Thank you."

He was beginning to think that he might like it here.

UNDER JURISDICTION
Time Line/Summary Bibliography

An Exchange of Hostages
Andrej Koscuisko, having graduated from medical school, engendered a child, and quarreled with his father, reports to Fleet Orientation Station Medical for his training to serve as Ship's Inquisitor within the Jurisdiction Fleet.

Short story *Insubordination*
An unexpected confrontation between Joslire Curran and a student to whom he was assigned prior to meeting Andrej in *An Exchange of Hostages* shows Joslire a way to gain a degree of autonomy from the constraints of his governor.

Prisoner of Conscience
Three and a half years later, Andrej—currently serving on the Jurisdiction Fleet Ship *Scylla*—is detailed to the Domitt Prison at Port Rudistal to process prisoners of war.

Short story *Prisoner of Conscience, Ghost Epilogue*
Prisoner of Conscience left antagonist Mergau Noycannir en route to the Domitt Prison to take control. She finds Andrej in charge instead. The discovery does not sweeten her temper.

Novella *Jurisdiction*
Having completed his four-year tour of duty on *Scylla*, Andrej returns to Port Rudistal (site of the Domitt Prison) to perform a Tenth Level Command Termination. Security Chief Stildyne and bond-involuntary Security assigned, Jurisdiction Fleet Ship *Ragnarok*, take the handoff from *Scylla*, and escort Andrej to his new ship of assignment.

Novella *Quid Pro Quo*

It is several months after Andrej's assignment to the *Ragnarok*. Robert St. Clare takes one, or rather four-and-thirty, for the team; Andrej uses the incident to make a devil's bargain with Captain Lowden to protect his bond-involuntary Security assigned from further imposition.

Angel of Destruction

Bench Intelligence Specialist Karol Vogel is the protagonist of this novel, set a year or two into Andrej's tour of duty on the *Ragnarok*.

Novelette *Pizza and Beer Theatre! with Cousin Stanoczk*

Damage control required to address incident at an insignificant waystation reunites Cousin Stanoczk with Bench specialist Karol Vogel to rein in Mergau Noycannir's excesses, and is the last straw for First Secretary Verlaine.

Short story *Intimacies*

As far as he can tell Security Chief Stildyne never loved anybody in his life—except his younger sister, perhaps, and she's dead. At a service house, he tries an experiment, a strategy to manage the unfamiliar situation in which he finds himself; but you didn't hear it from me.

Hour of Judgment

Andrej has completed his four-year tour of duty on the *Ragnarok*, but circumstances force him to elect a second tour of duty. Meanwhile, someone's put a contract out on Andrej's life, and Bench Intelligence Specialist Karol Vogel has been tasked with its execution.

Short story *Night Breezes*

There are two undercover resistance operations at Port Burkhayden working to frustrate Bench tyranny. They'd both like to stop a Fleet pursuit ship from catching up with a Nurail refugee transport before it can escape to Gonebeyond space; the solution lies in the hands of a gardener, and the daughter of one of the port governor's principal allies.

The Devil and Deep Space

It hasn't been long since Andrej extended his assignment to the *Ragnarok* by another four years. His son, Anton Andreievitch, is eight years old; so Andrej decides it's high time he took leave to go home and get married.

Vignette *Labyrinth*

Andrej's father has come a long way since he forced his son to accept the rank—and the responsibilities—of a Ship's Inquisitor. In this vignette we see "first contact" between the Koscuisko prince and Andrej's son, recently the inconvenient offspring of a gentlewoman, now the first-born child of the sacred wife of the Prince Inheritor to the Koscuisko familial corporation.

Warring States

About a year has passed since the *Ragnarok*'s "mutiny in form" (at the end of *The Devil and Deep Space*). The Jurisdiction's Bench itself stands on the brink of disaster, and things are really starting to get a little out of hand with the *Ragnarok*'s command-and-control environment.

Blood Enemies

Andrej Koscuisko came to Gonebeyond to apologize to Brachi Stildyne. For a full year circumstances—and the custodial guardianship of the Nurail of Safehaven—have conspired against him. In this novel, his finally-successful effort to escape and find his people puts his people, his Malcontent "Cousin" Stanoczk, and the future of all of Gonebeyond Space itself into critical danger from which only an unimaginable crime can possibly save them all.

Novella *Stalking Horse*

With Jurisdiction space thrown into political turmoil after the events of Warring States, criminal activity has exploded. The Malcontent, working in conjunction with Bench Intelligence Specialist Irenja Rafenkel at Chilleau Judiciary, needs Andrej's help to set a plot in motion that will destabilize the black market in torture vids so that it can be fragmented, contained, and destroyed.

Crimes Against Humanity

Andrej is with the Langsarik Coalition as it moves against a thriving slave trade that's been raiding undefended settlements in Gonebeyond to supply its market. His conflicts with a man he blames for the death of Joslire Curran—and with an old, old friend—threaten to distract him from the realization that someone has set a dangerous, genetically engineered virus loose in a refugee hospital, with himself as its intended victim.

WHO ARE ALL THESE PEOPLE,
AND WHERE DID THEY COME FROM?

⊕

Crew of the Jurisdiction Fleet Ship *Ragnarok*

Jennet ap Rhiannon (Captain) (Hour of Judgement)
"Two" (Intelligence Officer) (novella "Jurisdiction")
Dierryk Rukota (supernumerary) (The Devil and Deep Space)
Gille Mahaffie (acting Chief Medical Officer)
Ralph Mendez (First Officer) (Hour of Judgement)

Andrej Koscuisko's Security

All of Andrej's security with a major role in this story first
appeared in the novella "Jurisdiction;" with the exception of
Robert St. Clare, who first appeared in "An Exchange of
Hostages."

Garrity
Godsalt
Hirsel
Kerenko (Lek Kerenko)
Pyotr (Pyotr Micmac)
St. Clare (Robert St. Clare)
Stildyne (Brachi Stildyne)

Everybody Else

Hilton Shires (Langsarik battle commander) (Angel of
　　Destruction in Baen omnibus Fleet Inquisitor; Blood
　　Enemies)
Danyo Pefisct (Inquisitor, deserter) (An Exchange of Hostages
　　by reference; short story Insubordination, printed in Baen
　　omnibus Fleet Insurgent)

Jils Ivers (Bench specialist, seen with Karol Vogel in every novel but An Exchange of Hostages, printed in the Baen omnibuses Fleet Insurgent and Fleet Renegade; other material in Baen omnibus Fleet Insurgent)

Karol Vogel (Bench specialist, see entry for Jils Ivers, above)

Bat Yorvik (Bench Judge) introduced here, Bench-level Judge on remote assignment)

Yogee Gascarone (Gonebeyond Space's Surgeon General) (introduced here, friend of Andrej Koscuisko from medical school on Mayon prior to series debut An Exchange of Hostages)

Medith Riggs (*Fisher* Wolf's cargo handler) (Into Gonebeyond, short story web-published by Baen in March 2017; subsequently, novella Stalking Horse, Baen omnibus Fleet Insurgent)

Janforth Ifrits (A former bond-involuntary once reporting to Brachi Stildyne)

Ekaterina "Kadrinnij" Felsanjir (Dolgorukij intelligence operative) (novella Stalking Horse, Baen omnibus Fleet Insurgent; I suspect she and Andrej may be on intimate terms, but there's no evidence in sight)

Names and Terms

Azanry (planet)—Andrej's home world

Aznir—ethnicity of Andrej and his family, topmost class of Dolgorukij

Bench (the Bench)—overall term for interplanetary government, government offices, etc.; not operational in Gonebeyond

Bond-involuntary—a Security slave with an implanted "governor," condemned to participate/perform torture of enemies of the Bench; stolen from the Bench by Andrej Koscuisko in the novel "Warring States"

Dasidar and Dyraine—Dolgorukij cultural icons ("Prisoner of Conscience")

Dolgorukij (the Dolgorukij Combine)— system of origin for Andrej Koscuisko, Fisner Feraltz, Cousin Stanoczk, Lek Kerenko, others

Fisher Wolf—the Malcontent's thula, currently crewed by Andrej Koscuisko's escaped bond-involuntary Security troops, first appearing in "The Devil and Deep Space"

Gonebeyond space—a no-man's-land, once beneath official Bench notice, now developing itself into a new peer government

Judiciary—one of nine geographical units under Jurisdiction

Jurisdiction—overall term for system of government characterized by legalistic structure, increasingly harsh methods of control

Langsariks—pirates/commerce raiders framed for terrorist acts in the novel "Angel of Destruction" whose relocation/escape to Gonebeyond space was facilitated by Karol/Garol Vogel in that novel

Malcontent—the secret service of the Dolgorukij church (An Exchange of Hostages, by reference)

Ragnarok—Jurisdiction Fleet Ship of assignment for Andrej Koscuisko in the novels "Hour of Judgement," "The Devil and Deep Space," and "Warring States;" technically mutinous, lurking in Gonebeyond waiting for its status to be resolved

Thula—an elite courier characterized by its speed and high-end navigation and interception abilities. This novel introduces the thula *Haspirzak*, personal courier of the Third Judge Nantik Parline, Haspirzak Judiciary.